Capitalism and Development

American University Studies

Series IX
History

Vol. 119

PETER LANG
New York • Washington, D.C./Baltimore • Boston
Bern • Frankfurt am Main • Berlin • Vienna • Paris

Marcial E. Ocasio Meléndez

Capitalism and Development

Tampico, Mexico
1876–1924

PETER LANG
New York • Washington, D.C./Baltimore • Boston
Bern • Frankfurt am Main • Berlin • Vienna • Paris

Library of Congress Cataloging-in-Publication Data

Ocasio Meléndez, Marcial E.
Capitalism and development: Tampico, Mexico,
1876–1924/ Marcial E. Ocasio Meléndez.
p. cm. — (American university studies. Series IX, History; vol. 119)
Includes bibliographical references and index.
1. Tampico (Tamaulipas, Mexico)—Economic conditions. 2. Tampico
(Tamaulipas, Mexico)—History. I. Title. II. Series.
HC138.T36o26 330.972'12—dc20 91-43586
ISBN 0-8204-1717-3
ISSN 0740-0462

Die Deutsche Bibliothek-CIP-Einheitsaufnahme

Ocasio Meléndez, Marcial E.:
Capitalism and development: Tampico, Mexico, 1876–1924/
Marcial E. Ocasio Meléndez. ñNew York, Washington, D.C./Baltimore; Boston;
Bern; Frankfurt am Main; Berlin; Vienna; Paris: Lang.
(American university studies: Ser. 9, History; Vol. 119)
ISBN 0-8204-1717-3
NE: American University Studies / 09

The paper in this book meets the guidelines for permanence and durability
of the Committee on Production Guidelines for Book Longevity
of the Council of Library Resources.

To my mother Amparo, Madrina Gertrude,
Emmanuel, Melody,
David C. Bailey and Leslie P. Rout. Jr.

TABLE OF CONTENTS

LIST OF TABLES

LIST OF ABBREVIATIONS

AGNPPM	Archivo General de la Nación. Papeles Presidenciales de México.
AMT	Archivo Municipal de Tampico.
CACT	National Archives. Consular Papers of the Tampico Consuls.
CRUSE	Department of State. Bureau of Foreign Commerce, *Commercial Relations of the United States with Foreign Countries.*
HMM	Daniel Cosío Villegas, *Historia Moderna de México.*
NA.DCT/84	National Archives. Despatches of the U.S. Consuls in Tampico, 1824-1906. Record Group 84.
NA.DCV/84	National Archives. Despatches of the United States Consuls in Veracruz, 1823-1906. Record Group 84.
POET	*Periódico Oficial del Estado de Tamaulipas.*
RDRIAM	U.S. Department of State. Records of the Department of State Relating to the Internal Affairs of Mexico, 1910-1929. MC 274.
RUCRF	*Report Upon the Commercial Relations of the United States with Foreign Countries for the Year ...*
USCR	*United States Consular Reports.*
USRCCM	U.S. Department of State, *Reports From the Consuls of the United States on Commerce, Manufactures, etc., of their Consular Districts.*

ACKNOWLEDGMENT

Many are those who assisted, encouraged, and gave me constant support and advice in this wonderful, yet long research and writing process. First, I wish to thank the Faculty, Development and Awards Committee of the University of Michigan-Flint, who helped me financially for this project. To my colleagues of the History Department at the University of Michigan-Flint, especially Leslie Moch, I am indebted for their words of encouragement and wisdom. Similarly to Gordon Stewart and Joseph Konvitz from Michigan State University, who have always given me their continuous support. The project could not have been completed without the outstanding assistance and help of my friend Father Carlos Gonzalez Salas, who as Tampico's official historian and loved man-for-all seasons, opened many doors for my research both in official and private sources in the city and at Tamaulipas State Capital of Ciudad Victoria. A special thanks go to Stella González and Jorge Garibay, who guided and assisted me at the Archivo General de la Nación in México City; and also to its former director Alejandra Moreno Toscano. The AGNM is blessed with a group of wonderful, courteous and helpful employees. Very close to this project were my friends Thomas Benjamin, a constant voice of encouragement, and Gertrude G. Bauer (Madrina), who provided intellectual and material nourishment whenever it was necessary. Special thanks go to Jossie Pellot, who helped with the typing and setting of the manuscript. However, this project began with the encouragement and support of my two former mentors at Michigan State University, David C. Bailey and Leslie B. Rout, Jr., who read and advised me on it before departing from our midst. To their memory, I dedicate this work and to my family go my deepest thanks for their patience and understanding of what it means to bring forth an intellectual offspring.

PREFACE

This study highlights the political and economic history of Tampico, a major Mexican port city. It traces and explains its urban development and growth between 1876 and 1924, a historical moment encompassing the Porfiriato and the Revolution. The city evolved dominated by an urban spirit formed since its foundation. It helped its residents make the best use of the material resources available to them by national and international forces and to make Tampico a powerful regional center. Yet, after 1920, development stagnated, and Tampico suffered a constant loss of its semi-independent regional influence becoming a tool for national integration and international interests.

Tampico was founded in 1823, immediately becoming an important port, but it was not until 1876 when its commercial growth took a steadier course. By 1920, it challenged the traditional main port of Veracruz, becoming México's fifth largest city, and the world's first international oil port. When compared to other Mexican cities, Tampico's growth occurred within the context of local events, but also of national and international incidents. Argentine historian José Luis Romero has defined "national" cities as those founded after independence, and Tampico fits this definition. Its history and organization point to a paradigm of colonial urbanism, influential upon the new urban life that characterized the Mexican nation after 1821. However, Tampico's historical evolution conforms to the development of similar "national" Spanish American cities. Many of these also grew into regional semi-autonomous centers, eventually forced to become integrated to their nations because of their economic importance.

Porfirian collaborators and revolutionary leaders alike attempted to modernize México between 1876 and 1924. The process disrupted Mexican society's old patterns, and was characterized by constant and growing alterations in the daily experiences of many Mexicans: on land control, industrial production, and labor development, finally leading to a terrible civil war and to a new political system. These conflicting changes and results are the subject of a growing historiography of the Porfiriato and the Revolutionary periods. Yet, urban studies for both have deserved little attention, except minutiae of either historical moment within the context of México's largest cities.

Important colonial urban centers such as México City, Puebla, Guadalajara, Monterrey, and Veracruz have deserved national attention from chroniclers, social scientists, and historians. Other Mexican cities, whether colonial or national, were of particular interest only to local historians until the forties. It was in these other cities, however, that many important changes occurred consequently affecting regions or states in unique ways.

The study of these urban centers has increased Mexican historical knowledge and understanding. City formation in México and throughout Latin America has followed local, individualistic, and inorganic forms inherited from the colonial period. Most of the earliest colonial cities were founded independently of the metropolitan authorities, although dependent on royal recognition; an idea rooted in medieval cities' development. These "free" cities were the result of individual enterprise or of royal grants and orders. Christopher Columbus founded Isabela in northern Hispaniola as his viceregal capital. His brother Bartolomé moved its residents south of the island founding Santo Domingo de Guzmán to take advantage of the nearby gold mines. Juan Ponce de León founded Caparra in northern San Juan (Puerto Rico) with permission from the governor of Hispaniola. Eleven years later its residents moved the town against the wishes of the Conquistador and the Hispaniola government. Hernán Cortés founded the Villa Rica de la Vera Cruz, as a seat of local control that empowered him to explore and conquer the Aztec empire, thus opposing orders from the governor of Cuba. Other

Conquistadors followed similar models or founded cities so that they could be remembered in history. In almost all cases, the city was a necessary element of the Conquest. This formation of cities was carried out independently from each other, although certain ties were established with earlier successful settlements that attained power as seats of royal officials; bishops, governors, and Audiencias.

The models for this inorganic system of cities can be found in medieval Christian Spain, especially during the Reconquest of the peninsula from the Moslems. It allowed "conquerors" to establish centers of legal power to control adjoining territories in order to justify their actions to the Crown. These also served as military bases to continue attacks on their enemies. Many jurisdictions overlapped. Thus, these legal entities, when coupled with the geographical features of distance and terrain, made many of them inaccessible to the official hubs of royal power. Far from the authority of some religious or Crown officer, towns became semi-independent units in a format that encouraged autonomy, especially when controlled by a powerful local elite represented in the "cabildos," who challenged external authorities except those acknowledged previously.

The history of Latin America's national cities continued the colonial trend of semi-independent status in its relationship to the nation owing to the lack of really political or military control by the new central governments. These young towns attained a regional importance and power that could only be suppressed or controlled through the imposition of strong national governments. México presents a most interesting example of such a case.

The history of México between 1822 and 1876 shows a constant failure by the central government to impose direct rule over most of its territory. This lack of control occurred, among other factors, because of the ideological struggles between national leaders, over the type of political system to be adopted for the nation, a system that could serve national needs but not those of most Mexicans. The government's major urban concern was México City, on the assumption that the nation's reputation would be strengthened by the capital's beauty and comfort. Worried more about political, economic and military issues rather than on the creation of a strong urban network that would help the nation's improvement, leaders' continued wrangling led to a relative autonomy of urban centers and regions of the country.

The Huasteca, a semitropical area spread among five different eastern Mexican states was one of these semi-autonomous regions. Tampico became its port city serving regional interests by design of its founders. Yet, not much of its pre revolutionary history has been written. The city's historian, Carlos González Salas, constantly publishes books and newspaper articles about the city. Other authors also use the local press to write on Tampico, but their historical concerns are heavily centered in the post-Revolutionary period, that is, after 1920. Only two major chronicles of Tampico exist. One, by Juan Manuel Torrea and Ignacio Fuentes (1942), covers specific topics of the city's history since its foundation; the other, by Joaquín Meade (1977), is rich in information spreading from the colonial period to the 1930s. Leif Adleson also wrote an excellent study of Tampico's labor movement between 1915 and 1919. Yet, none of these sources provides a comprehensive historical analysis of the city's development.

This study of Tampico interprets its origin and development, postulating that an urban "spirit," has prevailed over time, which has characterized city residents since its foundation. The data analysis leads to the thesis that the growth and development of Tampico (1823-1924) were the result of the willingness of its residents to seek, accept, collaborate, and guide external economic and political forces toward such objective. These attitudes strengthened local capitalism with a resulting powerful position vis-a-vis the national government. This "Geist," or collective ideology, endured until the 1920s, accepted and nurtured by all residents at every social level. This "spirit" emphasized urbanization, city beautification, commercial growth, preventive health and sanitary measures, capital accumulation, better communications system, and encouragement of competition. It was filled with a strong capitalist ideology.

The 1876-1911 Díaz' regime fostered principles similar to those advocated by the Tampiqueños. The Porfiriato opened México to foreign investors, and encouraged national development and modernization, guided after 1880 by the ideological presence of Comtian positivism. Tampico's leaders moved into the maze of national politics to protect, and promote their urban goals. The city's excellent port location on the Mexican Gulf, and the similarity between national and local goals led to an easy acceptance of the Porfiriato, of foreign enterprises, and to a collaboration with those forces for the construction of an important physical infrastructure between 1876 and 1900. In 1901, and luckily for the city, oil was discovered in large quantities in the nearby Huasteca region, once the new facilities were finished. Thus Tampico could renew its role as the natural outlet for the Huasteca, and making it México's major oil exporter for the next three decades. The resulting prosperity brought a host of new forces into the local and regional political power structure, and gave Tampico a prominent presence in the national and international scene.

The analysis shows that the "Geist" continued undiminished throughout the revolutionary period and well into the 1930s. Nationalism encouraged by the Mexican government, especially during and after Alvaro Obregon's presidency (1920-1924), integrated the disorganized nation. City views, supported by labor and capital alike, and by its political leadership ruled Tampico. The urban "geist" was strongly attacked once the national government began to institutionalize the

"Revolution" the late 1930s and early 1940s. The "new México" sought to eliminate Tampico's old urban "spirit."

Two major goals permeated Tampico's evolution between 1823 and 1924. One was capitalist growth and the other was the city's modernization. Capitalist growth meant capital accumulation, promotion of trade and business, and continued control of a large hinterland - partly acquired in the last years of the colonial period - that exported minerals and agricultural products, while city's businessmen served as middlemen for imports. Modernization, on the other hand, was seen as physical growth. It implied urban expansion and planning, construction of new port facilities, newer connections by land to the rest of México - whether by roads or railroads - and by sea to North Atlantic ports and to the rest of the Americas. Modernization also meant the development of an infrastructure that would attract investments, new businesses, and tourists. The city had to resemble the great cities of North America and Western Europe, in appearance, sanitation, hygiene, and health services. Yet, these were essential services for the local population because of its location amid lagoons, rivers and jungles. Furthermore, another major concern was behind these goals: to compete and overtake Veracruz, México's premier port city since colonial times. The goals were partially achieved with the help of Federal representatives for the 1876-1920 period, all strong supporters of local capitalism and of Tampico's modernization plans.

Three groups labored to keep the urban "spirit" alive in the community: business, labor, and foreign residents. The business community was made up of Mexicans and by a group of foreign merchants, many from the United States, who had made Tampico and México their home, marrying locally and forming a progeny of Tampiqueños. The city's labor force was small for a long time, mainly involved in service jobs to commerce, to port and land transportation businesses.

However, it grew fast after the 1880s when railroad works reached Tampico, and even faster after the discovery of oil in the Huasteca. Both business and labor groups, advocated modernization, and better economic conditions. Although strange bedfellows, they collaborated to attract foreign enterprises and brought pressure on local, state and national politicians within their own sphere of influence in order to attain their urban goals, simultaneously with those of their own class or their individual personal gains.

Foreign residents, whether entrepreneurs or agents of foreign companies, made up the third group that played a role in Tampico's development. A foreign presence began with the city's origin, yet its strongest influence was felt in the 1880s with the arrival of railroad officials and related companies. By the first decade of the twentieth century, more foreigners in the city were associated to oil companies that wanted to use it as their entrance into the Huasteca hinterland or the Mexican market. Most of them were United States citizens, but also Europeans and Asians arrived. Slowly, Tampico began to function as an American port in México, a valuable beachhead for North American expansion in the national marketplace at a time when Veracruz was the beachhead for Great Britain. Foreign investors and their agents promoted the port's modernization through their investments, their pressures on federal government officials to receive special treatment that benefitted the city, and by their local support of the Tampiqueños' "Geist" to advance and to make their city a richer and more satisfying place to live. Their own selfish reasons fitted perfectly with those of the local population.

The combination of these groups' interests with major local and national ideological aims, and the resulting achievements and disillusionments, make Tampico an urban subject worthy of study, and an example of Latin American national ports' urban history. It is during this period that new cities on the continent, especially in countries such as Brazil,

Argentina, and México, began to assert their freedom from the control of the old colonial primacy centers, growing in importance as regional hubs and thereby influencing national economics and development. It is also a period characterized by the outward thrust of American capitalists; most of whose foreign investments were made in the neighboring countries of Canada and México, eventually spreading to the Antilles, Central and South America. Yet, this expansion faced them with the dominant capitalist power in the Americas: Great Britain. The rivalry that ensued between the two economic powers was used by several Latin American politicians, whether at local or national levels, to benefit both their region or country's development and their own economic and political status.

The above elements are part of this analysis on Tampico. In the study, people appear against the backdrop of local achievements to develop their city, notwithstanding the economic failures and the political turmoil brought about by foreign and national forces. They also appear against the backdrop of national and international events that had great significance for their city's economy and for their daily lives.

The first chapter is a brief history of Tampico from its foundation until 1876. It describes the earliest appearance of the urban "spirit," and how it was encouraged by events that made the city a focal point in the nation. A second chapter deals with the Porfiriato, and how the presence of Porfirio Díaz at the national helm brought new visions for the nation and for Tampico. Railroad lines, new port facilities, more shipping lines, and increased trade were symbolic of the modernizing vision of the federal bureaucracy.

The railroad companies' attempt to control Tampico is the theme of the third chapter. Their plans to link U.S. markets using the Mexican crossing, were marred by the Pánuco River's conditions; it required constant dredging and the construction of jetties that would open the bar at the river's entrance to allow large ships to enter the port and meet the terminus of the railroad line. Local, state and federal support was given to one railroad company until the jetties were constructed, but by then, plans had changed.

Chapter four focuses on oil in México, its growing world importance, and on the two entrepreneurs who made Tampico an international oil city: Weetman Pearson and Edward L. Doheny. Petroleum reorganized the sources of power and the type of development sought by local forces by changing the economic base of urban and regional income.

The Revolution and its impact on the city are the theme of chapter five. During the revolutionary years, Tampico was jealously guarded by all the revolutionary parties interested in the port and its wealth. It was also protected by foreign governments, interested in the safety of their citizens' oil companies in the Huasteca and Tampico. It was the parallel occurrence of the First World War, and the concomitant increase in petroleum's importance, which enhanced the city's international significance as a secure source of the valuable liquid. Thus, collaboration emerged again between local, national, and foreign forces in and around Tampico to promote the city's safety and share in the profits.

Chapter six discusses Tampico after the Constitutionalist forces took the city. The urban situation is examined under a new political reality based on nationalism, constitutionality and centralism. A parallel "oil boom" occurs in the Huasteca that influences the city; large labor immigration, greater U.S. concern for Mexican oil owing both to fear of low production at home and through the powerful oil lobby in Congress opposed to México's nationalist Constitution and its reforms.

As Tampico struggled under all these new conditions, its "urban spirit" was forced to modify itself because labor and capital faced one another in a debate over more benefits. Chapter seven describes how Tampico's municipality was divided to create a new town. Again it was another instance of collaboration among all competing parties in the city:

labor, municipal government, state and federal governments, and the oil companies. Ciudad Madero, the new town, satisfied the wishes of the labor force because now they would receive lands, and had their own political jurisdiction. The success, however, was not to be long termed.

This analysis of development based on the evolving combination of forces that shaped Tampico's urban milieu for the 1876-1924 period shows how the original "spirit" yielded to the forces of nationalism and foreign interests. Tampico exemplifies what was occurring at other major ports of Latin America during these years. The book suggests that local and regional collaboration was crucial to urban evolution; and contradicts the popular notion of urban growth as a peripheral result of imperialist North Atlantic economic forces. It also proposes that historians ought to concentrate on the study of internal and external forces in the Latin American city itself in order to understand its urban development. Although the global political and economic context is crucial, it does not direct the evolution of the Latin American city. This book also provides suggestions for further studies on the relationships among urban groups with external political and economic forces. Such bonding studies can lead to a better understanding of Mexican and Latin American urban life and history.

PROLOGUE

MAN OVERBOARD!

> The various towns and cities near this Port are in revolution, communications to all parts by land out. It is feared that this City will fall at any moment. We have no security and the American citizens as well as the French and English have appealed to me for protection. It is my opinion that an American gun boat should be sent here...
> U.S. Consul Edmund Johnson, 1876.

Federal troops in Tampico were on alert since March 1876, watching all ships arriving at the Port. Residents went about their daily chores, apparently with little concern over the new revolution started three months earlier along the Río Bravo del Norte, on their own state's northern border with the United States. Revolutions and wars had been a common feature of the nation for the past fifty three years, and few Tampiqueños expected any changes from this new rebellion.

General Porfirio Díaz, hero of Puebla during the War of the French Intervention (1862-1867), and twice-defeated presidential candidate, had rebelled again, now against president Sebastián Lerdo de Tejada. Díaz rebelled under the Plan of Tuxtepec, signed at Palo Blanco, a ranch in northern Tamaulipas, on 21 March 1876.[1] By 2 April, his troops took the border city of Matamoros, but under the constant siege of federal troops hastily despatched from México City, they abandoned it by 19 May. A confident Díaz took refuge in the United States knowing that his rebellion had spread throughout the nation. His followers, especially those in the important and populous central states, wanted his immediate return to México. Whether purposely or not, rumors spread about Díaz' whereabouts in the U.S. and to the method and seaports that he would probably use to reenter the country. Based on these rumors, President Lerdo tried to prevent Díaz's return, and proclaimed martial law in all states adjacent to the U.S., and also those along the Mexican Gulf.[2]

Brigadier General Jesús Alonso Flores, commander of the Tampico federal garrison, was in a most difficult situation. He was vocally loyal to Lerdo's government, but many of his officers differed from him. One of his most skilled and popular officers, General Juan de Haro, declared for Díaz, and left the city with his troops, setting up a rebel stronghold in the nearby town of Pueblo Viejo from where he began to prepare an attack on Tampico as his forces increased rapidly, especially from federal garrison defectors. U.S. Consul, Edmund Johnson, reported to Washington that many of the "lower classes are constantly leaving the city to join him."[3] The comment points both to General Flores's predicament, but also to Díaz's growing popularity.

Flores faced the reduction of his garrison. By late April, he had only 300 men left, most of whom were farm hands seized by force, and compelled to serve in the ranks. Their loyalty to the service or to the principles it stood for were highly questionable. Furthermore, as the rebellion grew, incoming despatches told Flores that Tampico was rapidly becoming the last federal stronghold in the state and in the Huasteca. Most towns and cities in the states of Tamaulipas, San Luis Potosí and Veracruz had already joined the rebellion. By the end of May, Tamaulipas governor, General Servando Canales, announced his defection to Díaz and decided to attack Tampico.[4] Still, Flores stood loyal to President Lerdo, probably as a measure to allay some local fears.

Tampico's business community shared the General's anxieties, but not necessarily his loyalty. Armed attacks and street fights were feared, and also the possibility of rioting and pillaging, all of which would imply destruction of businesses, forced loans, or even ransoms. Hence, business leaders joined General Flores, seeking quick alternatives to the desertion problem and to the possibility of an attack.[5] They met with the **presidente municipal** or mayor of Tampico and with the General to devise a plan that would preserve order under any future eventuality. Lerdo's government was not popular among these businessmen because many of them had supported Díaz's candidacy to the presidency in 1872. The Benito Juárez government then took strong economic measures against the port, hurting businesses and the city's livelihood. These leaders, although not forgetting their grievances against the government, worried over their homes and businesses, and over their city. The plan devised suggested their real concern.

The city government – included a **cabildo** or council and a mayor whose members since 1823 had been businessmen or professionals – decreed on 28 April that all able-bodied males between the ages of 16 and 50 had to report to General Flores for immediate duty. They also created a special fund to pay for a "vigilante" force that would protect businesses from looters. Both the U.S. Consul, and his vice-Consul, Luis de la Lastra, scion of one of the wealthiest families in the port, urged Washington to send gunboats for the "protection of foreigners resident in Tampico."[6] Their request was heeded, and on 4 May, the **USS Shawanut** entered the Pánuco river, and anchored opposite the city. All these measures brought some relief to the tense situation faced by the leaders, but the siege by rebel forces continued.

Three more warships anchored offshore on the Gulf during the first week of June. The flotilla was under the command of Admiral William E. Leroy, who was very busy receiving visits from General Flores, the consuls, the mayor and other city notables, all seeking his intervention to prevent the rebels from taking Tampico. But, the Admiral ignored their pleas; he clearly stated that his ships were there solely to safeguard the departure of American merchant vessels from the port, and that any military action of his ships or men would violate various international treaties. Verily, by 8 June, the three ships offshore left for Veracruz, leaving only one at Tampico.[7]

Meanwhile, General Díaz had arrived at New Orleans with the intention of returning to México as soon as possible. On 18 June, he bought two tickets under false names: one for himself, as the Cuban Dr. Rodríguez de la Boza - disguised with a wig, a heavy beard, dark glasses, and a large, fake belly - and for a companion, the American "Dr. Jones." They were passengers in the steamer **City of Havana**, owned by the Alexandre and Sons Company of New York, en route to Tampico and Veracruz.[8] Once aboard, both men kept to their cabin for the three days journey to Tampico. On 21 June, the steamer, as customary for ships with drafts that could not cross the sand bar at the Pánuco's entrance, anchored three miles offshore on the Gulf. Two Mexican ships, the gunboat **Independencia** and the trader **Constante**, were anchored nearby. Shortly after the steamer's arrival, the small steam tugboat **Irún** came out of the river pulling several boats loaded with federal soldiers on their way to Veracruz. On board there were also clerks, customs officers, passengers, and visitors for the **City of Havana**.[9]

One can only suspect the amazement of those aboard the ship, when suddenly, a naked man ran out of a cabin, and jumped off the steamer. It was Dr. Rodríguez de la Boza, who was apparently trying to swim ashore through the shark-infested waters, probably to avoid recognition by the boarding troops. The ship's captain, Samuel Phillips, immediately ordered a rescue operation, while passengers and visitors wondered about the incident. The ship's mail clerk, Manuel Gutiérrez Zamora, was told by "Dr. Jones" who the swimmer really was, and asked for his assistance. Gutiérrez Zamora called on Alexander K. Coney, the ship's purser to help them save the General. Meanwhile, Díaz was rescued against his will by the sailors, who brought him back to the ship. Then, Coney took him directly to his cabin avoiding all the people that had arrived. He tried to get the **USS Awattara**, leaving the port to join the flotilla at Veracruz, to take Díaz with them, but the ship's captain refused. Luckily, Coney and Gutiérrez Zamora kept the General secretly on board until the **City of Havana** arrived at Veracruz two days later.[10]

General Díaz's safe arrival at Veracruz, an essential event for México's historical future, was brought about by the support given him by the two officers. Their reasons for helping the General can only be inferred from the available sources. Gutiérrez Zamora seems to have been an admirer and advocate of the General, and was rewarded with honors and official positions for himself and his relatives. Coney's assistance was led by monetary or ideological reasons. Díaz might have represented the Mexican people; knowledge that could have reached him after several visits to México aboard the **City of Havana**, but he was also generously rewarded, which might have been the main reason for his actions.

Military officers visiting the **City of Havana**, heard of the event and told General Flores upon their return to Tampico. However, for him it was unimportant. A lunatic who swam naked daring sharks was of no real consequence when the city was under a siege. This lack of interest on the event allowed the **City of Havana** leave Tampico's jurisdictional waters, and to land safely in Veracruz. Tampico remained in the throes of anguish and economic collapse as the pro-Díaz forces blockaded land exits and disrupted the city's trade. However, this first Tampico Incident, as it has been called, became part of the Caudillo's myth in Porfirian laudatory historiography.[11]

Tampico remained close to General Díaz's heart for the next thirty-four years. He visited the city on various occasions, and gave it federal support to build a modern port and municipal facilities, done in Tampico earlier and much more extensively than at any other Mexican port. Furthermore, Porfirio Díaz's second wife, Carmen Romero Castell, native of the Tamaulipas' town of Tula, was related to one of Tampico's leading families, descendants of the Spanish engineer that had planned the port in 1823. Her uncles served as mayors, state and federal senators and representatives. One of them, Juan B. Castelló, was the state's last Porfirian governor.[12]

Historian Adalberto J. Arguelles argues that the general's patronage significantly hastened the economic development of Tampico and of the state. The city's business and political community, although scared of the revolutionary turmoil of 1876, supported Díaz and his regime as long as their interests met. Thus, they played a singular role during the Porfiriato, in Tampico, in the Huasteca, and at the state level.[13]

From Tampico, Díaz reached Veracruz, and from November 1876 until May 1911, he took control of México, originating one of the nation's most fascinating historical periods. The country's economic development complemented the growth and expansion of the financial and industrial sectors of Western Europe and North America.[14] "The combination of internal security, government concessions and subsidies, cheap and docile labor, and the natural resources of the country attracted..." foreign investments which totaled about one billion dollars by 1910.[15] Mining, railroad, and later petroleum, received the largest investments. Díaz' government and foreign businessmen confused capitalist priorities with México's national goals: subordinating the latter to the former. Within this economic atmosphere, Tampico searched for a loophole and asserted its presence.

The city was a natural port for México's northeast. Its economic hinterland included some major mining centers such as Zacatecas, Querétaro, Guanajuato, and San Luis Potosí. For many years, San Luis Potosí's officials believed that their capital could compete with México City as the major center for storage and distribution for the northern part of the nation if Tampico was its port, just as Veracruz served the nation's capital.[16] Most important for Tampico was its proximity, within 150 miles, to some of México's major oil deposits. These elements played an important role in the city's development, and deeply influenced its history. The Porfiriato started a new age for Tampico, and its economic growth continued uninterrupted between 1910 and 1940.[17]

The Tampico Incident of 1876 connects the city and the man who ruled over the nation for the next three decades, where he was the federal government. A government that could impose reforms and advance modernization, within its own definitions and without the slow and languishing methods of democracy. Thus, Tampico benefitted in its capitalist spirit, and its leaders were ready to tackle the capitalist revolutionary movements that would affect their city.

NOTES

1.México's independence in 1821 came after the Plan de Iguala was drafted as a pact and as a declaration of principles. Since then, most Mexican revolutionaries followed the tradition of Plans that presented the motives for their rebellions, and some even included the steps to be followed if the revolt was successful. The Plan of Tuxtepec was proclaimed on 10 January 1876 by Colonel Hermenegildo Sarmiento, while Porfirio Díaz was in the U. S. fleeing from federal troops. Then he crossed into Tamaulipas, and at the Palo Alto ranch reformed and reissued the plan. It accused Lerdo of serious political crimes, and treason. It refused to recognize his authority, and named Porfirio Díaz as leader of all rebel forces in the Republic, also recognized all state governors that would adhere to the plan. See Alberto M. Carreño, *Archivo del general Porfirio Díaz. Memorias y documentos*, v. 12, 96-100; Laurens B. Perry, *Juárez y Díaz: Machine Politics in Mexico*: 203; Mariano Cuevas, *Historia de la Nación Mexicana*, 968.

2.National Archives, Documents Consulate at Veracruz, Group 84, Number 183, Letter 11 April 1876, Consul Trowbridge to Assistant Secretary of State (hereinafter NA, DCV, #, date,); Carreño, XII, 267; Perry, 261.

3.Díaz had many supporters in Tampico. They mutinied, and on 11 June 1871, Federal General Sóstenes Rocha attacked the city. Close to 250 rebels were killed, and about 110 federal soldiers died during the battle. Three hundred thirty prisoners were taken, and three hundred were wounded. Rocha threatened civilians against supporting Díaz, still he won half the city's votes in that year's presidential election. NA, Documents Consulate Tampico (hereinafter DCT), 84, 16, 24 June 1871, Consul Henry A. Badham to Assistant Secretary of State; Gabriel Saldívar, *Historia Compendiada de Tamaulipas*, 251; Daniel Cosío Villegas (ed.), *Historia Moderna de México. La República Restaurada. La Vida Política* Vol. I, 163, 185, 270, 588-595. (Hereinafter HMM, vol. no., pages); Perry, 264.

4.Juan Manuel Torrea e Ignacio Fuentes, *Tampico. Apuntes para su historia*, 231-232; Carreño, XI, 320-21 and XII, 36, 156, 208-209.

5.NA, DCT, 84, 116, 14 April 1876, Consul Johnson to Assistant Secretary of State; Carreño, XII, 252; Perry, 269-270, 281.

6.NA, DCT, 84, 117, 28 April 1876, Consul Johnson to Assistant Secretary of State; Perry, 265. NA, DCT, 84, 14, 29 August 1873, Consul Johnson to Department of State.

7.The other U.S. warships were the **USS Hartford**, **USS Swattara**, and **USS Marion**. The **Swattara** replaced the **Shawanut** on the river.

8.The *City of Havana* was one of six steamers chartered by the Alexandre and Sons Line of New York, reputedly owned by President Lerdo through the Cárdenas Company. Beginning October 1874, this line connected the ports of Tampico, Tuxpám, Veracruz, Campeche and Progreso with New Orleans and New York. The annual subvention paid by the Mexican Government to the company for mail and passengers was $100,000 pesos. NA, DCV, 84, 6122, 10 December 1874, Consul Trowbridge to Assistant Secretary of

State; *La Reconstrucción* (Tampico), III, 1, 10 octubre 1874, 1; *The Daily Picayune* (New Orleans), 44, 228, 10 September 1880, 3:1; 292, 13 November 1880, 1:6.

9.This account is based on the story of one witness, Manuel Gutiérrez Zamora, "El salvamento de Don Porfirio frente a la Barra de Tampico." *Historia Mexicana*, 5, (julio-septiembre 1955), 68-86. Among visitors aboard the *City of Havana* that day was Cándido Rosa, a clerk at one of the important stores in town, who was city councilman (1878, 1879, 1885, and 1888), and also a mayor of Tampico for the years 1886, 1891, 1892, and 1894. Although no linkage has been established between his visit to the ship, and his successful career under the Porfiriato years, his staunch Porfirismo in 1876 makes that visit somewhat suspicious. AMT, Acta (Minutes) del Gobierno Municipal, 1878, 1879, 1885, 1886, 1888, 1891, 1892, and 1894. Also Carlos González Salas, *Del reloj en vela*, 218.

10.José López Portillo y Rojas, *Elevación y caída de Porfirio Díaz*, 117; Vidál Covián Martínez, *Cronología histórica de Tampico, Ciudad Madero y Altamira, Tamaulipas y de la expropiación petrolera*, 7; Nemesio García Naranjo, *Porfirio Díaz*, 195; Cuevas, 969-970; *HMM*, I, 879.

11.The Porfiriato has an extensive historiography. Two useful texts are Cosío Villegas, *Historia Moderna de México*, and Thomas Benjamin and Marcial E. Ocasio-Meléndez, "Organizing the Memory of Modern Mexico, Porfirian Historiography in Perspective, 1880s-1980s," *Hispanic American Historical Review*, 64, 2 (May 1984), 323-364.

12.The Castelló family was linked to Tampico since its foundation. Salvador Castelló planned the city in 1823. Manuel Romero Rubio, a Tamaulipas soldier during the War of the French Intervention, Liberal politician, ambassador to the United States, and Minister of Finance under President Lerdo married Salvador's sister, living in Tula and later in México City owing to his diplomatic career. His daughter, María del Carmen Romero Rubio Castelló married Porfirio Díaz on 5 November 1881. Her cousin, Salvador V. Castelló, was Tampico's representative at the State legislature in 1882, and mayor in 1883. He also served as councilman in 1877, 1879, and 1881. He was an important businessman: State agent for the Banco Mercantil Mexicano, and owner of a tugboat company which handled loading and unloading of merchandise. His brother, Juan B. Castelló, was Tampico´s councilman in 1878 and 1880, andserved as Guanajuato's Federal Congressman in 1882, yet assisting Tampico whenever he could. In 1896, he was the city's representative in the State Legislature, and served as the last Porfirian governor of the state. *AMT*, Minutes for the period 1878-1910.

13.Adalberto J. Arguelles, *Reseña del Estado de Tamaulipas*, 2; Leopoldo Zea, *Dos ensayos de Leopoldo Zea*, 80.

14.Fernando Rosenzweig, "El desarrollo económico de México de 1877 a 1911." *El Trimestre Económico*, 24; also his "El comercio exterior," *HMM*, II, 711; Luis Nicolau D'Olwer, "Las inversiones extranjeras," *HMM*, II, 973-1185; Cleona Lewis, *America's Stake at International Investment*, 173, 201-203.

15.By 1904, U.S. capitalists had invested 503 million dollars in México, rising to $1,044,600,000 dollars by 1911. Mira Wilkins, *The Emergence of Multinational Enterprise: American Business Abroad From the Colonial Era to 1914*, 613-614; Don M. Coerver, *The Porfirian Interregnum: the Presidency of Manuel González of México, 1880-1884*, 187-190; Luis Nicolau D'Olwer, *HMM*, V, 1090-1105, 1125-1130; Robert V. Kemper and Anya P. Royce, "Mexican Urbanization Since 1821: A Macro Historical Approach," *Urban Anthropology*, 8:3/4, 1979:270; Mario Gil, *Los ferrocarrileros*, 10-13.

16.Frederick A. Ober, *Travels in Mexico*, 419; NA, DCT, 84, 96, 28 February 1890, Consul Greathouse to Assistant Secretary of State.

17.Luis González Treviño, "Indices de geografía económica y social del Estado de Tamaulipas," *Boletín de la Sociedad de Geografía y Estadística*, 59, 5-6 (septiembre - diciembre 1944): 317.

It goes without saying that what distinguishes a town from a village is not size, but the presence of a soul. A mass-soul of a wholly new kind – whose last foundations will remain hidden from us for ever – suddenly buds off from the general spirituality of its Culture. As soon as it is awake, it forms for itself a visible body. Out of the rustic group of farms and cottages, each of which has its own history, arises a totality. And the whole lives, breathes, grow, and acquire a face and an inner form and history. Thenceforward, in addition to the individual house, the temple, the cathedral, and the palace, the townfigure itself becomes a unit objectively expressing the form-language and style-history that accompanies the Culture throughout its life course.

Spengler, *The Decline of the West*

1

BIRTH AND DEVELOPMENT

> The city is like a work of art. Its space is not only organized and constituted, but also modeled and shaped according to this or that other group's requirements, ethics and esthetics, that is by their ideology.
>
> Henri Lefebvre, *Espace et politique*

México's urban history is old. Its pre-Hispanic societies built cities on its coasts and central plateau.[1] The Spanish Conquistadors brought to the New World an urban design acquired through Iberia's long civilizing process that goes back at least to the twelfth century before Christ. The Mexican urban system was continued after the Conquest, reformed with Spanish and European elements, and spread throughout the territory later integrated into the Viceroyalty of New Spain. Cities such as Guadalajara, Mérida, Puebla, Oaxaca, Querétaro, Guanajuato and Monterey were founded during the long colonial period (1521–1821). Few port cities were created owing to both the geographical nature of the coasts which have few natural harbors, and to the requirements of Spanish mercantilism that concentrated all its overseas trade in just a few ports of the colonies. Veracruz, a port on the Gulf of Mexico, created by Hernán Cortés under the political circumstances of 1519, faced east to Spain and Europe; and Acapulco, a magnificent natural harbor on the Pacific Ocean, became the center for the Asian trade of New Spain and of Spain. These two legal ports served New Spain for three hundred years, and connected México to both Europe and Asia.

The Bourbon reforms of the XVIII century changed the strict mercantilistic policies of the Spanish Crown, and increased the Viceroyalty's economic productivity. The expansion of trade accentuated the need for more ports both on the Gulf and Pacific coasts of New Spain. The rebellion of the North American English colonies and the French Revolution had minor effects on the reforms, yet the ascent of Napoleon

Bonaparte to imperial power in Europe created havoc within Spain and its colonies, especially after 1808. The seizure of the Spanish king, and the imposition of a Bonaparte on the Spanish throne gave way to demonstrations of affection to the old regime, but by 1810, nationalist rebellions erupted in the colonies creating an economic upheaval that, especially in México, disrupted traditional routes for exports and commerce.

The Pánuco River became an alternate route for Mexican mineral exports, and discussions to build a town on its shores began by 1800. It was accomplished on the second decade of the nineteenth century. Tampico was this town, and its development began after Mexican independence, and continued to be intimately connected to national milestones. However, the young country would not be ready to perceive its national goals until late in the century. Tampico's residents worked for their city and region within the constraints of a weak national authority, of foreign attacks, and in the constant turmoil of the times. It is in this period that a trend appears placing local interests on a higher scale among the residents's priorities. The uniqueness of Tampico among Mexico's port cities began at its foundation, and evolved past the 1910 Revolution.

The Port on the Pánuco, 1823–1876

Tampico was founded as a trade center by its original settlers, on 12 April 1823. Most of them were residents at the nearby colonial town of Altamira, twenty miles north of the Pánuco's shore. Both settlements were located in the former Province of Nueva Santander, which after 1825 became the State of Tamaulipas of the United States of México.[2] At the southern end of a lagoon connecting with the Pánuco River, and in the Province of México, later State of Veracruz, was another colonial town called Pueblo Viejo. In the late eighteenth and early nineteenth centuries both towns were rivals for the control of the Pánuco River's trade. These towns might have remained sleepy villages had not the War of Independence (1810–21) given a great boost to the region's commerce. Armed bands disrupted land connections between northern and central México's mining centers with the official port of Veracruz. As a result, *conductas*, large caravans of mules loaded with silver, were driven towards the Pánuco River shores, whence European and United States's ships would take their cargo. This sudden traffic of wealth created an economic boom for both Altamira and Pueblo Viejo, and their commercial leaders began to vie for better arrangements to increase their profits when unexpected events developed.

The Viceroyalty of New Spain as well as the other major units of the Spanish American Empire were shaken by the political turmoil produced by the Napoleonic invasion of Spain in 1808. In an effort to free México from the Spaniards, Miguel Hidalgo, Ignacio Allende, José María Morelos, Guadalupe Victoria and Vicente Guerrero, creole and mestizo leaders of New Spain, led thousands of natives against the combined power of Spaniards and creoles. The viceregal armies were victorious between 1816 and 1820, but could not control the colonial territory. Hidalgo, Allende, and Morelos were captured and killed by 1815. Other rebels, especially in the southern provinces, carried on their patriotic struggle.

Unstable conditions prevailed throughout New Spain. Highwaymen and rebels disrupted land transportation, and Veracruz, too far away from the major mining centers, was unable to send them the basic production materials arriving from Spain. In 1815, the Viceroy ordered all shipments of mercury - essential to silver mining - to be diverted from Veracruz to Altamira near the Pánuco, thus providing a faster and less dangerous path for the needed mineral. In a completely unrelated action, the Viceroy ordered the establishment of a customs house in Pueblo Viejo, suggested by some of its residents, influential at his Court. Altamira merchants deeply resented this action on behalf of their neighbors, and vainly pleaded to have the customs house transferred to their town. Yet, the influence of the Pueblo Viejo merchants was too strong at the moment.[3] Spanish events, however, continued to mold the Viceroyalty's political situation, affecting the result of the Independence War.

In 1820, a military revolt among royal troops at Cádiz sent to fight American rebels forced King Ferdinand VII to restore the 1812 Spanish Constitution, abolished upon his return from French imprisonment in 1814. Its liberal provisions were rather inimical and upsetting for the creole and Spanish elites, for the Catholic hierarchy, and for many military officers of New Spain. These groups decided pragmatically to join the independence movement led now by Vicente Guerrero. On 24 February 1821, General Agustín de Iturbide, creole commander of the viceregal army, met with Guerrero, and together proclaimed the Plan de Iguala, a statement of principles under which Mexico became independent. Support for the Plan was almost unanimous throughout New Spain, and Spanish troops in Acapulco, Veracruz, and México City quickly surrendered. A new viceroy sent from Spain, Juan O'Donojú, arrived at Veracruz and realizing the impossibility of recovering the colony, signed a treaty recognizing Iturbide. He also arranged the departure of Spanish soldiers gathering them at the fort of San Juan de Ulúa in Veracruz, whence they were to return home. On 28 September 1821, Iturbide proclaimed Mexico's independence.

The Madrid government, however, did not support O'Donojú's action and ordered its navy to blockade Veracruz. Troops at the fort of San Juan de Ulúa attacked the port, and the large trade carried through it came to a halt. Merchants, traders, and the México City leaders decided to use alternate Gulf ports such as Campeche, Soto La Marina, Altamira and Pueblo Viejo. The last two, especially, received the bulk of the trade because exporters of silver and agricultural products, mainly from northern México, found the Pánuco ports safer and more accessible to their markets, located mostly in the United States. Only in 1822, more than one hundred vessels left Pánuco ports with over sixty percent of their trade slated for U.S. Gulf and Atlantic ports.[4]

More trade meant more profits, especially to merchants nearer the customs house. Altamira merchants, desperate to stop what they considered a great harm, decided to counteract Pueblo Viejo's control of the river's trade. They firmly decided to build a new town on the northern left shore of the Pánuco River, in a place earlier inhabited by Huastecan Indians, and known as *Alto de Tampico* (Old Tampico's Bluff). The location was closer to the river's mouth than either Altamira or Pueblo Viejo, and at an excellent spot for piers and wharves because it lays right across from where the Pánuco is at its widest and deepest. Thus, in 1821, Altamira leaders called on the new national government for permission to carry out their plan. However, a chaotic administration beset with innumerable problems arriving from all quarters of the territory, torn with governmental strife, and with almost no experience in the affairs of state, could not respond rapidly to their quest. The Altamiranos, however, found a sudden solution to their problem in 1822 when a military coup erupted against Iturbide, indicative of the chaotic conditions in the country. They helped the revolt and won a city for themselves.

General Antonio López de Santa Anna, commander of the national forces in Veracruz, and at the time an advocate of republican federalism, rebelled against the monarchy installed by Iturbide, now self-proclaimed Emperor Agustín I. The rebellion began in December 1822, when Santa Anna proclaimed the Plan de Casa Mata, and was immediately supported by independence and republican leaders. The plan called for a federal republican type of government.

From Veracruz, Santa Anna sailed with a number of men to Altamira arriving on 19 March 1823. He expected to assemble more troops in the Huasteca, and to obtain economic support from the wealthy merchant community in town. The Altamira businessmen, aware that Santa Anna's needs could be useful for their plans, asked his approval for their projected city. General Santa Anna was shown a blueprint of the new town and was told of the benefits of that it would bring the region. He gave his provisional consent, until he would officially be in control of the government, and received in exchange, the merchants' economic support for his "cause" of freedom. Santa Anna left Altamira to begin his long career as Mexico's strong man, and the new town on the river was built as wished by the Altamiranos, who as a sign of gratitude to the general named it Santa Anna de Tampico.[5]

The blueprint shown to General Santa Anna followed the traditional grid plan used by Spaniards in the design of their colonial cities. Salvador Castelló, a Spanish engineer, merchant and resident of Altamira, designed the plan for Tampico. The urban center revolved around a main square, where the official buildings, church and city hall, would be built. However, as customary for river and port cities planned by Spaniards, another square was made facing the river. Provisions were also taken for the future construction of piers. This plan covered an area of 3,436 hectares or 7,559.2 acres, with four east-west streets and six north-south streets that ended at the river's shore. Lots within city blocks were divided among Altamira merchants first, who had decided to move "en masse" to the new town. Lots were also given free of charge to other Altamira residents, who had given either time or money to clear the land for the project or who had helped build a road connecting the new town to Altamira.[6]

The city was set on a rocky, peninsula-like bluff overlooking the Pánuco and Tamesín rivers from a height that averages twelve to sixty feet, depending on its proximity to the rivers's shores. Two lagoons also border on the planned urban center. To the west, the Chairel Lagoon – the Tamesín River runs through it – empties into the Pánuco which flows around the city's south and southeast.[7] To the east, the Carpintero Lagoon borders the city, meeting the Pánuco through the Cortadura Channel. This lagoon developed into a major source of health hazards and pollution for the residents.[8]

The Pánuco River is one of México's longest, and its basin covers a large inland area. It flows from the mountains near México City, and meanders through the tropical forests of the Huasteca. Its last twenty kilometers serve as a natural political boundary between the states of Veracruz (south) and Tamaulipas (north) until it reaches the Gulf of Mexico. Its deepest and widest spot fronts Tampico about thirteen kilometers from the mouth. Both opposite shores along this final segment of the river grew in population and were urbanized after the city was built.

The Huasteca, a tropical, swampy, and mostly low-lying area, with countless species of plants and animals, as well as with some fertile and productive lands, limits Tampico's center and its municipality to the north, west, and south (across the river). This hot and humid jungle, teeming with myriads of insects, snakes, and other threatening fauna, made human habitation almost unbearable. Thus, the city was isolated by the natural milieu surrounding it, and its geographical terrain created a natural barrier for urban expansion that lasted well into the second decade of the twentieth century. Humidity is usually very high in Tampico owing to the lagoons – Chariel, Carpintero, Tamiahua and Pueblo Viejo – and the two rivers, which represent a constant threat of epidemic diseases such as yellow fever. Nevertheless, they are useful for rapid communications and trade with villages and towns of the region and upstream rivers. Furthermore, they are excellent hatcheries of fish, lobsters, crabs and shrimp. Marie France Prevot, a French geographer, observes that Tampico was founded on the only possible site capable of human habitation in the area. Thus, the geographical and environmental characteristics of Tampico were relatively beneficial to its development as it was not easy for other regional towns to compete with it in terms of their less healthy, unbearable or inadequate location.[9]

There are almost thirteen kilometers (about eleven miles) between Tampico and the mouth of the Pánuco River on the Gulf of México, which measures about three hundred meters wide. For centuries, this entrance was partially blocked by a formidable sand bar. Vessels with a draft no deeper than eight feet could pass the bar during high tide. Moreover, *nortes* (northers), strong and gusty cold winter winds that blow in the region between November and March, made extremely difficult the entrance or exit of ships, even with skilled local pilots manning the incoming or outgoing vessels.[10] Hence, up until the last decade of the nineteenth century, most ships had to unload their cargo on boats offshore on the Gulf for transfer to Tampico. The 1879 United States's Consul in Tampico reported that vessels "owing to the shallowness of the bar are unloaded at sea, three or four miles distant from the custom-houses, by the slow means of lighters." [11] This sand-bar was a major hindrance to the port's development.

The river networks were fundamental for Tampico's trade with its hinterland. Small crafts can navigate the Pánuco River for almost two hundred miles upstream entering the States of Veracruz and San Luis Potosí. The Tamesín River is also navigable for several miles upstream into Tamaulipas. West of Tampico, the Pánuco meets the Tamesín where its silt formed some islands that divided both currents for several hundred meters right across from the city. These river islands were used by Tampico merchants to build piers and warehouses, and for cultivation. Some years after they were used for more port facilities, and for the railroad station, without affecting the original city plan.[12] These communications made Tampico a most useful depot or warehouse after independence for imports and exports of the Huasteca region which covers five eastern states: Tamaulipas, Veracruz, San Luis Potosí, Hidalgo, and Querétaro. The city's hinterland reached further inland as far as Michoacán and Monterey, and even México City. Geography favored Tampico to become the natural port for México's northeast and for the Huasteca. If economics and communications helped its development, politics assisted its birth.[13]

Santa Anna's revolutionary success eliminated Pueblo Viejo's influence in México City. Altamira merchants did not rely only on the General's approval of their foundation plan. They also moved rapidly into the new power structure created by the federal system at the state and national levels in order to legalize their action, and to impede their former competitors any political move that could alter their plans. Thus, almost immediately after the city's official foundation in April 1823, the federal government (probably at the request of Altamira's envoys) decreed various measures that benefitted the port allowing it to attain immediate national recognition. In September, Tampico was granted permission to operate a **Receptoría Marítima** (Maritime Warehouse) - an institution that could receive and distribute imported goods. Veracruz and Pueblo Viejo delegates in México City fought this grant because the **Receptoría** could tax articles, and receive payments for them in a fashion similar to a customs house. Thus, the **Receptoría** could bypass the authority of the customs-house at Pueblo Viejo. Almost one year later, in November 1824, the Federal Congress designated Tampico as a **puerto de altura** (first class port), meaning it could serve Mexico's foreign trade and introduce foreign products in the country, thus reaffirming the power already given to the economic structure of the city. Furthermore, President Guadalupe Victoria approved the construction of the federal building that would house the Maritime Warehouse, and gave Tampico de Santa Anna an edge over its competitors in the Huasteca.

The battle, however, continued because the customs-house was still located at Pueblo Viejo. The Tamaulipas delegate to the 1826 Federal Congress, Pedro González Paredes, asked for its transfer from Pueblo Viejo to Tampico, owing to the conveniences of the new site. A presidential decree of 10 February 1827 granted his request; and marked the Tampiqueños' success. Pueblo Viejo representatives realized that Tampico win would eliminate their economic advantage decided to fight their enemy on the Pánuco. They requested Congress for permission to found a town across from Tampico, that was named Mata de la Morena - today Mata Redonda. Permission granted, they moved homes and businesses to the new location. But it served them poorly. Soon they recognized that Mata was no match for Tampico, and that their stubbornness was bad for business. Then, most of them moved to Tampico.[14] Luck, planning, and political influences, although not necessarily in that order, became part of the Tampico success story.

The Tamaulipas State government, influenced by Tampico's wealthiest residents, and by the potential economic advantages that a major port would bring to state revenues, aided and gave legal recognition to all actions on behalf of the city. In September 1826, Tampico's government was granted **ejidos**, rural lands that historically were part of the municipal realm either for communal service or for its native population. Furthermore, on 15 December 1826, State governor Lucas Fernández, gave Tampico the official title of **Ciudad** (city), an action that recognized an administrative territory known as **municipio** over which city officials would have control, following the Spanish colonial tradition. Thus, in Tampico, municipal lands and ejidos were part of the same grant given by State authorities.

The municipio (municipality) would be administered by a city council headed by a mayor, with headquarters in the urban center. The city and its municipality were divided into urban and rural boroughs, popularly known as ejidos. Tampico's geographical location did not permit a large municipal area - only 46 square kilometers. This territorial limitation added to the importance of the municipality's urban center and to its commercial nature, not allowing for the formation of a strong rural landholding or agricultural class, and also helping to define more accurately what pertained to the city proper versus its larger municipal features. Tampico is an example of a city defining the land or countryside. Thus, by the end of 1826, that is, three years after its foundation, Tampico had acquired some of the elements that would allow it to grow and develop into one of México's major ports.[15]

Other important elements necessary for the city's growth were of a different nature. The United States and the major European powers recognized México's independence, intent in filling up the economic void left by Spaniards. Consular agents were immediately named to those cities of commercial importance such as Mexico City, Guadalajara, Puebla and San Luis Potosí, and the traditional ports of Veracruz and Acapulco. Tampico, however, was also included, an acknowledgment of an international status recognition. The city's first consul, W.A.P. Ingraham, named by the United States in 1823 died within a year, and George P. Robertson replaced him in 1826. In the same year, Richard P. Bowden, was named British Vice-consul. Monsieur G. Tuger, a French resident and merchant, became France's commercial agent at the port. Five years later, representatives from European countries that had established commercial relations with México, were named to Tampico. Their presence brought the city a business and commercial renown which satisfied the founders' goals and propelled a local pride and interest in the protection of commercial values. These agents also served as important cultural links for many Tampiqueños.[16]

Numerous foreigners migrated to México, especially to port towns intent in profiting from business ventures, and maybe seeking a more adventurous life in the "tropics." Tampico was somewhat special because almost everyone in town was an immigrant. Most city "fathers" came from Altamira's municipality They were later joined by those from Pueblo Viejo and other nearby towns in the Huasteca. Furthermore, the "local" Mexican and "foreign" population of Tampico increased with newer immigrants constantly arriving in the numerous ships coming to town after 1823. The sixty four original settlers from Altamira swelled to more than sixteen hundred by 1826.[17]

Tampico's early history is also imbued by a nationalistic pride based on events, where not only the safety and honor of the city and the nation were involved. The last battle for independence, where Mexicans triumphed over Spaniards, finally forcing them to accept the separation of their richest colony in the New World, occurred at Tampico. President Vicente Guerrero, upon taking office in 1829, and aware that Spain planned an attack on México, decreed the expulsion of all Spaniards still resident in the Republic. The Spanish government, furious over the treatment received by its nationals, and expecting a collapse of the country owing to its recent internal turmoil believed that they could recover their profitable American colony, and decided to send a military expedition from Cuba under the command of General Isidro Barradas.

By July 1829, three thousand Spanish soldiers landed in an area south of the Pánuco River's mouth. Rapidly moving across land to Pueblo Viejo and Mata de la Morena, they reached Tampico. In August, the city was attacked and seized after some fighting. Meanwhile, President Guerrero had called upon his only Division General, Antonio López de Santa Anna, to repel the invasion. He sailed from Veracruz to the Pánuco, landed his men, and attacked the city held strong by the paniards. The Iberians, however, were tired, sick, and demoralized after their long haul through the Huastecan jungles and swamps, and could not endure a long fight against external and internal enemies - even resident Spaniards had attacked them in Tampico. Finally, on 11 September 1829, General Barradas surrendered to General Santa Anna in an elaborate ceremony that took place in the largest and better built house in town, right across from the harbor square. Ironically, the house was owned by Benito Castilla, a wealthy Spanish businessman and one of the city's founders. After the ceremony the square was named **Plaza de la Libertad** (Freedom Square) in memory of México's struggle for independence. This victory in Tampico gave Santa Anna the recognition that lead to his political supremacy ruling the nation eleven times between 1833 and 1855, and he was thereafter called **Vencedor de Tampico** (Tampico's Champion). For the city's residents, but especially its merchant community, the victory linked Tampico to a national event, a most welcome advertisement.[18]

Commercial and urban development in Tampico took place rapidly after Barrada's defeat. The city council discussed and implemented rules for architectural uniformity, squares's ornamentation, and sanitation and health services, keeping in mind attractiveness and safety for both residents and visitors. They reasoned that a good image of the city would provide more visitors and increase business. New houses and public buildings were rapidly built as well as pier facilities across from the Plaza de la Libertad, on both the Tamesín and Pánuco shores of the city. Already by 1835, Tampico had 231 houses made of stone, bricks or wood, and 1,201 **jacales** (huts) built mostly along the shores. There were also twenty one warehouses, seventeen clothing stores, sixty four mixed products stores, nine restaurants, two pharmacies, two candle-making operations, seven billiard-rooms, fourteen artisan shops, nine tailor shops, nine shoe stores, three barber shops, and thirty four other small businesses. These commercial enterprises serviced an urban population that had grown to more than 3,000 residents, and also thousands more from the nearby villages and rural areas as well as hundreds of visitors constantly arriving in town.

Tampico grew in political and commercial importance. New consulates and commercial agents from Prussia, Oldenburg, Hamburg, Sardinia, Austria, and Sweden joined the United States, England and France. Furthermore, the powerful city representatives in the State capital of Ciudad Victoria won for Tampico the honor of being capital of the state's southern district. This newly-created administrative unit brought state, district, and federal courts to the city, as well as bureaus of other state and federal units, which were managed and serviced by a host of lawyers and other bureaucratic professionals. These services enhanced Tampico's preeminence in the region, and state.[19]

Yet, the unstable political and economic conditions of México curtailed and disrupted the city's development. Rebellions, some of them occurring near the city, plus the attacks and invasions of México by foreign powers were at the heart of these obstructing circumstances. Five different revolutions began in or around Tampico between 1835 and 1840. In 1836, Texan ships failed to take the port during that rebellious state's war of independence from México. The "Pastry War" with France in 1838 also disrupted local life owing to French attacks to take the city, but the worst was yet to come.

On 20 May 1846, U.S. warships blockaded the port. After a long siege, American troops disembarked and occupied the city on 14 November, after General Santa Anna had ordered the withdrawal of Mexican forces from the town. This Yankee occupation lasted for two years during which the economic life of the city slumped because communication lines to the hinterland were disrupted and also internal commerce shifted to smaller national ports. Besides, few articles for export were available to the city's merchants, and the municipality's political life suffered under the control of a U.S. military commander, whose views were basically of a logistic nature. It would be interesting to delve deeper into this period because of its impact on city life and on residents, perhaps encouraging the regional spirit already present in Tampico. For example, after the U.S. invasion was over, the federal government ordered the closing of the port on four different occasions between 1848 and 1863, citing local political problems. The truth, however, was that federal leaders really wanted to punish Tampico's population and its political and commercial leaders for the support given to some of the nine revolutionary movements that developed during those years, or because town notables had endorsed either Liberal or Conservative policies and leaders, at the wrong time, when the opposite was in power in the capital.[20]

To make matters worse, the sand bar at the river's mouth grew larger. To remedy the situation, the federal government, in great need of the Tampico customs house income, moved the facility from the urban center to a point nearest the Pánuco entrance, a borough named La Barra (the sand bar). This federal action hurt the city's economy: merchants had to build new warehouses closer to customs, and piers were rapidly built for the boats now loading and unloading at this new facility, eleven miles downstream from Tampico. It was hard for stevedores, who were forced to move closer to their job, or pay for transportation to the new site. Thus, a small hamlet named La Barra grew around the customs facility, but without an urban environment.

In 1860, Manuel Gardette, Tampico's **Jefe Político** (political boss) – a governor's appointee with control over the municipal council and the southern district militia – stated that public buildings in Tampico were collapsing, that the city had no financial credit, and that streets and sidewalks were in need of repairs at a time when the municipal treasury had lost most of its income, mainly from property taxes and tariffs on imports and exports passing through municipal territory. The situation was further aggravated when on 23 November 1863, French troops invaded Tampico as part of Napoleon the Third's attempt to dominate México. Both the French Emperor and his trusted Marshall Achille Bazaine considered Tampico a valuable prize and a supply base from where attacks could be launched against the patriotic forces fighting the invasion in the Huasteca and in northern Tamaulipas. The city became a fortress and military headquarters until 31 July 1866, when French troops abandoned the country. Mexican forces captured Emperor Maximilian in 1867, and executed him at Querétaro. Thus ended the French Intervention and the abandonment of Tampico by the French. Their defeat brought both Tampico and the nation a political freedom unknown before, but economic conditions had worsened.[21]

Economic woes (1866-1876)

The political life of the city, despite the difficulties endured since its foundation, was relatively unchanged through time. Elections were held yearly for City Council positions that usually went to the most prominent members of the community; businessmen and professionals. A certain continuity of families and traditional ideas were particularly useful to maintain an urban spirit, attuned to commerce and capitalism and encouraged since the city's foundation. The councilors were interested in orderliness and fomented urban ornamentation. The impression of Tampico among some visitors in 1870 was that of a very particular small city. It was described as follows:

> Its streets straight, measured by cord, offer a model of symmetry. Most of its houses have that modesty seen in towns which are built hastily and in the midst of revolutions. Palaces, both in town and at La Barra, are few and belong to the rich merchants. Commerce and not agriculture, although fertile lands abound near the city, is the principal occupation of the Tampiqueños.[22]

The city, however, was much more. Tampico grew by 1870 to

one hundred thirty blocks along thirteen East-West streets and eighteen North-South roads. Two new plazas, one for conductas and another to the north, appeared. New buildings included a well-built city hall, a large Catholic church, and a new Presbyterian temple with an American minister. It had three hospitals: the Civil or Municipal, a military Infirmary, and a private clinic owned by a local Spaniards' organization. There were two cemeteries, one for Catholics and the other for non-Catholics. A central market building was under construction close to the piers on Riviera Street, that was considered Tampico's main commercial avenue where most major stores and warehouses were located. Two well kept municipal roads, one east to La Barra and the other north to the town of Altamira, connected the city and its environs by land. But, this outward appearance was fictitious.

There was a constant disrupture of the city's commerce owing to armed bands in the near areas, and many businesses were bankrupt or closed. Population decreased as people left seeking work elsewhere. Accordingly, municipal finances collapsed forcing lay offs, a growing indebtedness, and a loss of credit. The customs-house income that had financed federal projects in town, paid salaries, and helped state and municipal treasuries was given as security on foreign loans by the national treasury, thus drying up another economic source for the city.

A former governor of Tamaulipas and Tampico resident, engineer Alejandro Prieto, wrote in 1873 that Tampico's annual average trade dropped to $870,072.00 pesos, only 12% of its 1842 total of almost $7,000,000 pesos. The city's military buildings were in ruins, and even the bullfight and cockfight arenas were closed owing to the difficult monetary situation. The municipal income had not improved since 1868, when it had been $946.00 pesos for the whole year.

Business leaders felt that three factors, other than those above, had increased the economic difficulties. One was the poor economic policies of the federal government under Presidents Benito Juárez and Miguel Lerdo de Tejada. Another was Tampico's dependence on U.S. markets - started early in the century - which were in a depression since 1870. Probably, the worst factor was Tampico's isolation as a port. Ships increased in size yearly, and so was the sand bar at the Pánuco's mouth that did not allow their entrance. The few and poorly-kept roads that connected Tampico to the large cities of San Luis Potosí, México, Ciudad Victoria, and Tula (Tamaulipas's most important agricultural center) were in great need of repairs, and during the rainy season became impassable. Community leaders were at a loss over what to do about the lack of investments and the poor connections that were ruining the life of their city.[23]

National politics also affected this situation of disorder and disorientation. Many city businessmen who liked Porfirio Díaz had supported his presidential candidacy against Lerdo de Tejada in 1873-74, mainly because the federal government under Juárez and Lerdo had benefitted Veracruz and Mazatlán over Tampico. Both ports were declared **puertos de depósito** (clearance ports), giving them a monopoly over the foreign trade of the nation; they also received the silver **conductas** thus taking away from Tampico its largest export since the beginning of the century. Now that México was opening to the world's commerce after its long years of turmoil, the main port of Tampico was being punished by the federal government. Besides, other ports had begun to compete for Mexico's foreign trade. On the Gulf, two Yucatán ports, Progreso and Sisal, became important exporters of **henequén** (agave plant and fiber), and importers of foreign products. Also, the small towns on the United States-Mexican border began a profitable overland trade between the two countries that lowered prices of imported articles, thus substituting Tampico's influence in northern México.

The economic crisis also had an impact on the city's social

problems that were detailed in the Municipal Council Minutes or **Actas**. There was an increase of public drinking and use of marijuana (which had been sold freely at pharmacies until the aldermen decided to stop it). Sanitation and health services suffered owing to layoffs, which brought alarm to municipal physicians worried over the possibility of an epidemic such as the dreaded yellow fever. Moreover, many urban proprietors sold their houses and lots in order to get some money. The only buyers were the rich city merchants, who expanded their economic control over the town, and increased the social imbalance already present.

The 1876 Tuxtepec Revolution of General Porfirio Díaz had an immediate and negative effect on the town. City officials loyal to President Lerdo de Tejada would not allow the Díaz group any power or actions in city affairs. Furthermore, the rebellion stopped whatever little trade was still conducted with the hinterland. Rebel armies encircled Tampico as the last important city in the state that had not joined the rebels, and where the federal garrison and the city government remained steadfastly in favor of the central government. It was the lack of revenues, however, that brought a confrontation between the federal military commander and the business community. Under the impact of the economic reverses, and with no money for his troops, General Jesús A. Flores, exacted two loans from the merchants by instilling fear among them with the reasoning that the lower classes were "ready to join the invading party merely for a chance of plundering the wealthy of any nationality." U.S. Vice-consul Luis de la Lastra expressed the elite's fears when he called on the U.S. to send a man-of-war to Tampico that would protect them from pillage, yet no explanation was given as to whose pillage, because the general exacted four more forced loans from the businessmen, the last one based on an advance on the 1% of the following year's tax.[24] Notwithstanding the loans and "loyalty" to the Lerdo government, General Flores and his garrison soon switched sides, declaring for Porfirio Díaz immediately after he had triumphantly entered México City. The national revolution won, but the people of Tampico were not sure they shared its success.[25]

The economic situation of the city became desperate. Its exports dropped from $118,630.99 pesos in June 1876 to only $8,951.30 by September of the same year, The city treasury had no money to pay its employees, and many were laid off or continued working without any compensation. Of thirty policemen, only seven remained to patrol the city. In November 1876, twenty eight businesses closed their doors, including one of the oldest and most important import-export firms in town, Obregón and Successors. Streets were kept dark at night because there was neither money for kerosene nor employees to service the lamps. U.S. Consul, Edmund Johnson, reported that "the local conditions of this Port, in a mercantile point of view, is (sic) truly disheartening." [26]

Once the federal garrison favored the rebellion, the "loyal" city council was deposed and replaced by Díaz's supporters, many of whom had been in power during 1874, year in which they had supported the General's bid for the presidency. Elections for a new city council were planned for January 1877. The new mayor and aldermen were expected to cope with the economic crisis and with the problems associated to the city's capability to remain competitive with old and new competitors.

Thus, Tampico entered the Porfiriato. This national city born on the shores of the Pánuco River, in the Mexican Huasteca, whose primary objective was to become the commercial hub of its region, and whose urban spirit was based on capitalist premises was the center of great regional and international activity in its first fifty three years. Its commercial goals were rapidly attained as recipient and exporter of goods and wealth for the northern section of the country, and its importance was recognized by international governments. However, the city suffered the consequences of México's political instability, and paid dearly as the nation was invaded and subjected to constant plundering of its territorial and financial resources. Furthermore, Tampicos's business class supported the wrong party - beneficial to their interests - on several occasions, bringing upon them the wrath of the federal government.

It is important to realize that, although a class structure developed in the city between those who had and those who did not have, a similarity of interests kept them together in a stronger bond than the problems dividing them. The city was in the center of an extensive jungle environment, surrounded by swampy lands, rivers and lagoons. Agriculture within the municipality constituted a minute portion of the economic life of the city. It was so small that Tampico was an importer of agricultural foodstuffs to feed its residents. Thus, the primary activity of the city was trade, and engaged in all services needed to make it successful and profitable. The poorest groups knew that their livelihood was linked necessarily, just like that of the wealthy merchants, to a capitalist undertaking. Thus, the elements that made up this capitalist spirit had the appropriate environment to thrive among all residents. Even though, each class sought to benefit as much as possible from the profits available, they also realized how important it was to make sure that their actions would not hurt the prospect of Tampico's development.

The Tuxtepec Revolution came at a most difficult time for the city, but for some residents it also brought great hopes. General Díaz established a Tampico connection through his second wife, and through his adventurous return to conquer México. Maybe now, the federal government would come to the city's rescue.

NOTES

1.See the following works, among others: Sabloff, Jeremy A., *The Cities of Ancient Mexico: Reconstructing a Lost World* (N.Y.: Thames and Hudson, 1989); Ciudad Ruíz, Andrés, *Las culturas del antiguo México* (Madrid: Alhambra, 1989); Prem, Hans J., *El antiguo México: historia y cultura de los pueblos mesoamericanos* (Barcelona: Plaza y Janés, 1986); Séjourné, Laurette, *Un palacio en la Ciudad de los Dioses, Teotihuacán* (México, D.F.: Instituto Nacional de Antropología e Historia, 1959); Culbert, T. Patrick (ed), *Classic Maya Political History: Hieroglyphic and Archeological Evidence* (Cambridge: Cambridge University Press, 1991); Voorhies, Barbara (ed), *Ancient Trade and Tribute: Economies of the Soconusco Region of Mesoamerica* (Salt Lake City: University of Utah Press, 1989); Bove, Frederick and Lynette Heller (eds), *New Frontiers in the Archaeology of the Pacific Coast of Southern Mesoamerica* (Tempe: Arizona State University Press, 1989); Healan, Dan M. (ed), *Tula of the Toltecs*: Excavations and Survey (Iowa City: University of Iowa Press, 1989); Berrin, Kathleen (ed), *Feathered Serpents and Flowering Trees: Reconstructing the Murals of Teotihuacán* (San Francisco: Fine Arts Museums/University of Washington Press, 1988); Wilkar, Richard and Wendy Ashmore (eds), *Household and Community in the Mesoamerican Past* (Albuquerque: University of New Mexico Press, 1988); López Ramos, Juan Arturo, *Esplendor de la antigua Mixteca* (México, D.F.: Editorial Trillas, 1987); Castro Leal, Marcia, *Tzintzuntzan, capital de los tarascos* (Morelia: Gobierno del Estado de Michoacán, 1986); García Moll, Roberto y Daniel Juárez Cossío (eds), *Yaxchilán: antología de su descubrimiento y estudios* (México, D.F.: Instituto Nacional de Antropología e Historia, 1986).

2.Altamira was founded by José de Escandón in 1749 as part of the Spanish drive to conquer Northern México, begun in the sixteenth century, but which had not advanced past the River Pánuco shores. Toussaint, Manuel, *La conquista del Pánuco* (México, D.F., 1948); Chipman, David E., *Nuño de Guzmán and the Province of Pánuco, 1518-1533* (Glendale, CA, 1967); Meade, Joaquín, *La Huasteca Tamaulipeca*, 3 vol. (Ciudad Victoria, 1977-78), Volume I deals with the establishment of towns in the region. González Salas, Carlos, *Tampico, Mi Ciudad* (Tampico, 1982): 28-32; *Reloj en Vela* (Tampico, 1983): 29-32; Torrea y Fuentes, *Tampico* :102-103; Lemoine Villicaña, Ernesto, "Proyecto para la colonización de Tamaulipas en 1616," *Boletín del Archivo General de la Nación* 2:4 (1961): 569-582; Parodi, Claudia "La fundación de Santisteban del Puerto y el arribo de Garay al Pánuco: comentarios históricos y lingüísticos," *Historia Mexicana* 27:4 (abril/junio 1978): 616-636. Formation of Tamaulipas see O'Gorman, Edmundo, *Historia de las divisiones territoriales de México* (México, D.F., 1966): 15-19.

3.Meade, II, 10; Ward, Sir Henry George, *Mexico: Second edition enlarged with an account of the mining companies, and of the political events in that Republic to the present day* (2 vols.) (London, 1929), I, 267, 319, 322, 325, 326, 346. For conditions of the period see Navarro García, Luis, "Las provincias internas en el siglo XIX," *Anuario de Estudios Americanos*, 21, (1964): 332-333, 365; Brading, *David, Mines and Merchants in Bourbon Mexico, 1763-1810* (Cambridge: Cambridge University Press, 1971); Hammill, H.W. Jr., *The Hidalgo Revolt: Prelude to Mexican Independence* (Gainesville: University of Florida Press, 1966); Timmons, H. W. *Morelos of Mexico, Priest, Soldier, Statesman* (El Paso: Texas Western Press, 1963).

4.Meade, II, 24-27. Veracruz was not threatened until 1825, however, the port had been closed to all trade since 1821; Bancroft, 44. The trade with the United States through Tampico was not a result of a British policy as suggested by Tulio Halperin Donghi in his excellent *The Aftermath of the Revolution in Latin America* (New York, 1973), 57.

5.Meade, II, 29-31; Archivo Municipal de Tampico, *Actas de fundación de la Ciudad de Tampico de Tamaulipas y asignación de ejidos* (Ciudad Victoria, 1898). Hereinafter AMT, *Aft.* Also see Velasco y Mendoza, *Luis, Repoblación de Tampico* (México, D.F., 1942). The city's name was changed later to Tampico de Tamaulipas, Tampico de Santa Anna, and finally Tampico.

6.For the use of the grid plan in Spanish American cities see Hardoy, Jorge E. "La forma de las ciudades coloniales en la América Española" in Solano, Francisco de (ed), *Estudios sobre la ciudad hispanoamericana* 2nd. ed. revised (Madrid, 1983), 315-344. Also Chueca Goitía, Fernando and Torres Balbas, Leopoldo, *Planos de ciudades iberoamericanas y filipinas existentes en el Archivo de Indias* 2nd. ed. (Madrid, 1981); Sendegui, G. de, "City Planning in the Spanish Colonies," *Americas* 29 (February 1977): 1-12; Stanislawski, Dan, "Early Spanish Town Planning in the New World," *Geographical Review* 37 (1943): 94-105. For a detailed description of the Tampico plan and the lots granted see AMT, *Aft.*

7.The city is located at 22°16' north latitude and 97°49' west longitude. See article on Tampico in *Enciclopedia Espasa Calpe* (Madrid, 1926); Galindo y Villa, Jesús, *Geografía de la República Mexicana. Geografía física* (México, D.F., 1926), vol.I, 116-119; González Salas, *Tampico...*, 76. The Tampico municipality covered an area measuring 45 square kilometers. See Collins Rojas, Carlos, *Estudio del puerto de Tampico y desarrollo futuro* (Tésis de ingenieria, Universidad Autónoma de Veracruz, 1969), 8.

8.Dorbecker, Nano, "Laguna del Carpintero," *Boletín de la Sociedad Mexicana de Geografía y Estadística* 59 (1944): 225-233. The Cortadura Channel opened in 1837 under the name of Iturbide Canal, and made the city a true peninsula amid the surrounding waters. The Canal was built to force the Pánuco waters into the Carpintero Lagoon as a way to clear it and change its damaging nature. See González Salas, *Del reloj en vela*, 38.

9.Prevot, Marie France, *Tampico, geographie urbaine* (M.A. diss. Centre Nationale de la Recherche Scientifique, Paris, 1972), 14. For a description of the region see Vázquez de Espinosa, Antonio, *Descripción de la Nueva España* (1630) (México, D.F., 1944) and Von Humboldt, Alexander, *Ensayo político sobre el reino de la Nueva España* (1811) (México, D.F., 1966) 31, 41, 183, 295, 299. Nineteenth century descriptions can be found in Poinsett, Joel Roberts, *Notes on Mexico made in the Autumn of 1822 accompanied by an Historical sketch of the Revolution and Translations of Official Reports on the present state of that country* (Philadelphia, 1824), 205-209; Lyon, G. F., *Journal of a Residence and Tour in the Republic of Mexico in the year 1826 with some account of the mines of that country* 2 vols. (London, 1828). Also see Calderón de la Barca, Frances, *Life in Mexico* (1843) (Hudson, N.Y., 1970), 531-532; Norman, Benjamin M., *Rambles by Land and Water* (New York, 1845), chapters 7 and 8; Berlandier, Louis and Rafael Choval, *Diario de viajes de la Comisión de Límites* (México, D.F., 1854), 171, 218-223.

10.The Tampico Municipal Archive has numerous documents describing the effects of *nortes* on shipping. Wrecks occurred constantly at the bar whether by high tides, unskilled captain's orders, or by the effects of the winds on ship's sails.

11.NA/DCT/84, 10, 15 April 1879. Consul Cassard to Assistant Secretary of State.

12.A channel was opened during the U.S. occupation of Tampico along the Tamesín river west of the city. The Yankee commander ordered these works to keep the city's idle population busy - paying them a good salary - rather than having them as possible local enemies. The channel was to have some military purpose, never really stated. See Meade, II, 109. Yet, the Tamesín's silt covered the channel and formed the islands that were called Pitahaya, Zapote, and Moralillo (later Muelle). During the 1880s, the three islands were divided into lots and granted to city notables. Covián Martínez, 13.

13.For more details on the Huasteca see: Bassols Batalla, Angel et al., *Las Huastecas en el desarrollo regional de México* (México, D.F., 1977); Andrade A., Aníbal, *Huaxtecapán, el estado huasteco* (México, D.F., 1952); Baldizan, E., *La Huasteca potosina* 2 vols. (México, D.F., 1946); Meade, Joaquín, *La Huasteca, época antigua* (México, D.F., 1942), *La Huasteca veracruzana* 2 vols. (México, D.F., 1962), *La Huasteca poblana* (México, D.F., 1951), *La Huasteca queretana* (México, D.F., 1951); Péan, Guy Stresser, "Ancient Sources on the Huasteca," in Wauchope, Robert (ed), *Handbook of Middle American Indians* (Austin, 1971) 2, 582-602; Menéndez, Hilario, *La Huasteca y su evolución social* (México, D.F., 1944). For attempts to make Tampico center of a Huastecan state see: Meade, *La Huasteca Tamaulipeca*, I, 13-19 and II, 30-36; Norman, 99-100; González Salas, *Del reloj en vela*, 34-40. General A. Moctezuma, leader of a revolution in 1832, promised the creation of a Huastecan State with Tampico as its capital in order to get the support of the region's residents. A few years later, the leaders of another revolutionary movement proposed a similar plan; see Soto, Manuel F., *El nuevo estado. Necesidad de formarlo inmediatamente (de partes de Tamaulipas, Hidalgo y Veracruz)* (México, D.F., 1856) and Meade, *ibid*, II, 80, 118. Also see Alba, Rafael de, *Tamaulipas. Reseña geográfica y estadística* (México, D.F., 1910), 3.

14.Archivo Municipal de Tampico (hereinafter AMT), Expediente 65 "Receptoría Marítima," (1826); Meade, *Huasteca Tamaulipeca*, II, 41, 51; Torrea y Fuentes, *Tampico*, 95, 101; González Salas, *Tampico, mi ciudad*, 60.

15.Tampico's first mayor, named by the residents after moving from Altamira was Felipe Lagos. He was one of the six members of the State of Tamaulipas's Congress in 1826. Two other men from Tampico also held important administrative positions in the State's administration. AMT, Expediente 61 "Oficios," 2 August 1826. Yet, it was Lagos's influence that determined the recognition of Tampico as a "city." AMT, Expediente 58, 15 December 1826; Expediente 62, Decreto 48, "Determinación de ejidos y límites para Tampico," 23 September 1826. Contrary to the image of the ejido as a rural holding for the Indian population, its Spanish origins were associated to municipal lands granted by the kings. The urban center itself was already divided by 1826 into the *barrios* (boroughs) of La Riviera, Espartal and Salud. As population grew other boroughs were created.

16.AMT, *Aft.*, 1826, 1830. Also NA/DCT/84, 29 May 1824, Letter to Secretary of State; AMT, Expediente 61, 2 August 1826; Expediente 66, 6 December 1826. See Penot, Jacques, *Primeros contactos diplomáticos entre México y Francia, 1808-1838* (México, D.F., 1975), 69.

17.AMT, Expediente 51, 'Padrón general de la municipalidad," octubre 1826. See AMT, *Actas* (Minutes) 1826, 1827, 1828.

18.Escobar y Rivera, Manuel María, "Campaña de Tampico de Tamaulipas, año de 1829," *Historia Mexicana* 9:1 (julio/septiembre 1959): 44-96; NA/DCT 84, n.n. George Roberts to Secretary of State, 10 August 1829, 4; Meade, *Huasteca Tamaulipeca*, II, 59-78; González Salas, *Tampico...*, 38; Miller, 206; Pereyra, Carlos, *Breve historia de América* (México, D.F., 1973), 650-51; Priestley, Herbert I., *The Mexican Nation. A History* (New York, 1924), 302.

19.AMT, Expediente 126, 1835; Meade, *Huasteca Tamaulipeca*, II, 89; Cosío Villegas, *HMM*, II, 290; Prieto, Alejandro, *Historia geográfica y estadística del Estado de Tamaulipas* (México, D.F., 1873), 280; González Salas, *Del reloj en vela*, 71; Moreno Toscano, Alejandra, "Patrones de urbanización en México, 1810-1910," *Historia Mexicana*, 22:2 86, 164-165; Meyer, Brantz, *México, lo que fue y lo que es* (New York, 1844) (México, D.F., 1983), 396-97.

20.AMT, *Actas*, 13 noviembre 1839; Filisola, Vicente, *Memoria para la historia de la Guerra de Tejas* 3 vols., (México, D.F., 1849), II, 217-218; Nance, Joseph Milton, *After San Jacinto. The Texas-Mexican Frontier, 1836-1841* (Austin, 1963), 144-145; Barker, E. C., "Tampico Expedition," *Quarterly of the Texas State Historical Association*, 6 (1902-1903): 169-186. On the U.S. invasion of Tampico see Rives, George L., *The United States and Mexico, 1821-1848. A History of the Relations Between the Two Countries from the Independence of Mexico to the Close of the War with the U.S.* 2 vols, (New York, 1913), I, 306-307, II, 280. 292-93, 312, 656; Dufour, Charles L., *The Mexican War. A Compact History, 1846-1848* (New York, 1968), 215; Torrea y Fuentes, 217-222; Meade, *ibid*, II, 98-109, 131-155.

21.AMT, *Actas*, 1 enero 1860. The French intervention of México has an extensive bibliography. Among them see: Arnaíz Freig, Arturo and Bataillon, Claude, *La Intervención Francesa y el Imperio de Maximiliano. Cien años despues, 1862-1962* (México, D.F., 1965); Sheridan, P.H., *Personal Memoirs* 2 vols. (New York, 1887), II, 205-232. Also see Tischendorf, Alfred, *Great Britain and Mexico in the Era of Porfirio Díaz* (Durham, NC., 1961), 5.

22.Cosío Villegas, *HMM*, III, 46.

23.AMT, Expediente "Estado Corte de Caja General de ingresos y egresos del municipio para el año de 1868," Diciembre 1868; Prieto, 280-281. For the national economic policies under Juárez and Lerdo de Tejada see: Sinkin, Richard N., *The Mexican Reform, 1855-1876* (Austin, 1979); Roeder, Ralph, *Juarez and His Mexico* 2 vols, (New York,

1947); Perry, Laurens B., *Juarez and Diaz...*; Brantz Meyer, 396-397. U.S. Consul at Veracruz, M. Trowbridge, mentions that the difficult economic situation of the U.S. during 1873 had restricted its trade with Mexico, National Archives, Documents Consulate of Veracruz, 84, 6122, M. Trowbridge to Assistant Secretary of State, 30 September 1874. Plans to develop new roads linking Tampico to San Luis Potosí and Querétaro were started in the early 1870s. The road to San Luis was finished to meet the Tamesín River in 1878, but did not reach Tampico until the end of the century. The road to Querétaro opened in 1873, but it was impassable and in disrepair almost since its inauguration. See Martínez Covián, 14, 56; Cosío Villegas, *HMM*, II, 290-356; Coatsworth, *John H., El impacto económico de los ferrocarriles en el Porfiriato* (México, D.F., 1976), 30, 271; *RUCRF* 1877 (Washington, D.C., 1878), 746; *RUCRF* 1878 (Washington, D.C., 1879), 468; *La Reconstrucción* (Tampico), III, 9 abril 1878, 1. Transportation was problematic all over the nation. See Glantz, Margo, *Viajes en México. Crónicas extranjeras* (México, D.F., 1964), 26-27; Leal, Juan Felipe and Woldenberg, José, *La clase obrera en la historia de México. Del estado liberal a los inicios de la dictadura porfirista* (México, D.F., 1981), 56-64; Coello Salazar, Emilio, "El comercio interior," in Cosío Villegas, *HMM*, II, 772.

24.AMT, Expediente n.s., 15 julio 1877; Expediente n.s., 14 septiembre 1877; Expediente n.s., 30 septiembre 1877; Expediente 1171, n.d.; Expediente 1265, n.d.; *RUCRF* 1876 (Washington, D.C., 1877), 49, 765-766.

25.NA/DCT/84, 135, Luis de la Lastra to Assistant Secretary of State, 13 October 1876.

26.NA/DCT/84, 135, Luis de la Lastra to Assistant Secretary of State, 3 November 1876; 143, Edmund Johnson to Assistant Secretary of State, 1 January 1877.

2

HOPE AND DESPAIR: EL FERROCARRIL

> The Mexican people do not at present take any interest in the Panama Canal, as the railroad fever has taken hold of the minds of all thinking Mexicans...
>
> U.S.Consul A. J. Cassard, 1881

On January 12, 1877, Colonel Antonio Canales, representative of the Political Chief for the Tamaulipas Southern District, installed a provisional city council made up of the Porfiristas who held a similar position in 1874. They were nine businessmen presided by Gregorio Cortina, one of the city's major entrepreneurs. They decided to take advantage of their loyalty to Díaz by asking him for immediate assistance to help solve the difficult economic situation of Tampico. At their first meeting it was resolved to send an envoy to México City. Their choice was Colonel Ramón Obregón, chief of the Corps of Engineers and member of one of the city's wealthiest families. His task was to explain Tampico's problems to the President, and to implore his aid. However, after his arrival to Mexico City, Colonel Obregón discovered that he was not alone in his task. Most cities, regions, and individuals "loyal" to Díaz, immersed in similar problems, had also decided to send envoys.

Meanwhile, the provisional city council asked the state governor to appoint as judges to the Tampico courts, the same men who held those offices in 1874. The governor granted their request with a provision that their tenure of office would end by January 31. The judges were needed to oversee the January 21 elections, for which some bitter quarreling arose between two factions made up of pro and anti–Porfiristas. The pro–Díaz group won the election through corruption, with some help from the judges, and with the ominous presence of Federal troops in town. Complaints were filed immediately at the state capital that were not answered until December 1877, when the "elected" officials were finally ousted and replaced. These illegal officials were **Presidente municipal** Gregorio Peláez, who was accompanied by councilors José R. Osorio, Luis F. Llorente, José de la Luz González, Juan M. Maraboto, Salvador V. Castelló (uncle of Mrs. Porfirio Díaz) and Federico F. Shutz. The group waited expectantly for news of Colonel Obregón's trip, but it was a failure because he had not seen the President. A different method was needed to approach Díaz. On March 15, the council sent a letter to the General asking him to decree that Tampico would be a **puerto de depósito** (warehouse port) like Veracruz and Mazatlan, but there was no answer.[1]

Unknown to Tampico leaders, the federal government was planning great changes in the economic policies that had characterized past Mexican regimes. A new spirit of progress and modernity, of economic growth and development, took hold of the President and his cabinet. The regime, according to Leopoldo Zea, represented the new order aiming to enrich the nation, based on the wealth and advancement of the best and ablest Mexicans, as other great nations of the world had already done.[2]

A new national plan was in the making, where port cities would be highly important for its success. By 31 August 1877, the Tampico customs-house was ordered to renew the payment of 1.3% of its income to the city treasury. This was a measure of some relief for the difficult municipal economic situation, even though the amount received at first was rather limited. The economic malaise was, according to Tampico leaders, based on two main reasons. First, an extensive contraband trade was carried out regularly through the **Zona Libre** (Free Zone) during the past fifteen years siphoning away trade that might have come through Tampico. The second involved external actions: seventy eight percent of Tampico's trade was with the United States, and when in 1876-77 that country's merchant marine increased its freight charges, an immediate drop in the city's trade ocurred, which affected negatively the customs-house income. The city's budget for 1877 was a mere $2,567.00 pesos, with an outstanding debt of $16,000 pesos. By November, the treasury had only fifty five cents on hand.[3]

The city council could not solve the economic problems and its election had become a big political issue. Tamaulipas' legislature decided on the illegality of the January election, and ordered the removal of the mayor and city council members. Instead, they sought an "amparo" – a Mexican legal protection or stay – that allowed them to finish their tenure of one year in office. Thus, political problems effectively hindered the Tampico-Ciudad Victoria relationship for that year. Yet, 1878 brought some relief to Tampico.

Carlos Diez Gutiérrez, governor of San Luis Potosí, met in mid-January with several entrepreneurs seeking the construction of a railroad line between his capital and Tampico. Some meetings were held afterwards, implying that some arrangement would be formalized for the construction of the railroad. The governor was very interested in developing land communications with Tampico, and work continued on a road that would join the port and San Luis Potosí.[4]

The federal government was also attentive to Tampico's communications, and started construction of the Chijol channel connecting the Pánuco and the Tamiahua Lagoon, a large body of water lying along the Gulf coast southeast of Tampico. The channel, inaugurated on 15 June 1878, permitted faster connections with Tuxpam, a Veracruz port located about one hundred and fifty kilometers south of Tampico. Other federal projects involved the construction of a large pier started in June and took several years for completion, and the opening of the river's sandbar.

Natural calamities, health, and economic problems continued to disturb the port and its residents. On 17 August, a tropical storm destroyed the work done on all three projects, and floods wrecked the shacks of the poorest families living near rivers and lagoons. To make matters worse, yellow fever and smallpox epidemics decimated the municipality. Tampico's status as the healthiest Gulf port, partly owed to the measures established by its elite's interest in health and sanitary conditions, had badly deteriorated owing to the difficult economic situation of 1877. A new yellow fever epidemic killed about 20% of the city's population in 1879.

Besides these natural catastrophes, citizens were in great need of currency. All public and commercial services, trade, and businesses were affected. The city's merchants developed a plan, with the council's consent, to use commerce's IOUs as money.[5] Tampico's financial health was of paramount importance for the Huasteca and for the State. The governors of Tamaulipas and San Luis Potosí worried over the situation together with officials in México City. The city had national importance, not only for its trade and commerce, but also as a judicial, bureaucratic and military center with headquarters for naval and army units. The salaries of all the federal and military employees in the city and the region came from the resources obtained through its customs- house. The state also relied heavily on Tampico's income to support its treasury. Thus, the economic situation of the city jeopardized all state and regional productive actions.

It was necessary to pay more attention to Tampico's development, and to secure some of the markets it had lost. Better roads and means of communication with the port were essential, and had to be built. Agricultural exports from the city's hinterland, such as istle, fustic (yellow dye wood), sarsaparilla, coffee, sugar, and pelts, were in danger of being lost without good land communications. Those in existence were in constant need of repairs. Smuggling across the northern border towns had affected Tampico's exports, and the successful operations of the Mexican

National Railway - linking Veracruz with Mexico City - had detoured the silver "conductas" back to that city, thus, taking away Tampico's most profitable export and source of profits. For the past fifty years, roads connecting the mining towns to México City had improved, and the British railroad had made it easier to ship silver via Veracruz. However, by 1877, the price of silver dropped considerably in international markets because of the glut created by the discovery of the Nevada deposits. A decline in silver exports ensued, and also a great fear for its future value when several European countries and the United States debated the role that silver would play in their currencies.[6] These new problems created more headaches for the Tampico community.

Thus, when it was announced that Díaz's **Ministro de Fomento** (Secretary of Development), General Vicente Riva Palacio, would visit Tampico on 2 March 1878, there was general expectation and excitement. His arrival with a number of "personas científicas," (scientists or technicians) to inspect various federal projects and the construction of the road to San Luis Potosí, led Tampiqueños to envision a "thousand hopes, a thousand advantages, and a better future."[7] Elegant dinners and a grand Ball were prepared as part of the reception given the visitors by the business and political community. General Riva was kept busy between visits to the renewed federal projects and meetings with all the important businessmen and consuls in the city. Finally, someone from the federal hierarchy had listened to the plight of Tampico. Riva Palacio's visit was very useful. Back in México City, and in April 1878, he met with representatives of the Tamaulipas and San Luis Potosí governors, and signed an agreement approving a concession to build a railroad between the cities of Tampico and San Luis Potosí, the line endorsed by Governor Diez Gutiérrez. Now Tampiqueños could foresee a brighter future with the arrival of the train.[8]

Railroad projects and the city

General Antonio López de Santa Anna granted an exclusive concession to the Mosso Brothers on 22 April 1885 for the construction of a railroad line between México City and Tampico, but the project was never started. Another failed project ocurred in 1865, when a proposal made by the Mexican imperial government to build a railway between San Luis Potosí and Tampico financed by French capitalists was annulled by a victorious Benito Juárez.[9]

Not long after, the U.S. Minister to México, General William S. Rosencranz, urged the Juárez government to seek closer ties with North American railroad companies, in order to strengthen communications between the two countries. On 28 March 1869, he asked permission from the Mexican government to have two trunk lines built: one between México City and Tampico, the other between the capital and Antón Lizardo, an excellent Gulf site south of Veracruz. Rosencranz wanted to press "American enterprises up to, and within México wherever it can profitably go...(that) will give us advantages which force and money alone would hardly procure. It would give us a peaceful conquest of the country."[10] Yet, his plans had to wait until more capitalists from his country would be interested to invest in México. Despite the lack of investors, the news about the Rosencranz plan and the city's future prosperity brought Tampico not loads of dollars, but a "large number of strolling vagrants from south Texas and Tuxpam (also Americans)...(who) are very persistent in their demands for assistance and relief."[11] These North Americans - mostly Southerners - were not Rosencranz's investors, but became an immediate part of Tampico's social problems.

The concession granted to build a railroad line between San Luis Potosí and Tampico would have connected initially the towns of Ciudad Valles o del Maíz (Corn City), an important San Luis Potosí state agricultural center, and Tantoyuquita, a small town lying on the Tamesín

River's shores. From it, boats would transport trade and passengers to Tampico. On 5 May 1878, a group of engineers arrived at the port to begin surveying the line. Materials and equipment were ordered from England and the United States, whence these were to be shipped to Tampico, thus creating jobs at piers, and generating a host of other service-related chores and enterprises. The construction of the line included the hiring of hundreds of workers and the use of many carts to haul the materials from Tampico's piers three hundred miles inland to Ciudad Valles, where the construction would start. The project began immediately, with positive effects on the port. During 1879, one hundred-one vessels entered Tampico, fifty-six of them from the United States loaded mostly with construction materials. Trade increased so rapidly that the city council had to rent a warehouse to assist in their safety, and to take advantage of charging for all arriving imports. The Tampico "Junta de Comercio" (Board of Trade), a private business organization founded in the 1830s, also began construction of a new and larger warehouse for its members's use.[12]

News of the port's prosperity spread throughout the Huasteca bringing numerous Mexican immigrants, both entrepreneurs and laborers, to cash in the future riches that railroad and pier activities would provide. Between 1879 and 1881, a series of projects involving Tampico were presented to the municipal, state, and federal governments for their approval. Charles S Gunter, an American immigrant, wanted to build a channel connecting the federal pier - located on one of the islands across the city - to the shore below the Plaza de la Libertad. Another project presented by Benito Zorilla, a wealthy Spanish resident, was the construction of a trolley pulled by mules from the piers to the northern residential areas.[13]

In late nineteenth century, modernity implied industry, jobs, communications, new constructions, railroads, and other elements diversified by the perception of the social groups. Modernity had finally arrived in Tampico. The increasing popular feeling was that economic conditions had changed for good, and forever. New technology was to assist the modernization process. In 1870, a concession for a submarine cable between Tampico and Galveston, Texas was granted to a North American company. In 1878, a station was built for the cable at the small village of La Barra, but the system was never finished. A new cable company organized in New York in 1880 conceived a more ambitious plan to connect South America and the United States through relay stations, one of which was to be in Tampico, the most important link between Matamoros and Veracruz. The system was built and completed by 10 March 1881. On its inauguration, congratulatory messages were sent from New York to President Díaz and to the governor of Tamaulipas. Out of the La Barra station a similar message was sent to New York's mayor. Not long after, a second cable line was installed between Tampico and Havana, Cuba. The importance of this new communications systems was hailed as a major step to improve trade relations between the United States and México. A third cable line system from Galveston through Tampico to South America began in 1881.

Soon also telephones appeared in Tampico. Daniel Fernández, a local merchant, asked the city council for a concession to build a telephone system. Although limited in its coverage because it served only City Hall and several business firms, it was approved and inaugurated on 17 May 1881. Soon, two other telephone systems were approved by the city council. One was owned by Juan José Viñas, the Spanish Vice-consul and a very wealthy resident businessman; the other belonged to the Mexican Central Railway Company, and connected its offices that were scattered throughout Tampico. When in May 1883, D.S. Haines - an American entrepreneur - asked for a telephone and telegraph concession, it was rejected by the council because of the previous concessions.[14]

National transportation reforms also assisted in Tampico's development. Porfirio Díaz decided in 1880 to leave center stage, and allowed his yeoman, Tamaulipas-born and intimately connected to Tampico General Manuel González, to become México's president for the 1880-1884 period. Soon after, great news reached the city, when newly appointed **Ministro de Fomento** (Secretary of Development) Porfirio Díaz – decided to renew the practice of paying subsidies to passenger lines so that they would include México in their routes. Steamship companies such as the Alexandre & Sons of New York together with lines from Spain, France, Germany and Great Britain, signed contracts with the government to stop at Tampico and at other Mexican Gulf ports.[15]

A lighthouse for the Pánuco's entrance was planned in the 1870s, but neither the permit nor the money for the structure were granted by the federal government. Now, the increase in the port's maritime traffic during the railroad works required its immediate construction, and a new request was made to México City that was denied again. Instead, permission and materials were granted to build a lighthouse at the Gulf island of Lobos, which lies between the Panuco's mouth and Túxpam. The ship carrying the materials for that installation had an accident near the river's entrance in 1882. The port authorities were notified of the incident, and measures were taken to assist it the ship. However, the salvage crew realized the ship's cargo, and advised city councilors, who immediately gave orders to have the ship towed into the harbor. Once the materials were unloaded and secure in Tampico, the mayor called on the federal authorities to allow them to keep the lighthouse on the excuse that the port needed it more than Port Lobos. México City accepted the Tampico fait-accompli and granted the permits and tax-exemptions for the construction of the lighthouse. Tampico businessmen contributed with money for all the other materials needed for the works. The structure was built rapidly, and was finished by 1 February 1883. Minister Porfirio

Díaz congratulated the city for the successful completion of its lighthouse.[16]

Many newcomers came to the city trying top cash in the economic prospects that seemed so real to all. Mexicans and foreigners arrived, increasing Tampico's population, and forcing its expansion. Even with epidemics such as yellow fever and smallpox, the city increased to 6,996 inhabitants by 1879. Most immigrants moved into the poorest neighborhoods where they built rows of shacks on empty and marshy lots in the periphery of the urban center. An indication of the changing urban economy was a petition made by bakery owners to the city council asking for a rise in the price of bread. They had two reasons for this plea: salaries had gone up without any price increases on the price of bread since 1856, and higher demand for their product forced them to seek more employees, but they could not find them to work in their stores owing to the need for workers at piers and at various city warehouses.[17]

The federal projects also brought money to city coffers. Municipal expenses diminished because some of its service units, such as the Municipal or Civil Hospital, had found enough paying clients to provide for their expenses, i.e. the railroad companies signed a contract with the hospital to provide health care to its employees. Income also increased at the customs-house between 1879 and 1882. The 1879-1880 revenues rose to $432,235.61 pesos, but those for the 1882-83 year jumped to $1,009,759.16 pesos, an increase of more than 50%. Tampico received from its 1.3% in customs–house allowance an increase that went from $5,619.55 to $13,126.87 pesos in those three years. By 1881, the city was able to pay most of its $16,000 pesos debt, reducing it to only $3,639.85 pesos. Thus, a renewed confidence in Tampico brought its officials and business leaders hopes that their modernization dreams could be attained.[18]

It was rumored in early 1881, and later confirmed by México City newspapers, that plans were being drawn to build a jetty system in Tampico similar to those already in operation both in Europe and the United States. When built, these jetties or **escolleras** would finally allow ships to enter the Pánuco without all the inconveniences that the sandbar created. It was a simple, but expensive, system. By providing an enlarged mouth to the river, the silt carried downstream by the current is moved further out into the Gulf to deeper sites. Thus, the sandbar is eliminated and ships with deeper drafts can enter the river. In March 1881, the New Orleans *Daily Picayune* announced the departure for Tampico of Captain Joseph Eads, one of North America's foremost engineers, who had built the Mississippi River's jetties. He was in charge of a group of engineers that would survey Tampico's harbor under a mission for the U.S. government. His arrival in Tampico, happily welcomed, encouraged city leaders to believe that once the project was approved and underway, their city would finally take over Veracruz, México's major port.[19] It should be noted that most of these infrastructural projects, port surveying, and jetties, were really part of the railroad company's plans underway in México that were supported by the federal government.

American railroad entrepreneurs were among the first to take advantage of the new economic policies implemented by President González and Minister Díaz after 1880. This opportunity for capital investment by railroads came luckily when companies were bitterly fighting over expansion in the American Southwest. One of the most aggressive firms was the Atchison, Topeka and Santa Fe Company. Its management began to extend their tracks to the South faster than any other railroad in the United States, and México became part of their southern expansion plan. The company's aim to enter México was to provide an alternate route to reach the American West. According to S.F. Van Oss, an 1890s expert in railroad investments, "we clearly perceive one great purpose – the intention to make the Atchison the great connecting link between Mexico, Southern California, the Rockies, and the entire Southwest."[20] Yet, the Atchison plans were marred by competition from other powerful railroad groups such as the Gould-Dillon, the Pierce-Huntington, and the Morgan-McComb, all of which had similar aims. By 1880, several rail lines neared the Mexican border. Agents from known and not-so-well known railroad companies travelled to México City, to state capitals, and to the major urban centers, seeking federal, state and municipal concessions and tax-exemptions. Many were granted, but the lack of investment capital or investors, and in some cases lack of good publicity about these projects, led to many failures. Moreover, the objectives of the major U.S. railroad companies changed to satisfy or avert new domestic conditions, and several decided not to complete their original plans. Despite these problems, some companies did enter México, and built important roads and networks.[21]

Robert B. Symons, the Atchison's agent in México, won a concession from the Ministry of Public Works on 11 May 1880, to build a line between El Paso, Texas and México City. Immediately a new company was incorporated in Massachusetts, affiliated to the Atchison, and named the Central Mexican Railway. Its first task was to supervise the construction of the road, and to manage it. The president of the Central Mexican Railway was to sit on the Atchison's board as one of its vice-presidents. Symons also requested the concession for two trunk lines to the ports of Tampico on the Gulf and San Blas on the Pacific, to be built prior to the completion of the main line. The request fulfilled one of Atchison's objectives: to cut the distance between U.S. oceanic shores by using México as a shorter route. This plan included use of a fleet of steamers, company-owned, to travel between New Orleans and Tampico, where products from the East coast would be transferred by train to San Blas, via San Luis Potosí. At the Pacific port, another fleet of steamers would receive the products for the California coast. Yet, before the line to Tampico was finished, a management reorganization owing to a change of investors at the Atchison headquarters in New York eliminated the plan. The Symons's concession included a Mexican government subsidy of $9,500 pesos per kilometer or about $15,200 dollars per mile. The subsidy was to be paid from a 6% receipt taken by the nation's customs-houses. Importers' duties increased by 6% more to insure construction of this new Mexican railroad.[22] Thus, México was paying for a railroad network that would profit only foreign investors, and not the nation.

The strong presence of the Atchison Company in México was well planned. Its agents visited the governors of the states through which its roads would run, especially Tamaulipas and San Luis Potosí. They also visited Tampico authorities to enlist their support when requesting federal and state concessions, and also seeking local grants. There was general surprise in governmental circles when in September 1880, an obscure official at the Public Works Ministry granted a concession for the San Luis Potosí-Tampico line to the Southern Pacific Railroad Company, owned by the Huntington group. Newly named Minister Díaz quickly intervened upon request from the involved state governors and from Tampico officials, and reversed the award on 5 December 1880, on behalf of the Mexican Central Railway. He also announced his plan to visit Tampico in the near future. Those events point to the powerful influence that the Atchison was gaining in the economic activity of the city, and the Huasteca, with the support of the local, state and national elite. The port was an important link in the Atchison, Topeka and Santa Fe Railroad plans for its Mexican venture.[23]

Díaz's announced visit to Tampico raised great expectations. In an 1880 farewell speech, outgoing **Presidente Municipal** (mayor) Julio R. Osorio, stated that the economic situation had remained extremely disturbing, although some improvements were noticeable. He also expressed Tampico's elite wishes by saying that

> Our hope lies in the construction of the railroad line that will connect us with the capital of the State of San Luis Potosí, and also in the channeling of the Sand-Bar at the entrance of this Port. Yet, only great entrepreneurs under the shadow of the present government of the Republic can make such grandiose works...soon, our new Minister of Development and Public Works, citizen General Porfirio Díaz will honor our city...there is much we can expect from this distinguished visitor.[24]

The mayor was keenly aware that only foreign capital could undertake such expensive projects; but, he knew that the Díaz regime had to support and protect them. To the Tampico business community, Díaz's patronage was an absolute requirement for the city's development.

On 27 April 1881, Minister Díaz arrived at the port, and was received with great celebrations. That night, a banquet and dance were held in his honor. During his speech, he affirmed the use of his influence "upon the Supreme Government so that measures to enlarge and enrich this Port will be taken."[25] On the 28th, Díaz ordered a federal dredger to be sent toTampico. It would clear the channels connecting the Chairel and Chijol lagoons with the Pánuco so that these waterways would be open for Tampico's trade with other areas of the Huasteca. He also ordered the Port Captain to provide a full report of the facilities, properties, and islands that lined the shores of both the Pánuco and Tamesín rivers as a first step to plan the port's development. Thus, Díaz's presence in Tampico, and his continued interest after leaving the city had a strong influence and was a motor for the city's growth.

Before federal authorities received the report wanted by Minister Díaz, a problem developed over jurisdiction of the Pánuco River islands located right across from the city. Surveyors for the Mexican Central Railroad line arrived in Tampico under the direction of the road's superintendent, engineer Santiago Harrington. They were followed by a large shipment of equipment sent from England which created a flurry of activity at the port. Mr. Harrington asked the city council - and

Tampico's Federal District Court - for the cession of the two large islands on the Pánuco, called Zapote (later Muelle) and Moralillo. On 2 May 1881, Presidente Municipal Luis F. Llorente transferred the islands in perpetuity to the railroad company, without consulting the other members of the council nor the federal court. State and federal authorities were appalled, and rejected this action on the principle that these islands were not under Tampico's domain, but were national lands. Llorente was accused of trespassing his political authority and benefitting personally from this action. Tamaulipas's governor ordered his immediate removal from office in late August, but he held to his post until 15 September, date of his letter of resignation. A plausible reason for this delay can be found in the federal government's new ideology which protected investors. Although the authorities opposed Llorente's action, they did not want to interfere with the railroad company's project, which if cancelled would hinder both local and national development. Therefore, the Tampico Federal Court allowed the city government to cede the islands asked by the company not on perpetuity, but for an indeterminate number of years.[26]

The problem with the islands brought about a heated confrontation between two sectors of the Tampico business community. Several of its members owned lands in these islands, and saw both the Llorente and federal actions as violations of their property rights; they had been deprived without due notice or compensation. Others, not directly affected, argued that the mayor could not dispense of lands considered part of the national domain. Still, a third group supported Llorente's action and the federal court's ruling, based on their support of foreign capital which was necessary for the city's and progress. If these foreign capitalists were not given the resources and facilities, modernity for both city and nation would be unattainable. This discussion at the local level is indicative of one of the main problems of late nineteenth century

México and elsewhere in Latin America. Local business and political forces had to make a choice - owing to their lack of capital for investments - between the integrity of the nation, its institutions, and the growth and future economic development that foreign enterprises and capital would generate.[27] The December 1880 elections were the battleground where opposing forces faced each other for control of city politics and ideology. However, the New Year soothed the debate as news arrived that Tampico was being considered as a branch or terminus for other railroads, for new investments, and implying that the river-islands' problem would not hinder Tampico's future.

Three concessions for railroads to run via Tampico were granted by both federal and state governments. One of these grants brought great interest because it would link Tampico directly with the U.S. border. It was awarded in 1881 to the New York, Texas and Mexican Railway, also known as Count Telfner's road, to connect Tampico and Galveston, Texas, with stops at Ciudad Victoria, Matamoros, and Brownsville. By December, company engineers began surveying the route, but in January 1882, the concession was sold to a Mr. Héctor De Castro. Lack of investors forced De Castro to stop the project. A second award was received by the Jay Gould–Degress group, under the name of Mexican Oriental Interoceanic and International Railroad. The line would start at Laredo, on the U.S. side of the border, then enter México through Tamaulipas and cross Nuevo León and San Luis Potosí states, bridging the Pánuco River about sixty miles west of Tampico. The port would be connected to it by a branch line somewhere along its way to México City. This line's fate was similar to Count Tefler's for similar reasons: lack of investors and change of plans. By 1882, the only successful railroad award was held by the Atchison, Topeka and Santa Fe company.[28]

Despite failures, the concessions were a possibility for the future, and Tampico residents needed to believe in it. The roads would fulfill the long-demanded communications for the port to compete with the northern border cities and with Veracruz, and to serve its former hinterland. The continued economic recovery which followed the rumors and news of railroad concessions supported residents' perceptions. Immigration continued strong when the Mexican Central Railway began using its steamers to bring workers from New Orleans and Galveston; Mexicans continued streaming into the city. Editorials from Tampico's newspapers encouraged immigration, and called upon residents to give new arrivals the best possible welcome; they also appealed for the creation of new jobs. Already in 1882, railroad works employed about 4,000 men.

This population increase led to a physical expansion of the city. New facilities and homes appeared both in the downtown and in the periphery of the urban core. The Continental, a new hotel owned by Americans, opened near the main square. It had reasonable rates, and an excellent restaurant headed by an experienced French chef.[29] But, the demographic growth also created problems for the public services. Tampico's government did not have the capital nor the resources to build new facilities needed for its residents and for the newcomers.

Local entrepreneurs tried to fill in these urban needs. Tampico lacked an aqueduct. A town without running water could not fit the image of a modern city, and Enrique Castillo, a young local businessman, supported by U.S. investors, won a permit from the city council to build a plant on the Tamesín River that would deliver water to city houses through underground pipes.[30] Other Tampico businessmen were involved in the telephone and telegraphic systems of the city.

National banks, recently formed with foreign capital, came to the assistance of Tampico's economic and financial activities. These institutions began to branch out throughout the country urged both by federal and state governments in need of their services. In June 1882, Salvador Castelló, one of the city's leading businessmen and uncle of President

Díaz's second wife, became the Tamaulipas agent of the Banco Mercantil Mexicano, with headquarters in Chihuahua. That same year, the federal government ordered the opening in Tampico of a branch of the Monte de Piedad, an official pawnbroker and savings institution, dating to colonial times to help the poor against usury. Other banks also opened branches in Tampico naming agents among the local businessmen. This banking interest is further proof of the impact that Tampico's railroad construction news had created in México City where the port was seen again as an economic center for the Northeast.[31] Although signs of prosperity abounded, the future was not as rosy as expected.

Challenges to economic growth, 1880-1890

México's ruling elite was excited over foreign investments entering México after 1880. For them, the country would attain its rightful place among the nations of the world. Many would be able to enjoy personal and national preeminence fitting their expectations for modernity. Still, some caution existed toward United States enterprises and capitalists. Mexican losses after the war with the United States had left a deep resentment, and fears of further imperial behavior by Americans had not disappeared from the general public nor from the leaders' minds. Some Tampiqueños shared these anti-American ideas, yet these had been somewhat ameliorated by the continued presence of U.S. nationals since the city's foundation in 1823. A less tense relationship existed in Tampico between North Americans and Mexicans, an attitude that became of paramount importance for U.S. investors.

The association between Tampico and the U.S. began early in the nineteenth century. The Pánuco was visited constantly by American ships long before Tampico was as a port. For example, fifty-two U.S. vessels entered the river between July and December 1822.[32] Furthermore, Tampico's first U.S. Consul was sent directly from Washington, rather than selected among local businessmen as it was customary among commercial nations. By the 1830s, a substantial group of American-born immigrants settled in Tampico, mainly from the recently acquired Spanish territories of Florida and Louisiana. Most of them had Spanish or French surnames, but held to their U.S. citizenship for a long time or for the rest of their lives. Probably, the 1829 comment of U.S. Consul George A. Robinson to the State Department that "there is a good deal of American property in this place" was related to this American presence in Tampico.[33] Robinson was replaced in 1832 by Franklin Chase. He was a trader and businessman, recently moved to Tampico, who held to the position until 1870. Chase was a significant participant, and a strong member of the business elite of the city, sharing and supporting the its spirit throughout all those years.[34]

Americans were the second largest group of foreigners, after Spaniards, in late nineteenth century Tampico. Of 338 foreigners in 1844, 46 were U.S. citizens. This number increased to 53 in 1855, and to 69 in 1867. (See Table 2). Interestingly, and in the words of Tampico's French Consul, a good number of them were "people of color." They occupied a middle class position owing to their occupational skills as mechanics, watchmakers, shoemakers, masons, carpenters and artisans. A few were professionals, including medical doctors. Documents show that Americans were well received and mixed at all social levels with the population. Other Americans had jumped ship, deserted, or were left behind by their captains. Railroad works attracted hundreds of men from U. S. Gulf port cities, and many served as stevedores, bulk-carriers, messengers or unemployed drifters. Few women were among these immigrants. Most of the males married Mexican women, settled down and remained in México until their death. A few took Mexican citizenship, and served in the city council at one time or another.[35]

By 1882, investments' growth in Tampico was also related to the large number of resident Americans. Consul Augustus J. Cassard declared that "the American colony in Tampico grew from (sic) not over twenty a year ago, and now there are residing in this consular district, at least 1200 U.S. citizens."[36] The number had increased owing to the arrivals on the Mexican Central Company steamers, who either came to work on the railroad or to join several immigrant colonies that had settled in the Huasteca or in southern Tamaulipas. However, the presence of this new group of Americans associated with the railroad was of great concern to Tampico residents. The company had labor problems with its Mexican workers in 1881 because the bosses would speak in English to them and they were paid less than American employees. To undermine their claims, the superintendent decided to bring in American laborers. In October, and at a construction site several miles west of Tampico, Mexican laborers rebelled against the American supervisors. A brisk fight ensued, but some friendly railroad officials managed to calm the workers. Still, the line superintendent called on the Tampico Federal garrison commander, General Jesús Alonso Flores, to protect the company and its properties. A detachment was sent immediately, but fighting continued between Americans and Mexicans, spreading to Tampico's streets. The municipal government alerted residents about the possibility of continued acts of violence, whereby creating more negative reactions against Americans. However, even with this difficult labor problem, the company had to finish the line on time, and decided to send for American laborers. Between January and February 1882, the Mexican Central steamer *Alabama* brought over 1000 men from New Orleans to Tampico, of whom at least half were blacks.[37]

This action released a non-expected Mexican xenophobia and racism, both at the port and in México City. Editorials in Tampico dailies criticized the arrival of these workers. They called upon the national government to force the railroad company to hire only Mexican workers.

In April, about two hundred men, mostly Black Americans, left Tampico. Consul Cassard called them tramps, who had failed to carry out given tasks and had become beggars and a nuisance to the community. The city council accused them of bad habits, of being armed, of disease–ridden, and also of irritating the community. Local newspapers reported that street gangs persecuted black Americans. Needless to say that all other workers who had arrived, left Tampico by mid-summer after facing these verbal and physical attacks from the citizenry, and at the same time having to withstand heat, malaria (in the jungles), lack of favorable living conditions, and lack of consular support. Thus, an intriguing chapter of labor problems and race relations was closed. [38]

American presence in other commercial or business activities, however, overcame these difficulties, and had positive consequences for the city. In June 1882, a leading newspaper reported that "Shakespeare and Byron's language is becoming indispensable among us owing to the coming of the Americans. Already several major commercial houses are setting a pair of hours daily for their employees to learn English."[39] The editorialized Americans did not work for the railroad, but were entrepreneurs who had invested in the city, and were opening new facilities in town. Among these were the American Hotel and Restaurant, the restaurants and bars opened by Lee Schatman and William Lee, and the small shops of John Tucker, M.C. Johnson, and Albert F. Brown. There were also the physicians J. W. Bryant, Warren, Braverman, Roberts, and Emilio Robert. Furthermore, a trilingual newspaper, *The Two Flags/Las Dos Banderas*, appeared in town with articles written in English, Spanish and French.[40]

Consul Cassard claimed in February 1883 that ties between Americans and Tampiqueños had reached a high point again after the city council offered a grand ball and banquet for the American colony of Tampico. It was the first such event ever held in México, and its objective was to erase the bitter discontent left by the "rough railroad workers."[41] Americans were welcomed as long as they acted according to the mores of the town's elite, and as long as they brought financial capital and new businesses. Interestingly, the racial tone seen before needs further research and explanations as it disappears from the sources. Foreign residents seem to have held similar racial views as those of the Tampico "notables."

The sudden impact of the railroad and of American investments was short-lived. The Mexican Central Company deadline to finish its main line El Paso-Mexico City was rapidly approaching, and beset by labor shortages, the management took its Tampico branch line workers over to its main project in 1882, thus stopping all work in the Huasteca. This action led to a decrease of services provided by the city to its large working population. It also placed the city's economy under great strain again, but now compounded with other problems.[42]

Tampico's economy declined until 1889 when again new measures and events restored the situation to its 1881 condition. It was partly due to the actions of the Mexican Central Railway, and because of the competition rapidly growing from the border towns. Tampico's customs-house income dropped in July 1883, from second to fifth position in the nation after those of Veracruz, Mazatlán, Progreso, and Paso del Norte (later Ciudad Juárez). Major difficulties began when the Mexican Central stopped all its Tampico works in December 1883; thousands of workers were idled with no other jobs available in the region. No other railroad projects were underway because most had failed or had been paper creations. The city was awash with unemployed men. Furthermore, Italians from the nearby Cerritos immigrant colony strayed into town begging and seeking assistance to go to Veracruz and back to Italy because the project was a total failure. It was a very difficult time to help them in Tampico. By January 1885, customs-house receipts were mortgaged by the federal government to 90% of their value with the city treasury losing most of its customs' allowance. The tramway system, which had increased its routes for the past two years, was on the verge of bankruptcy; indicating the difficult situation prevalent in the city. Its owner, Mrs. Zorilla, asked the city council for a tax relief. Cars and tracks needed repairs, and fewer passengers used the system. On the other hand, a shortage of basic commodities forced the city council to impose price controls, thereby increasing hoarding, which led to higher prices. The crisis was accentuated by a constant emigration from the city reversing the beneficial effects of past years. Loans were taken to pay for municipal expenses, and many businesses closed their doors. The mood was grim among residents and accusations were made against Americans, especially the Mexican Central Company, for betraying its promises. Yet, the biggest culprit was the Free Trade Zone, an economic system created along the US border that started successfully, and grew as trade increased between the two countries once the rail lines were completed.[43]

The Free Trade Zone was born out of the economic plight of the Tamaulipas' border towns right after the Mexican War (1846-1848), and especially after the U.S. Congressional Act of 30 August 1852, which stated that export products were to be held on the U.S. border until conditions for their export into México were favorable. The Tamaulipas State Congress, retaliated with the Act of 17 March 1858 creating the **Zona Libre** (Free Trade Zone) along its side of the border. All foreign goods were exempted from paying Mexican federal duties (not state or municipal) that were "intended for the use of the frontier towns of the State, for the ranches in their jurisdiction, or for trade between the towns."[44] However, lack of federal control over the border allowed for an open smuggling that hurt both national and state treasuries. Still, the Zone did not have a direct national impact until after 1876.

The 1870 Federal Congress voted to keep Tamaulipas's Free Zone operational in its search for new sources of revenue and trade. Minister Matías Romero Rubio, an efficient assistant of the Juárez government, advocated measures to prevent abuse and smuggling in the Zone, when these became endemic in the Tamaulipas's border towns. Regulations existed, but were poorly enforced. Most of the trade continued in the hands of smugglers, and commerce had little effect over the national market. When General Díaz came to power in 1876, his administration used the Free Trade Zone to increase Mexican-American trade and commercial relations. Border towns in other northern states (Coahuila, Sonora, Chihuahua) asked the federal government to create a national Free Trade Zone. Furthermore, the arrival of U.S. railroads to border sites, increased the potential for large trade between the two nations. Products could now be received or sent faster and more cheaply through the northern border towns than through the Gulf or Pacific ports of México. Smuggling continued on a large scale, and the Free Zone towns increased their legal and illegal revenues at the expense of cities such as Veracruz, Tampico, and Mazatlán. Table III shows how the various Gulf ports's customs-houses (*) lost their incomes while the border towns increased theirs. On 24 January 1885, President Díaz signed a new tariff law that extended the Free Trade Zone along the whole U.S.-Mexican border, thus legalizing what was already an accepted situation.[45]

The Free Trade Zone became Tampico's worst enemy. Painfully aware of this situation, the city council, and the newly formed Chamber of Commerce, sent a delegation to México City to meet with President Díaz. The General was told how Tampico's natural Tamaulipas markets of Ciudad Victoria and Ciudad del Maíz, were supplied with contraband goods from the border. They also asked for federal help in five major areas: remedies against smuggling in the border towns, resumption of the Mexican Central Railroad branch line to Tampico, canalization of the sandbar at the Pánuco's mouth, transfer of $2,000 pesos from the

Tampico customs-house to the city for the construction of a **Lazareto** (sanatorium) offered by the government since 1884, and the availability of a federal dredge to clear again the Chijol Canal which communicates with the Tamiahua Lagoon. They also wanted Díaz to force the State government to finish the road between the town of Tula and Tampico.[46]

President Díaz gave a warm welcome to the commission, and prudently listened to their petitions, but, he told them that strenuous times faced the nation owing to the international situation, and that not much could be done at the moment. He pledged, however, to do for Tampico the utmost within his power once the national financial situation improved. He vowed to call on the Mexican Central management to continue the Tampico branch line, to finish the federal pier (also under construction by the railroad company), and to give the money for the sanatorium. The envoys returned to Tampico not completely empty-handed, but with the President's promises.[47]

Distressing times continued in the city. In 1887, the French consulate closed its doors, and the U.S. also lowered Tampico's consulate status and raised those at the border towns. Beggars, fit to work but unemployed, roamed the streets; petty thievery also increased. By 1889, the customs-house fell to tenth place in the nation. Adverse weather conditions added their toll to the distressing economy. Floods covered the city's low areas leaving more than 600 families without shelter. A national fund drive to help victims was started in México City with President Díaz contributing $5,000 pesos to it. More storms and new epidemics also attacked the city, but changes neared again.[48]

In early 1888, the Federal government granted a concession to a group led by General Jerónimo Treviño and Mr. Emeterio de la Garza for the construction of a railroad to be built through Tamaulipas. The state governments of Tamaulipas and Nuevo León had already given their support to the project. It was a narrow–track road between Monterey and

Tampico via Ciudad Victoria. Once built, it would make Tampico the major port for the city of Monterey, known as the "Chicago" of México. One year later, on 29 September 1889, the company was sold to the Sociedad Anónima Belga de Caminos de Fierro en México (Mexican Belgian Railroad, Ltd.), with a clause that lengthened the time for construction beyond the original ten year clause.[49] Furthermore, a contract was signed on August 1888 between the Mexican Central and the Federal government to build the jetties at the Pánuco's mouth. The contract also gave Mexican Central the right to build piers, walks, dikes, warehouses and various other facilities to increase maritime traffic at the port.[50]

The rise of U.S. tariffs on Mexican ore minerals created great fear among mineral producers, who were mostly Americans. They decided to save money by investing in smelting foundries built in México from which the minerals could be shipped to the U.S. paying much lower duties. Most of the new smelters were located at Monterey and Aguas Calientes, and it behooved their owners that railroad connections were made with Tampico, which had the infrastructure to ship their production. Railroad connections became essential for this new aspect of the mineral industry. The renewal of railroad works by the Mexican Central, and the construction of the Belgian road, were signs that the difficult moment was passing. Rumors of future profits spread, and on 14 August 1889, another railroad company received a concession to build a line between Tampico and México City via Pachuca, an important mining town on Hidalgo State. Tampiqueños were delighted with the news, thus making hope more successful than reality.[51]

On 1 April 1890, **el tren** finally arrived. A Mexican Central Pullman reached Tampico from San Luis Potosí carrying the company's most important officials. Celebrations for the event began on the eighteenth of the month after Mexico City officials arrived by sea from

Veracruz. The celebrations underscored the future prosperity and the end of Tampico's isolation by land. The five day journey by coach from San Luis Potosí was now only twenty hours by train. For sixty seven years Tampiqueños struggled to establish an economic foundation to develop their city and their fortunes. National events and obstacles created by external forces and influences had slowed the promising start of 1823. Porfirio Díaz' presidency steered the country into a modernizing era fraught with development policies to aid the nation's growth. Yet, even with federal assistance, Tampico's economic condition needed the arrival of newer forms of transportation, and the building of a larger infrastructure to attract more businesses. After 1880, Tampiqueños expected their future to be linked to foreign entrepreneurs and to national industrial policies. Tampico's urban growth was consistent with these developmental issues.

NOTES

1.AMT, *Actas*, 12 enero 1877; 14 enero 1877; 15 marzo 1877; *RUCRF*, 1877 (Washington, D.C., 1878), 748. *La Reconstrucción*, (Ciudad Victoria), 3:71, 23 noviembre 1877, 3.

2.Zea, Leopoldo, *Dos ensayos de Leopoldo Zea* (Valencia: 1960), 79.

3.AMT, *Actas*, 19 enero 1877; 31 agosto 1877; 22 noviembre 1877. NA, DCT, 84, 166, 30 September 1877, "Yearly Report on the trade, etc. of the Port of Tampico for the Year ending in 30 September 1877," Consul Johnson to Assistant Secretary of State. *RUCRF* Washington, 1880), 468.

4.*La Reconstrucción* (Cd. Victoria) 3:77, 25 enero 1878, 4; 3:80, 23 febrero 1878, 4.

5.AMT, *Actas*, 21 enero, 7 mayo, 3 junio, 15 junio, 30 agosto 1878. *La Reconstrucción* (Ciudad Victoria), 3:93, 4 julio 1878, 4; 3:99, 29 agosto 1878, 3; NA, DCT\84, 10, 5 August 1879, August J. Cassard to Assistant Secretary of State; 18, 29 September 1879, August J. Cassard to Assistant Secretary of State.

6.AMT, *Actas*, 21 septiembre 1877; 20 agosto 1878; 22 enero 1880; *RUCRF*, 1879 (Washington, D.C., 1880), 449; *La Reconstrucción* (Ciudad Victoria), 5:10, 3 octubre 1880, 1; 7:42, 1 junio 1882, 3. The silver problem is discussed in Rosenzweig, Fernando, "El comercio exterior," Cosío Villegas, *HMM*, VII, 425, 647-657; NA, DCT, 84, 166, 30 September 1877, "Consul Edmund Johnson to Assistant Secretary of State; "Depreciation of Mexican Silver," and "The Mercantile Crisis and the Depreciation of Silver in Mexico," in *USCR*, 75, March 1877, 667-672, 672-678; "What's Bimetallism," *USCR*, 122, December 1877, 390-405; "The Silver Question in Mexico," *USCR*, 122, November 1890, 541-543; Pletcher, David M., "The Fall of Silver in Mexico, 1870-1910, and Its Effects on American Investments," *Journal of Economic History*, 18 (Spring 1958), 33-55; Secretaría de Fomento, Colonización, Industria y Comercio, *La crisis monetaria. Estudio sobre la crisis mercantil y la depreciación de la plata* (México, D.F., 1886).

7.The *Diario Oficial*, a federal government publication, of 8 March 1878, published a notice on the arrival and festivities held to honor Riva Palacio in Tampico, see *La Reconstrucción* (Ciudad Victoria) 3:83. 9 abril 1878, 3-4.

8.Historian C. González Salas wrote various articles on the visit using a long narrative document which I discovered in the Tampico municipal archive. See "Don Vicente Riva Palacio en Tampico," *El Sol de Tampico* (Tampico), 12:9, 16 agosto 1883, 2 septiembre 1883.

9.Florescano, Enrique y Lanzagorta, María del Rosario, "Política económica: antecedentes y consecuencias (en la época de Juárez)," in González, Luis et al., *La economía mexicana en la época de Juárez* (México, D.F., 1972); Báez Gallo, Gustavo, *Historia del ferrocarril mexicano* (México, D.F., 1874), 16; Covián Martínez, 30.

10.Pletcher, David M., *Rails, Mines and Progress: Seven American Promoters in Mexico, 1867–1911* (Ithaca, N.Y., 1958), 38-39. General Smith D. Atkins said a few years later: "The conquest of Mexico is a commercial, if not a political necessity. That country will never be developed or governed until we take hold of it. If we put property there, we must protect it, and if we do not put property there, it will always be a standing menace to our civilization. The immense national wealth of Mexico only awaits American enterprise for its development." *Daily Picayune* (New Orleans), 45 (95), 29 April 1881, 8:5.

11.After the U.S. Civil War, several colonies of Confederate refugees were founded in Central Tamaulipas and at Tuxpam. Many of the Tampico vagrants belonged to these colonies. NA, DCT, 84, 156, 30 September 1877, Consul Johnson to Asssistant Secretary of State.

12.*La Reconstrucción* (Ciudad Victoria) 3:77, 25 enero 1878, 4; 3:84, 19 abril 1878, 2; 3:91, 20 junio 1878, 4; 3:99, 29 agosto 1878, 4; Ober, *Frederick, Travels in Mexico* (Boston, 1883), 419; *RUCRF*, 1879 (Washington, D.C., 1880), 416, 468. Veracruz received in 1879, only 106 vessels, 47 from the U.S.

13.AMT, *Actas*, 27 febrero, 6 marzo, 12 marzo, 18 abril, 2 junio, 4 agosto, 6 noviembre, 8 diciembre and 26 diciembre 1879. Also see Expediente 153, "Contiene todo lo referente sobre la tracción del ferrocarril de esta Ciudad," 3 octubre 1879. In 1824, the federal government took under its jurisdiction all the lands in Tampico located between the Riviera Street and the Tamesín River shore.

14.AMT, *Actas*, 1 enero and 22 marzo 1880, 10 marzo 1881; Cosío Villegas, *HMM*, II, 529, 562; *Daily Picayune* (New Orleans), 44, 89, 23 April 1880, 3:1; 45, 39, 4 March 1881, 8:2; 44, 350, 12 January 1881, 3:2; 44, 121, 25 May 1882, 1:7; Covián Martínez, 33; *RUCRF*, 1880-1881 (Washington, D.C., 1883), 511; NA, Despatches from the Tuxpam Consulate, 48, 29 September 1881, Vice Consul Catlin to Assistant Secretary of State.

15.AMT, *Actas*, 22 julio 1880, 17 mayo and 23 junio 1881, 10 mayo 1883; Expediente 154, noviembre 1883; *Daily Picayune*, 44, 83, 17 April 1880, 5:7; 44, 27 May 1880, 8:2; 44, 292, 13 November 1880, 1:6; 45, 4, 28 January 1881, 8:3; *RUCRF* 1879 (Washington, D.C., 1880), 419.

16.*RUCRF* 1879, (Washington, D.C., 1880), 469; *Daily Picayune*, 44, 83, 17 April 1880, 5:7; AMT, Expediente 40, 5 febrero 1883; *La Reconstrucción* (Ciudad Victoria), 5, 1, 2 septiembre 1880, 3; Ocasio Meléndez, Marcial E., "El faro centenario," *El Sol de Tampico* (Tampico), 5 febrero 1983, 10:4-5.

17.AMT, *Actas*, 29 enero, 12 febrero, 21 octubre and 2 diciembre 1880; Expediente 46, "Bases relativas a los panaderos," noviembre 1881.

18.*La Reconstrucción* (Ciudad Victoria), 7, 70, 25 noviembre 1883; AMT, *Actas*, 30 septiembre 1881, 1 enero, 9 and 30 noviembre 1882, 15 abril 1883; NA, DCT, 84, 54, 28 November 1881, Consul Cassard to Assistant Secretary of State. In 1882, President Manuel González bought a house in Tampico for $4,000 pesos to serve for residential purposes. Others might have followed him to Tampico.

19.*Daily Picayune*, 4, 28 January 1881, 8:3; 45, 46, 11 March 1881, 3:4; Corthell, E. L., *A History of the Jetties at the Mouth of the Mississippi River* Second edition, (New York, 1881); NA, DCT, 84, n.n. 5 December 1882, Consul Cassard to Assistant Secretary of State.

20.Van Oss, S.F., *American Railroads as Investments* (Reprint) (New York, 1983), 565.

21.Wilkins, Mira, *The Emergence of Multinational Enterprises: American Business Abroad From the Colonial Era to 1914* (Cambridge: 1970), 114; Coatsworth, John H. *Growth Against Development. The Economic Impact of Railroads in Porfirian Mexico* (De Kalb, 1981); Anson, Arthur M. and Supple, Barry E., *Boston Capitalists and Western Railroads* (Cambridge, 1967), 287-306; Cott, Kenneth S., *Porfirian Investment Policies, 1876-1910* (Ph.D. dissertation, University of New Mexico, 1979); Leal, Juan Felipe, "La política ferrocarrilera de los primeros gobiernos porfiristas y las compañías ferroviarias norteamericanas," *Relaciones Internacionales* (México, D.F.) 5. julio/septiembre 1976, 14, 8-49; *Daily Picayune* 44, 3, 27 January 1880, 3:1; 4, 6, 30 January 1880, 7:1; 44, 226, 8 September 1880, 3:2; 44, 237, 19 September 1880, 4:1.

22.*Daily Picayune*, 44, 107, 11 May 1880, 2:3; 44, 237, 29 September 1880, 3:1; Cumberland, Charles C., *Mexico. A Struggle for Modernity* (New York, 1968), 214-215; Coerver, *Don M., The Porfirian Interregnum; The Presidency of Manuel Gonzalez of Mexico, 1880-1884* (Forth Worth, 1979), 198-199; Espinoza, Jorge, *Relaciones entre México y los Estados Unidos, 1870-1910* (México, D.F., 1951), 38-39.

23.*Daily Picayune*, 44,323, 14 December 1880, 8:2; AMT, *Actas*, 27 diciembre 1880.

24.AMT, *Actas*, 1 enero 1881.

25.AMT, *Actas*, 27 abril 1881.

26.AMT, *Actas*, 1 septiembre, 16 septiembre, 23 septiembre 1881.

27.Burns, Bradford E., *The Poverty of Progress. Latin America in the Nineteenth Century* (Berkeley, 1983).

28.*RUCRF* 1880-1881 (Washington, D.C., 1883), 511; NA, DCT, 84, 30, 23 February 1882, Consul Cassard to Assistant Secretary of State.

29.*Daily Picayune*, 46, 30, 23 February 1882, 2:4; *La Reconstrucción* (Tampico), 7, 74, 7 diciembre 1882, 5; 7, 80, 20 diciembre 1882, 2. On 14 March 1983, I interviewed Mrs. Milagros Ramírez Prom, 75 years old, who confirmed many of these details. Her family arrived from the Huasteca after hearing news of the need for workers in Tampico. Don Sabás Prom, her father, was a successful artisan, who organized one of Tampico's mutualist organizations. The process was quite similar for hundreds of families arriving monthly in Tampico. Men would come first, find jobs and homes, and then send for their families.

30.*El Semanario* (Tampico), 5, 10 noviembre 1882, 2; *La Reconstrucción*, 7, 48, 22 junio 1882, 3-4; AMT, Actas, 3 abril 1882.

31.Batíz Vázquez, José A., "Aspectos financieros y monetarios (1821-1880)," in Cardoso, Ciro (ed.) *México en el siglo XIX (1821-1910). Historia económica y de la estructura social* (México, D.F., 1984), 172, 179-180; Alfaro, Ofelia, "Historia de la banca. De la colonia a 1982," *Excelsior* (México, D.F.), 4 enero 1983, 5:1.

32.Meade, *Huasteca Tamaulipeca*, II, 10, 24-27, 33-36.

33.NA, DCT, 84, 4, 10 August 1829, Consul Robinson to Secretary of State.

34.See French, John D., "A U.S. Merchant Consul and the Foreign Community: Franklin Chase and His Friends and Enemies at Tampico, Mexico, 1861-1865," (M.A. Thesis, University of Pittsburgh, 1978).

35.Covián Martínez, 44; González Salas, *Tampico*, 74; French, 3.

36.NA, DCT, n.n., 19 May 1882, Consul Cassard to Assistant Secretary of State.

37.NA, DCT, 84, 49, 3 October 1882, Consul Cassard to Assistant Secretary of State.

38.NA, DCT, 84, 60, 20 February 1882, Consul Cassard to Assistant Secretary of State; 78, 14 August 1882, Consul Cassard to Assistant Secretary of State; *Daily Picayune*, 46, 30, 23 February 1882, 2:4; 46, 47, 12 March 1882, 3:3; 46, 74, 8 April 1882, 7:1; *El Semanario* (Tampico) 5, 200, 10 febrero 1882, 1-2; 5, 201, 17 febrero 1882, 1; 5, 202, 24 febrero 1882, 1; 5, 210, 21 abril 1882, 4; 5, 211, 28 abril 1882, 3; 5, 206, 17 mayo 1882, 1; AMT, *Actas*, 30 enero y 23 mayo 1882.

39.*El Semanario* (Tampico) 5, 217, 2 junio 1882, 4.

40.AMT, *Actas*, 13 abril, 4 mayo, 15 junio, 24 agosto, 23 diciembre 1882; 1 mayo 1883. Emilio Robert and his family came from the U.S. in the 1830s. He studied medicine at the Sorbonne in Paris, and returned to Tampico becoming one of its most distinguished members. He served as councilman on several occasions, and as director of the Civil or Municipal Hospital. One of his brothers was mayor of Barcelona, Spain, in the late nineteenth century.

41.NA, DCT, 84, n.n., 12 February 1883, Consul Cassard to Assistant Secretary of State.

42.AMT, *Actas*, 29 diciembre 1882; *USRCCM*, 30, April 1883, 520.

43.*USRCCM*, 39, March 1884, 66-67; "Exports of Mexico," *USRCCM*, 61, February 1886, 457; AMT, *Actas* 19 julio 1833, 10 enero 1884, 31 marzo 1884, 1 enero 1885; NA, DCT, 84, 106, 1 December 1883, 121, Cassard to Assistant Secretary of State; 20 October 1884, Cassard to Assistant Secretary of State; Creel, George, *The People Next Door* (New York, 1926), 275.

44.Van Oss, 300-302.

45.Romero Rubio, Matías, "The Free Zone in Mexico," *North American Review*, 154, May 1892, 462; "The Mexican Zona Libre," *USRCCM*, 133, October 1891, 206-208.

46.Martínez Jáquez, Oscar, *Border Boom Town: Ciudad Juárez Since 1848* (Austin, 1975), 19; Romero Rubio, 467; Vázquez, Josefina Z. and Meyer, Lorenzo, *México frente a los Estados Unidos. Un ensayo histórico 1776-1980* (México, D.F., 1982); AMT, *Actas*, 15 abril 1884, 20 febrero 1885, 15 abril 1885; *RUCRF*, 1879 (Washington, D.C., 1880), 468.

47.AMT, *Actas*, 20 mayo 1885.

48."Exports of Mexico," *USRCCM*, 168, September 1889, 94; Covián Martínez, 91.

49.Hernández Montemayor, 38-39; Covián Martínez, 14; *POET* (Ciudad Victoria), 21, 26, 29 febrero 1896, 1.

50.Collins Rojas, 134; Covián Martínez, 12; "Commerce and Trade of Mexico," *USCR*, 31, 104, April 1889, 711-750; Ballon, Maturin K., *Aztec Land* (Boston, 1890), 32.

51.Gómez Serrano, Jesús, *Aguascalientes: Imperio de los Guggenheim* (México, D.F., 1982), 56-57; NA, DCT, 84, 63, 6 September 1888, Consul Greathouse to Assistant Secretary of State; Barron, C. W., *The Mexican Problem* (Boston/New York, 1917), 22; *POET* (Ciudad Victoria), 21, 60, 19 mayo 1886, 1-3.

3

AN AMERICAN HARBOR, 1890-1905

> The shipping at Tampico is greater than that at any other port in Mexico. The shipping to the U.S. is greater than from any port in Mexico.
> U.S. Consul John Maguire, 1896.

The last decade of the nineteenth century was prosperous for the Mexican business elite. Their activities were supported by President Díaz, who had returned to power in 1884. The government was directed by positivist ideas, popular among Mexican professionals and bureaucrats, known collectively as Científicos. Their breed, trained in Europe and in the educational system developed by Juárez' Minister of Education, Gabino Barreda, wanted to advance México's international, political, and economic position in the world. Several political and economic measures were designed and decreed to attain those goals, especially to attract foreign investments, which flowed in competitively and unimpeded both from Europe and the United States.

A process of urban modernization throughout México accompanied the economic activity generated by those measures. This modernization was defined in physical and quantitative terms both in the capital and major cities of the country. The Federal District, San Luis Potosí, Monterey, Guadalajara, and Puebla inaugurated new technological amenities and improvements such as electricity, trolley cars, telephones, and improved sewerage systems.[1] As limited sectors of the nation's population increased their standard of living, others, especially the urban poor, inched forward – at times under desperate conditions – to participate in the "bonanza."

General Díaz imposed a sedate environment called by his apologists "Pax Porfiriana." It allowed a bolder and enterprising middle class to acquire a more noticeable presence in the affairs of the country, although secondary to foreigners in the national economy. Europeans controlled the major trading, merchandise, and financial houses of México; yet, U.S. entrepreneurs and merchants made rapid in-roads in the national export markets. Americans were under heavy criticism from many of their own consuls and commercial agents. They complained of the techniques and methods used with Mexican merchants. It was especially true about packaging styles and the credit system used by Americans which did not fit or satisfy Mexican customers. Europeans, however, served the market according to local styles and wishes.[2]

On the other hand, Americans had almost complete control over the railroad lines of México since the 1880s, and their manufactured products could compete favorably with their European counterparts. The United States had the advantage of being México's northern neighbor. Its industries and cities needed minerals and agricultural products. Cotton and hemp (henequén) were attractive fields for investments, and some observers, already thought of México as a complementary economic junior partner of the United States.[3] By 1892, more than half of all the ships entering or leaving Mexican ports were Americans, and over fifty percent of all Mexican trade was carried on with the U.S.[4] (See Table 4).

Two economic problems had forced greater federal government concern over the development of the nation's ports, especially Veracruz and Tampico. The nation's most important customs-houses suffered dearly when silver lost its preeminence in world markets, and as an international currency. The Mexican peso was based on silver and it was deeply hurt by this turn of events. Imports and exports suffered, and consequently most national development projects and investors' profits. The other problem was related to the needs of the new railroad companies that appeared throughout the country. Their losses or lack of immediate profits, owing mainly to lack of resources and internal trade, led them to a keen competition for roads and any other available source of earnings. One of these was their skill in securing ports for their exports and imports, which could then be moved at their own prices. Ports were negatively affected by the international situation, but became highly important for foreign railroad companies interested in exacting profits from the nation. Both problems undermined México's incipient capitalism, allowing for more foreign control of the economy.

The devaluation of silver in world markets was a problem for Mexican exports since 1870, but especially during the mid-1890s. At the most critical moment, trade slowed to a snail's pace. Furthermore, nature again would not help. Towns along the U.S. border suffered as a drought inflicted heavy damages to their agriculture forcing food imports. In 1891, John B. Richards, U.S. Consul at Matamoros, described the difficult situation

> Instead of having some produce to sell, all have to buy, and this state of things, has lasted for two years. People are starving all about, as there is no work Businessmen are living upon themselves in the hope that rains and railroads may reimburse them.[5]

Even William Jennings Bryan, defender of the silver currency, remarked that México was being crucified on "a cross of gold," thanks to the rising value of gold and the devaluation of silver in world markets.

Three years after the crisis began, the economic situation shifted in México's favor. By 1895, the silver currency became an advantage when trading with gold-currency countries. Payments in gold had reduced imports, and exports rose owing to their lower prices in world markets. México was paid in gold for products that were undervalued in silver, thereby receiving a higher profit in the trade-off.[6]

Notwithstanding the silver problem, it was the railroad network the one that defined the areas for accelerated growth as well as those where modernization was to be limited. It is said that "the construction of rail lines benefitted cities connected thereby with the capital and the major ports."[7] The development of these ports became a major priority for federal, state, and municipal governments as well as for the commercial communities in each town. The ports became an essential element of México's infrastructure for growth and modernization, and a tool for foreign control of the economy.

Notwithstanding the 1880–1895 financial crisis, the federal government did initiate various projects at Gulf and Pacific ports. By 1895, some of these projects were already finished or in their final construction stages; successfully allowing more ships to enter harbors and increase trade. The new works alleviated the economic worries through capital investment and through the labor productivity offered their respective regions.[8] Inadvertently to most Mexicans, the new facilities helped foreigners become more powerful within the nation. Not only were they investing a profitable capital, while accepting federal government's subsidies, but were also reaping a greater share of the benefits.

Tampico was part of this scenario until 1900. The railroad works gave the city a large publicity, attracting immigrants and increasing its fame. However, Tampico slowly drifted into the hands of the Mexican Central Railroad Company. The company controlled most of the city's communications and transportation systems by the 1890s. It became the major source of capital for the harbor and jetty works, the city's major employer, and was involved in the early successful exploration of oil in the Huasteca. It is valuable to examine how this company developed its control in Tampico.

The Mexican Central and the jetties

On 18 April 1890, the city officially inaugurated the San Luis Potosí-Tampico line with various festivities. The first train was received at the new station built on the Muelle Island. Two bridges were built over the Tamesín River connecting the island to the shore: one for the train, the other for people. This line allowed Tampico's cargo and passengers to reach Nuevo Laredo, on the main trunk line of the Central, within only three and a half days. It was an important day for San Luis Potosí, a city of about 65,000 inhabitants, site of growing U.S. investments, and a major distribution center for central and northeastern México. Although only one and a half day away, its leaders wanted to compete with the nation's capital. Now they could also boast of having their "own port" – Tampico – just as México City had Veracruz. For the Mexican Central, finishing the line was also an important issue.

Of all the concessions granted during the 1880s to build railroad lines across México, only two American companies won the most profitable routes stretching in a north-south line between the U.S. border and México City. One was the Atchison, called Mexican Central in México; the other was the Mexican National Company. Once the tracks were finished, company officials realized that these roads would not be profitable because they traversed long stretches of territory without population or trade of any sort. They also discovered that competition was going to be hard not only among themselves, but also with the British-owned Mexican Railway linking Veracruz to México City. This line monopolized México's busiest and richest port. Thus, it became essential for the American companies to establish competitive rates. It was especially important for the Mexican Central and its survival to have its own port similar to the Mexican Railway. Tampico could perfectly become that port on the Gulf, but it had a major handicap: the bar at the Pánuco's mouth would not allow the passage of most ships. It was perfectly clear that it had to be removed, and the fastest way was through the building of jetties. This enterprise signaled, for the first time in Tampico's history, the cooperation between federal, state, and municipal governments with a foreign corporation. The building of the jetties would help each partner accomplish its individual goals; and all contributed to make the works possible. Once finished the river harbor would be deep enough to allow a larger number of ships, of passengers, and trade into the city.[9] U.S. Consul General at Nuevo Laredo, Benjamin Sutton, wrote after a trip to Tampico, that officials "had very exaggerated ideas of a possible future for the city and think it destined to be a large city as well as a great receiving and forwarding port" once the jetties had been constructed.[10]

Indeed, optimism reigned in northern México for the future of the port. City officials, industrial and business leaders in San Luis Potosí and Monterey joined Tampico authorities in their hopes to reap greater benefits after the jetties were built. Plans for the construction of the Monterey and Gulf Railroad line – linking Tampico and Monterey via Ciudad Victoria – were advanced once the jetties' project was revealed. The leaders knew that the Mexican Central had problems reaching Tampico from México's major mineral and industrial centers. They also knew that the seaboard trade that had reached northern México through the port of Baghdad - near the border city of Matamoros - was being diverted by the Mexican National Railroad to the Texan port of Corpus Christi, which it served. The Monterey and Gulf Railroad officials, apparently urged by the federal government, sought to regain the trade back to a Mexican Gulf port, and figured that their line could provide a faster service for northern México from Tampico. However, it was an impossible proposition without the jetties. These structures would make Tampico a first class world port, with the benefits accruing to all those involved in their development and communications.[11] In 1895, Mr. Arthur Monnom, general manager of the Monterey and Gulf, stated that

> the policy of this company is to do all in their power to aid in the development of Monterey and its industries as well as those of Tampico and the entire route, as this policy can only tend to increase the value of their (bondholders) own investment.[12]

Thus, foreign railroad capitalists became allies of Mexican national and regional interests in pursuing Tampico's development that would also benefit them. The jetties, of course, were a most important element in the plan, even before their construction had started.

The granting of the contract to build the jetties had political connotations involving Mexican national priorities, nationalism, and fear of an American control of the economy.[13] The Central had asked the federal government for a contract to open the Pánuco bar since 1881. Then, the company had received the cooperation of the U.S. government by sending a harbor inspection team led by Captain Joseph B. Eads of Louisiana with a group of his engineering staff at the Louisiana Jetty and Lighterage Company. They surveyed the Pánuco River and the Gulf coast near its mouth.[14] The data collected was of great value for future U.S. operations in the Gulf.

One year after that study was finished, a new team, now of French engineers, arrived in Tampico for another river survey that included the bar and the harbor, but at the request of the Tampico City council. Behind this action was the opportunistic French consul, Monsieur Charles de St. Charles. He avidly sought to ingratiate himself with the local authorities, and it was rumored that he wanted a French company to build the jetties. St. Charles offered French financing, and engineering assistance. He was able to convince several city aldermen of his arguments, especially during the slowdown of the Central's operations in Tampico. The city council had no power to grant the jetties contract because all river and port works in México fell under federal government's jurisdiction. However, during one of the now common visits to the capital made by agents of the municipality in search for more money, it was asked of President Díaz to let the Tampico council make the final decision on the jetties' contract. The General refused this request, unwilling to relinquish federal power to any city or region.

Meanwhile in Tampico, U.S. Consul Jules Cassard feared that the Central would lose the contract for the jetties, not because of St. Charles's maneuvers, but owing to the Mexican Government's intention "of countervailing its (Mexican Central) preponderance in this section of the country."[15] Notwithstanding this alleged attitude, the Federal government granted the jetties' contract to the Mexican Central Company in August 1888.

For more than a year, financial problems held up the construction of the jetties. Finally in 1890, the Central hired the Louisiana Jetty and Lighterage Company, now headed by Colonel Joseph H. Hampson, to do the project. It involved the employment of more than three hundred Mexicans under the supervision of U.S. engineers and technicians. E. L. Corthell, famous for the construction of the Mississippi River jetties, was named chief engineer of the project. His professional expertise was an assurance of the quality expected of the construction. Assistant engineers of the project were Captain Joseph B. Eads, Major Harrington, Mr. T. Smith, Colonel A.F. Wronotwski (named resident engineer), and only one Mexican engineer, Emilio Lavit, a Tampico resident.[16]

The jetties consisted of two parallel walls built one thousand feet apart and extending over one mile out from the shore into the Gulf. These walls had a core of brush matting suspended from a trestle. Each mat measured from forty to eighty four feet wide according to depth, and sixty feet long. These were sunk at various levels and capped with stones. The trestle was built out and over the jetties with two tracks of railways and all the necessary equipment and sidetracks.[17]

Construction work advanced rapidly, and by 1892, the depth of the Pánuco's entrance had increased from eight to sixteen feet. When the project concluded the total depth reached thirty feet. The jetties were a very expensive enterprise. Until 1892, almost three million pesos gold had been spent on it. Since then, the upkeep and repairs of these works have required the expenditure of considerable sums by the federal government. Effects on Tampico were immediate. First, jetties' work attracted a large immigration from the surrounding area into the municipality. Widespread publicity had introduced the project as one that would hire hundreds, not for the construction itself, but for the new services, facilities, and industries that would be attracted to Tampico once the harbor was deepened. Again, the migration was larger than expected and lack of living facilities forced the newcomers to either live in multi-family shacks rented in swampy lots along the Carpintero Lagoon, along the rivers' shores or to build their own houses on lands further out north or east of the city center. Most of these houses were built on municipal or federal lands, mostly marshlands or empty lots, that were part of the concessions given to the railroad companies.

Numerous shacks and houses were also built along the seven miles of tracks laid out by the Mexican Central between Tampico and the northern jetty built at La Barra. One locomotive serviced that hamlet carrying men and materials to and from Tampico. It became the major form of transportation for workers and their families, who lived along the line. Thus, a population and suburbanization development occurred in the boroughs of Arbol Grande, Doña Cecilia, and La Barra. These growing suburban areas, distant several miles from Tampico's urban center, created the need for a variety of services. They developed new economic activities such as small stores and services. Yet, other activities competed with the old Tampico, i.e. the construction of piers for ships that could not be docked at city wharves. The Mexican Central built several warehouses at Doña Cecilia, while constructing similar facilities in Tampico, and at various other sites along the northern shore of the Pánuco. It planned to have all these depositories become bonded warehouses once the main pier and train facilities were finished in the city. Importers found the arrangement very convenient because workers lived nearby, thus lowering costs and expenses. Piers were also built all along the northern shore of the Pánuco. Soon, Doña Cecilia, Arbol Grande and La Barra had food shops, bars, and other stores to serve their residents.[18]

The Mexican Central had devised other plans involving Tampico's future. The company wanted to profit from its investment by all possible means. Miramar, the beach running north along the Gulf from the jetties and La Barra had excellent possibilities as a tourist resort. The project was discussed in Tampico receiving accolades from both the elite and the populace. First of all, there was already a railroad line connecting the beach with the city, and after 1895, a wagon train began moving people between Tampico and La Barra every two hours. Long before the arrival of the train, La Barra had been the summer resort for many wealthy Tampiqueños and foreign residents. Many had built beach houses, where they spent leisure time especially during the summer season. Furthermore, a small hamlet also grew up nearby, originally inhabited by lighterage workers and ship pilots with their families. In the words of an 1895 Tampico visitor, "the American and English colony ladies and gentlemen go to the beech (sic), to bathe and ride their bicycles up and down the beach sands." Thus, Miramar had already become a summer place for both the upper and lower echelon of Tampico's society, and had minimal facilities to serve non-residents. According to C.P. Bond of Boston, the Mexican Central wanted to make Tampico the Atlantic City of México. With that purpose in mind, "the company was to build at La Barra, on the beach, a handsome station, a magnificent pavilion, and comfortable bathing houses."[19] The project began to take shape with the available facilities and the good will of the Tampiqueños. Yet, financial problems affecting the Mexican Central's parent company and the increased competition from the other railroad lines in México, forced the company to postpone its plans indefinitely.

It was impossible for Tampico's trade to help the Central - it could not compete with other Mexican railroad companies - before the jetties were built. Freight trade from the port inland had remained relatively small compared to the one coming into México through the northern border towns and through Veracruz. Mr. Sutton, American Consul General in Nuevo Laredo, observed that in Tampico

> so far no goods to any amount have been carried through to San Luis Potosí or México City. A pay freight runs about twice a week but as yet causes only a small load, nearly all the freight carried is railway material and for the bar improvement.[20]

Profits for the Central and for Tampico's business community did not increase after train service began at the port. Most of the export-import trade at Tampico paid very low duties because its bulk was machinery or mineral ores. Although the bulk tonnage arriving at the port was larger than the one reaching Veracruz, its tariffs were lower. Besides, Veracruz had most of the luxury trade items which were heavily taxed.[21]

In order to get faster returns on its Mexican investments, the Central began an absurd rate war for the freight trade against its main competitors. In June 1892, the company dropped one fourth of its rates for hauling freight from Tampico, and from El Paso, to México City. This maneuver was part of a plan that envisioned control of the European trade that could be lured to come to Tampico away from the ports in southern Texas that were used to transfer cargo for México. Immediately, the Mexican Railway, Interoceanic and Mexican National companies, dropped their own freight rates. Yet, it was a short freight war when a combination of other elements intervened forcing its end. First, the price of silver dropped even further in 1893, forcing a new collapse of México's trade. Second, a poor harvest in the eastern half of the country reduced the freight carried by railroads to a minimum. Faced with these events, representatives from the four major competitors met in London, and formed a pool that set the rates for European articles entering México. The end result for the Mexican Central was higher losses than expected initially, with the disadvantage that it had now to keep its Tampico rates as low as those of Veracruz set by the British Mexican Railway.[22]

The competition that the Belgian line was expected to provide at Tampico never materialized. On 24 October 1891, the Monterey and Gulf Railroad finished its line to Tampico with the arrival of the first non-stop service Monterey-Tampico train at the Doña Cecilia Station. The city again celebrated the arrival with various ceremonies and festivities, but the honeymoon period was short. The line traversed a poor and uninhabited region of Nuevo León and Tamaulipas States with little or no freight available to either city at each end of the line. By April 1892, J.A. Robertson, Monterey and Gulf's general manager, was named by a federal court as receiver of the company owing to the line's bankruptcy. The railroad was turned over completely to representatives of the Belgian Syndicate of Bondholders, who held it for a few more years. The line's economic collapse eliminated it as a Mexican Central competitor until 1898, when it began to increase its cargo and earnings, again posing a threat against that company. Finally, the competition ended in 1903 when Rockefeller's Standard Oil Company bought both the Mexican Central and the Monterey and Gulf creating a transportation monopoly in the area and for Tampico. From then on, only one railroad line served the city.[23]

Mexican Central's position in Tampico was also assisted by President Díaz' policies to boost internal trade. In June 1895, a presidential decree allowed the importation of duty-free foreign merchandise through the northern border cities. Another decree followed giving the President authority to reform or annul any railroad, port or channel projects. Díaz was then able to stop the railway pool established in London, forcing the Mexican Central and the Mexican Railway to renew their rate war – a measure benefitting Mexican businesses – until

1896, when both lines' officials decided to renew their pooling, but now with the strong support of Standard Oil that was seeking to control the Mexican Central.[24]

The construction of the jetties and all other company maneuvers described, eventually brought a brisk trade traffic to the port of Tampico. There was a constant increase in the number of ships arriving daily in late 1895 with cargo for the Mexican Central. For example, between the 18th and the 20th of October, fifteen vessels arrived and left Tampico with 90% of their freight delivered by or to the Mexican Central.[25] Its General Manager, H.R. Nickerson, stated in an interview, that

> the amount of freight which arrives at the port is simply enormous, as it would amaze many in this city (Mexico City) to see the great number of freight trains which daily leave Tampico for the interior.[26]

By December 1895, the bar at the Pánuco's entrance had a depth of twenty five and a half feet allowing most ocean-going vessels to enter the port. Moreover, a channel had been dredged at the same depth all the way up to Tampico. And with no pooling

> a very large percentage of the business which heretofore moved exclusively via Veracruz, has now been transferred to the Tampico route with excellent results to the shipping public and with large gains for the Mexican Central.[27]

Tampico officials were delighted with all the new economic activity, and were most helpful to the railroad companies, especially with their port plans. Two years earlier, they had publicly complained against Mexican Central's failure to carry out the projects it had promised. They included the construction of a train station on the Muelle Island, the closing of the channel between the islands of Muelle and Moralillo, and the construction of bridges from these islands to the city's shore. Instead, the company had built the station at Doña Cecilia, a place closer to its warehouses, and did not even start the others promised. City officials had complained the federal government's construction of a new customs building in Doña Cecilia, after a mysterious fire burned the Tampico Customs House, located across Plaza de la Libertad, in March 1894. This federal action, "robbed" the city of its major and immediate source of income. Although Doña Cecilia was within Tampico's jurisdiction, the daily cargo traffic to and from the customs was needed for hundreds of workers living in city's core. Now other workers would benefit from it. Moreover, this cargo traffic shifted from the large commercial and trading houses of Tampico to its borough with fewer inhabitants and commerce, but where the Central controlled most of its economic life. The company owned or leased a sizable part of borough lands, owned a large warehouse, tracks, piers, and the train station. Still, even with all the criticism against them, company officials continued to have the support of local, state and federal officials.[28]

Complaints vanished after President Díaz ordered the construction of a new Customs House building and a very large pier, both to be located at the Muelle Island. Again, the contract to build these facilities was given to Mexican Central on 19 August 1895. The company would provide capital for the construction, and the federal government would repay it in installments. The contract exempted the company from all federal, state and municipal taxes on machinery and equipment for the project, and gave even more lands to the railroad. This new customs building – still a Tampico landmark – is a two story structure 300 meters long and 46 meters wide. The lower floor served as warehouse with receipt and delivery facilities, and customs offices occupied the second floor. The federal pier had a length of 350 meters and a width of 15 meters on the Pánuco side of Muelle island, where a maximum depth of 24 meters was reached. Rail tracks were built through the building to allow Mexican Central freight cars to pass directly through customs.[29]

A Boston traveller in Tampico declared that the new wharves and the customs building would bring to the city, the

> benefit of the most modern conveniences for the handling and discharging of cargoes, and will make the port of Tampico second to none in the North American continent in so far as the economic handling and quick despatch of goods are concerned.[30]

Thanks to the federal government, the Mexican Central Railroad Company became the largest employer in town. It is also clear that federal jurisdiction over the Muelle Island was virtually turned over to the company. By controlling the right of way to reach customs and the island itself, by constructing the customs building and wharf facilities, the company now had the power to determine which ships unloaded first and which cargo was to be kept at the island's warehouses or was to be sent elsewhere. The company became the great modernizing hope of Tampico's business community, the largest employer, and the major investor in the area. Thus, Tampico became Mexican Central's port.

The new Tampico

Once the river was easily navigable, investments made in harbor and transportation facilities began to pay off. Soon, the city had enough money to improve its beautification projects and for other plans to strengthen the urban infrastructure needed according to Tampico's commercial and social elite.

Receipts from exports between July 1893 and June 1894 reached $7,037,049 pesos. For the same 1890-1891 period, the receipts had amounted only to $486,930 pesos. In three years the difference was $6,550,119 pesos. This rise in exports was a bonanza for the city's treasury. Its share of the custom's receipts was exceptional. Moreover, it also increased its income from taxes paid by new and older businesses, and from professional services. Expenditures also decreased, and although in January 1894 there were only 42 cents left in the city's treasury, by December the surplus was over $6,000 pesos. Tables 5 and 6 show the growth in income for the city and for the federal customs. The figures also reflect how the recent urban growth benefitted the town's fiscal position.[31]

As the city's industrial base broadened, former State governor (1888-1896) and Tampico resident, engineer Alejandro Prieto, praised municipal administrations for their concern promoting new industries. He urged the 1896 city council to plan its future projects in light of two principles: the city's status as the state's most important industrial, tourist, and commercial center; and the possibility of becoming the nation's most important port if it was able to compete successfully with Veracruz. Tampico's mayor Arcadio I. Domínguez also expressed the need to plan adequately the city's future development. He invited the business community to help the municipal government in this enterprise, a call which had been a constant in the city since its foundation.

Still, some problems existed in this association between the private and public sectors of Tampico. One of them was the debate over the return of the city's original "ejidos"[32] that had been distributed among town notables. These lands were now needed to attract more investors and to provide space for more harbor development. They could also bring in more income through direct sales or leases. These ejidos, still under municipal control, were partitioned by Luis F. Llorente, the 1881 Presidente Municipal, among four individuals, and himself. The other distinguished grantees were two wealthy businessmen, José Aldama and Daniel Fernández; political figure José María Maraboto, congressman, State Congress' secretary, and Tamaulipas Secretary of State; and General Jesús Alonso Flores, commander of the city's federal garrison. A conflict existed over the interpretation of the lands' ownership which allowed Llorente to give them away as municipal, and not as ejido, lands. He also gave Mexican Central all lands on both Muelle and Moralillo islands. By law these islands were under the control of the federal government, yet México's federal power had been poorly enforced for decades. Individuals had taken over the islands without having any legal rights on the land. These lots' "owners" questioned Llorente's actions, and both state and federal governments were soon involved in the problem. The accused Llorente resigned with neither great damage to his reputation nor to his actions.

A group opposed to this land distribution won the 1886 election, and took Llorente and his four friends to court demanding the return of the ejidos, but the powerful presence of General Flores and his troops slowed down the judicial proceedings. The city council then annulled the grants as illegal administrative actions, but it was to little avail because the lands were not returned. Llorente and his 1881 council members decided to run for office again, and were powerful enough to make the December 1887 political campaign rather disturbing, and social turmoil intensified up until election day. Election proceedings were interrupted by federal troops when it was found out that the anti-Llorente group was winning. General Flores alleged that riots were occurring throughout the city. The governor named Llorente as provisional mayor until the electoral mess was cleared. As soon as he was back in office, Llorente repealed the annulment passed against his previous actions by the city council.

On 9 January 1888, Llorente resigned, after clearing himself legally and administratively. Yet, his enemies retook the Municipal Presidency and city council, and on 22 August 1888, again repealed his grants, and any other land sales which had taken place under his tenure. Some lands given to railroads or sold to private investors wer not returned, but city surveyors were able to recover those lots considered more important for future urban development, as was the case with lands along the Tamesín and to the north of the city. During the following years, city government continued its efforts to buy back the lands granted, and were very successful. Out of almost 100,000 square meters in valuable ejido lands, the railroad companies - Central, Monterey and Gulf - held 48,000; 24,000 were held by individuals, and the city, with none in 1882, acquired about 23,000 square meters.[33]

Another problem facing the municipality was the need for more income to provide for all the new expenses that the city had to assume as new businesses, a larger infrastructure, and a growing population expected in services and facilities. Table VII shows both Tampico's annual income and expenditures of Tampico for the 1895-99 period. The figures show that, although income rose, expenditures followed closely. Seeking solutions, the 1896 city council asked the federal government to increase the city's share from one and a third to two percent of customs income. Governor Guadalupe Mainero supported Tampico's request stating that "the second port (of the Republic) had to prove its status by showing the most outstanding features of modern civilization in its municipal services such as police, hygiene, comfort, and city ornamentation."[34] He was also referring to street lighting and pavement, sewerage, education, and social control, that is, keeping the poorest folks in check through police supervision. The city's income came normally from taxes on urban property, on professional and business enterprises, on imports into town, on a head tax, on entertainment (bars, billiards, dances, serenades, prostitution), on lenders, auctions and deeds, on fines imposed by the mayor, and on the rental of the public market floor space which was its second-largest local income (see Table 4). It was a joyous day for the city when on 29 May 1986 news arrived that the federal government had raised custom's share to two percent of the receipts. It meant at least 10,000 pesos more a month for the treasury, and the city could now have the cash to deal with some of the other local problems.[35]

Demographic growth had deeply affected municipal services. In

1887, the municipality had about 7,500 inhabitants; ten years later, the number increased to 12,000. New housing, sanitation and health services, burial sites,and better market facilities had to be provided. Moreover, this population growth occurred mainly in the boroughs of Doña Cecilia, Arbol Grande and La Barra, where residents could call for services as members of the municipality. In order for Tampico to be a modern city, it had to provide all those services.[36]

City and business leaders decided to continue their cooperation facing these difficulties. One of the first problems to tackle was the handling of the new public market facilities. Mr. Gregorio Cortina Basadre, city council member, important businessmen, and twice-elected mayor, with excellent connections to all the "right" people, bid for the construction of the market building in an area close to the Tamesín shore and the Plaza de la Libertad. His company's proposal stipulated that it would lease the floor space or stalls for the next thirty years,and the city treasury would receive a specific annual payment to be decided in the contract. At the end of the thirty years, the building would become city property. Cortina's company had the economic support of several U.S. citizens. He won the contract in 1896, and construction began immediately under the direction of engineer E.K. Pedrick. His sudden death detained the project for almost a year, when it continued under the direction of an American company with offices in México City directed by John Bannister and John A. Snell. They appointed J. H. Kain as the new chief engineer of the project.

The market building was an imposing structure with a width of seventy feet and a length of 280 feet. It was built of iron and steel with stone foundations, and was divided into 216 stalls, each with water facilities supplied by a tank holding 2500 gallons pumped in by a windmill. The new structure was a great addition to the city and a very profitable monopoly for Mr. Cortina Basadre and his partners.[37]

Also in 1896, the "shrewd" Cortina Basadre maneuvered City Hall to win the supply of "piped" water or sewerage to Tampico. However, the State government halted the concession, under its power to approve all municipal contracts, owing to complaints from worried Tampico citizens over Cortina's monopolies. The water contract was also forfeited by Abundio Iguera, who had a permit to build the sewerage system since 30 May 1894, however, after two years he had not started the project. The situation continued until June 1898, when Cortina, and his American partner Benezette Williams, presented two new sewerage plans to the city council. The partners would provide about $360,000 pesos or $180,000 dollars for the project. The concession they wanted allowed them to monopolize water services for the next forty years with a legal enforcement clause that would make all Tampico households pay a fee for water even if the liquid did not reach their home or if there were no sewerage connections to the houses. It was interesting to note that Mr. B. Williams was being financially supported by J. A. Robertson, who had served as general manager of the Monterey and Gulf Railroad and had important financial connections with the Mexican Central. Eventually, he served as the Central's general manager. Therefore, if the contract was granted to Cortina and Williams, the Mexican Central Company was going to control Tampico's water system.

In 1898, a new administration brought important changes to the city and different ideas about modernization and progress. The Presidente Municipal, Manuel J. Solórzano decided to change the rules of the game played where the Mexican Central was all-powerful. He and his councilors wanted Mexicans to have more control of the foreign capital arriving in Tampico, but still allowing for investments and innovations from abroad. Under his guidance, the city took away Cortina's concession to build the market. The municipality would build it at a cost of $155,000 pesos or $77,500 dollars. In order to pay for this investment, the city borrowed from the local branch of a national bank. Solórzano also rejected the Cortina-Williams plans for city sewerage, and asked the city engineer to prepare a new project to be built only with local capital and city government support. He had realized that, although Cortina Basadre was Mexican, by his reliance on external capital, he became an instrument and collaborator of the foreign community. The mayor's acts of national-socialist capitalism brought about a great debate in the business community.[38]

The situation in Tampico was indicative of a problem occurring throughout México that impinged on national and regional development. Tampico's business elite, although apparently in favor of any measures to increase their profits through the city's development, was divided on the roles of local and national entrepreneurs versus foreign investors. Solórzano and his group, most of them businessmen, represented a localist and nationalist position. They wanted their city to grow, but under their guidance. Without a large financial capital, they perceived the municipal government - now in a better financial condition than ever before - as the great entrepreneur or developer. The opposing group, strong supporters of private enterprise and laissez faire, represented by men such as Cortina Basadre and Llorente, considered city government as the vehicle to increase their personal fortunes through individual monopolies. They wanted municipal and ejido lands for profits, and wanted to control municipal services provided to residents to increase their economic power over the city and the region. The debate at the municipal level of the Mexican pyramidal governmental structure indicates that development issues were not the exclusive property of political philosophers or Ministers of State, but were also discussed throughout the nation.

By law, contract proposals had to be sent to the State governor for advise and consent, and officials at both Ciudad Victoria and México City severely criticized Solórzano's attitude because they supported private intervention in municipal projects. Governor Guadalupe Mainero addressed a strong letter to Tampico's mayor reprimanding him for his obstructionist's stance against private enterprise. He rejected the municipal plan for the city's aqueduct as well as the bank loan, thus dealing a blow to Tampico's governing group. The reaction from Ciudad Victoria and México City forced Solórzano and his friends to understand that policies at the higher echelons of the state and federal governments were collaborative with those individuals, natives or foreigners, who would promote modernization, development, and the capitalization of the nation's economy. They realized that their brand of local capitalism was doomed.[39]

Once the Solórzano plan failed, bidding for the aqueduct contract resumed. It was granted to an American, William Astor Chandler, who put the project under the direction of his countryman, engineer Donald H. Campbell. No one interfered this time. It took a long time to install the machinery and pipes in the city's central core, and in the upper and middle class residential areas that had started to mushroom to its north. In his annual report to the Mexican Congress of 1 April 1904, President Porfirio Díaz mentioned that 11,000 meters of iron tubing had been placed between Tampico and the Laguna del Camalote (northwest of the city and traversed by the Tamesín River) and another 9,000 meters had been placed within the city proper for its aqueduct. The distributing center was located at the "Alto de los Americanos" (American's Hill) – a promontory overlooking the Tamesín and the Laguna del Camalote, probably used by Americans during their 1846-48 occupation of Tampico – and where now elegant houses stood as homes for managers of foreign corporations in the city, and for the local and regional elite.[40]

Another city problem was the urban transportation system. The trolley company went bankrupt, owing to the poor condition of its infrastructure and lack of revenues, and as stated in the original grant, it as given to the municipal government. No local or foreign investors were available when this situation ocurred just before the train arrived in the city. However, population growth and the distance of some of the new facilities and residential areas forced a return of the trolley or urban train; besides, every modern city had a tram system. In September 1895, State Supreme Court Justice Rafael de Zúñiga, a resident of Ciudad Laredo, bid and won the concession to rebuild the Tampico trolley. Five months later, his son Rafael De Zúñiga, Jr. asked the city for permission to delay the construction owing to his father's sudden death; however, the project was never finished.[41]

Carriages, public wagons and the Mexican Central line to La Barra made transportation possible within the municipality. It took several years for city officials to find someone interested in investing on the trolley. The Mexican Central's management resented the appearance of any other competing transportation system within town. Finally in 1901, Enrique Bretón Camargo, a Tampico businessman, offered to take over the trolley concession, and to continue the same routes using mules to pull the cars. The tram lines stretched out from Plaza La Libertad, near the river, toward the northern and western boroughs. No route was created to serve La Barra because it would have competed with the Mexican Central. Mr. Bretón Camargo kept the system working until British interests bought it in 1911, changing it to an electrical system. New cars and equipment were bought in New York and London, and the tram system became an essential feature and element of Tampico's growing urbanization right after the turn of the century.

By 1900, Tampico was a city of 17,569 residents, with a high incidence of respiratory diseases, pneumonia and tuberculosis. Thousands lived in very precarious conditions, and the lack of proper health care and of a good diet increased the possibilities for a high mortality rate, especially among infants. Most of the population increase came from immigration, and some of these newcomers brought with them infectious diseases causing epidemics in the city. A high mortality rate created a problem for the available cemetery facilities, especially in a society where burials were a religious imperative. Located near the city's center, the only municipal cemetery in use dated from 1824, and by 1896, it had reached full capacity. Therefore, it became a matter of great importance for the city council to discuss the creation of a new and larger cemetery. Two problems emerged: the location for the new cemetery, and the cost of the land to be used. Both problems were argued and debated by various city administrations up to the first decade of the twentieth century. Meanwhile, several solutions were discussed to solve the problem. In 1897, city officials approached the Monterey and Gulf Railroad Company seeking the return of one hectare (2.2 acres) in Doña Cecilia borough to use as a local cemetery, but not only did management refused on grounds that all these lands were needed for further railroad development, but also complained to Governor Mainero. He immediately advised city government to stop interfering with the railroad lands. Another solution was to use the old Protestant cemetery, but both Catholics and Protestants alike protested immediately. Catholics argued that this land was not blessed, and Protestants were against having their dead mingle with Catholics. Tampico officials decided to build a new cemetery in 1899 at the site where the old Moreno Fortress stood, but debate over costs and other minor details detained the project until 1920. In the meantime, the old cemetery had to be enlarged several times until the new one was inaugurated.[42]

Electricity was another Tampico municipal service, important for its modernization. It also became a tug-o'-war between the public and local entrepreneurs and the foreign community. The first electrical plant in town was established in 1895 by Luis F. Llorente, already known for his illegal land grants. The plant originally provided electricity for street lighting, for City Hall, and for the plazas. Later on, houses began to be serviced. Its general manager was an American engineer, Mr. George Piggs.

However, many residents complained of the poor service provided, and Llorente's enemies in the council protested, but little or nothing was done to improve conditions or the facilities. In January 1897, Mr. Llorente died, and the will's executor decided to sell off the plant asking $27,000 pesos (14,000 dollars) for it. Mayor Solórzano wanted to buy the facility, and with the council's permission obtained a loan, paying $28,269.68 pesos for the plant, and making it a municipal company. But, Governor Mainero, whose views on municipal properties were known, forced Tampico's government to sell it back to private investors.

Jacob J. Hoagg, Joseph B. Hoagg, and William Bauer bought the plant three weeks later, and the concession to provide electricity to the city for only $22,000 pesos. The deal cost the city, thanks to the governor, the amount of $6,269.38 pesos, a debt it had to pay for the sake of laissez faire and private capitalism. The governor's action also allowed Tampico's electric power system to become a monopoly in the hands of American foreigners as long as demand for this service was low.[43]

Tampico's fast growth, however, positively affected local electrical service. On 5 July 1904, a new electrical concession was granted by the State government to the Compañía de Fuerza Eléctrica de Tampico, S.A., owned by Tampico businessmen Juan and Fernando Borde. The Llorente plant could not supply enough electricity for the growing demand needed at homes, businesses, and entertainment centers. Also new industries with electrical machinery arrived in the city, and needed a constant supply of electricity. The Borde Brothers' expectation was that their plant would fill in the gap, but it was impossible. Their capital was soon exhausted as the demand continued to grow, and the new plant had to be enlarged and modified requiring expenses beyond those expected. Eight years later, they sold their plant to a Pearson Company. Nevertheless, both electrical plants gave Tampico the image of a modern city, and provided electricity for municipal private residents, and for public services.[44]

A third public service facility monopolized in Tampico was the telephone system. Gregorio Cortina Basadre received a concession in 1896 to build a private telephone system serving subscribers. He also received a special contract for the system to serve City Hall, state and federal goverment offices, and to extend the company's service all over the municipality. But, again Cortina Basadre was only the local man for a larger company based in México City and owned by Americans. The Mexican Telephone System was attempting to create a national monopoly in México. The president of this corporation was Robert Colgate, of the Colgate-Palmolive Company. After 1896, any Tampico subscriber was connected to a telephone network of Mexican and United States cities. Mayor Solórzano also tried to take over this company, but again his action was confronted by Governor Mainero and governmental policies.[45]

Edward M. Rowley, an American, organized a company in 1897 that provided loading and unloading services at the Tampico port. Within one year, it had monopolized the whole waterfront, displacing local companies owned by various Tampico merchants, and also stevedores, who worked independently. Rowley created a whole new loading work system at the port that benefitted mobility of goods, and added a working component to the valuable infrastructure already shaping at the port. Any attempts by City Hall to take over Rowley's company or to compete with his monopoly were promptly discouraged by the state government.[46]

Thus, the years between 1895 and 1905 witnessed Tampico's development, a modernization of the port and the city. It was based on the railroads' presence and their attraction of more businesses. However, there was a unique feature of this growth. It was directed by the Mexican

Central with the basic capital, provisions, and the cooperation granted by local, state and federal governments. The attempts to "municipalize" (as in nationalize) essential city services by the Solórzano administration were nullified by the views and policies of state and federal officials, whose positivist views were strongly influenced by laissez faire ideas. For them, government had to remain peripheral to business enterprises, with only a supporting role to play. The record for this period does not indicate that Mayor Solórzano had any socialist leanings, but points to his belief that Tampico's income would increase if essential services to the community were under a municipal administration. The old capitalist spirit of the city brought forth an interest to place more control over foreign capital, whether foreign or Mexican, attempting to use local political forces to do it. However, Solórzano, as well as his successors in the presidencia, had to forgo their autonomous control of local politics and objectives. They had to (willingly or not) become collaborators, together with state and federal officials, of foreign capital especially represented by Americans, for modernization's sake. The city was forced to adopt the ideology of the nation.

Industrialization and its social effects

The railroads, the jetties, the opening of other communication facilities, and the improvement of city services for a growing population, gave Tampico the status of a city attractive for investments. The increasing presence of Americans at the port also made the city famous in the U.S. as a good entry point into the Mexican national market. The growth of exports from Zacatecas, Aguascalientes, San Luis Potosí, and Ciudad Victoria to the United States via Tampico made the city well known in trade circles, and gradually emerged as an important site for the location of industries.[47]

In 1893, only five industrial enterprises existed in the city, and their number grew from that year on. Mr. Edward Kemp, of the New York firm of Lanman and Kemp, received state and municipal tax exemptions in late 1896 for the construction of a plant that would produce balsam, Florida water, and other such products as Bristol Sarsaparrilla, Pectoral de Anacahuita, and Bristol Sugared Pills. It was established to serve the Mexican market, and eventually for exports to the United States. Also D.A. Bibb opened and managed a branch of the Consolidated Export Lumber Company. Its warehouse, wharf, and plant were located by the Pánuco on lands rented from the Monterey and Gulf Company. By 1900, the city's registered factories produced liquors, alcohol, preserved meats, fish and fruits, medicinal drugs, sodas, ice, furniture, soaps, and beer. There were also two foundries, one owned by Nicolás del Campo, one of Tampico's wealthiest men; the other owned by two Americans, Carl Haynes - agent for the New York, Mobile and Mexican Gulf Steamship Company - and W. Wiesel. Besides a refinery was built, partially owned by the Standard Oil Company, as well as timber warehouses, and several small tanneries. Records for that year register over four hundred other non-industrial businesses in the city.[48]

The financial sector also expanded during this period. Local banks opened competing with branches of national banks founded in México City, Chihuahua, and other major national cities. On 18 September 1895, a branch of the semi-private Banco Nacional de México opened at the port with strong support from the state governor, who encouraged all other cities in the state to make use of the Tampico facility. He also advised citizens that bills coming from the Tampico branch of the Banco Nacional were to be admitted as legal tender all over the state. Federico Schutz, long time German resident and wealthy businessman, was the Tampico agent for Banco de Londres y México, the only branch of this bank in the State of Tamaulipas which opened in early 1896. The Banco de Tamaulipas, a local bank, opened its doors in 1902 with a capital of over $2,000.000 pesos ($1,000,000 dollars). Its purpose was to serve the city, the state and the Huasteca region. Also a branch of the International Bank and Trust Company of America, opened in Tampico in the same year. However, on 19 October 1903, the bank's dealings attracted the attention of the Mexican fiscal authorities, who forced its closure for lack of capital. Two mutualist workers's organizations formed in Tampico during this period started **Cajas** or loan associations using their members's contributions. Their small size in financial terms did not pose any competitive threat to the Tampico banks, and were allowed to exist well into the century.[49]

The growth and development of the industrial, financial, and port sectors accelerated the need for an urban beautification project, which had been part of the city council's agenda for many years. The improvement of roads and streets was greatly desired, and the opportunity came in 1901 when an asphalt company established its headquarters in Tampico. The city signed a contract with the Tampico Asphalt Company to pave the main streets and avenues, a job that took several years to complete.

The **Resguardo Marítimo**, an old warehouse located at a very strategic place in the Muelle Island, was destroyed to make space for a garden area. Monuments to Mexican patriots were built for the city plazas that were also embellished with water fountains, benches, and bright electric lights for early evening or night promenades. The business community sponsored the opening of new schools because the city still lacked enough facilities for all school-age children in Tampico. On 4 March 1898, the new Apollo Theater opened to the public, and its owners began a policy to bring in the best possible entertainment for the Tampico public. The Municipal or Civil Hospital was enlarged and supplied with an X-ray machine in 1898, one of the first introduced in México. Furthermore, the municipal band was increased to twenty-eight musicians, who performed weekly from their bandstand in Plaza de la Constitución.[50]

Although a fire destroyed most of the newly built federal pier in 1898, its reconstruction was finished in time to be inaugurated together with the new Customs House on 16 October 1902. President Porfirio Díaz attended the ceremonies, and was highly pleased with the results of the project he had nurtured. A new train station was inaugurated on the Muelle Island, and two years later, the old wooden bridge "Porfirio Díaz" which traversed the Tamesín was replaced by a new iron bridge now named "Manuel Romero Rubio." [51]

Conversely, all those physical improvements brought unexpected problems. Trains and ships began to unload numerous fortune-seekers, adventurers, crooks, and women of ill repute. Several new businesses began to flourish in town that caused growing administrative and judicial concern. Judges, at the various local, state, and federal courts of Tampico, began to hear more cases involving foreigners, many of them Americans, accused of petty crimes and thievery. The growth of the Tampico police force was intimately correlated to the growth and protection of the industrial-commercial establishment. Worker's living areas in Doña Cecilia, Arbol Grande, and along the shores of the Pánuco and Tamesín rivers were considered by both the city council and the business elite as places in need of effective and constant police presence because of their potential for trouble. By 1904, the city had an "urban" police of 65 members with a commander, and a "rural" police with over 150 members, who patrolled the municipal roads and the boroughs.[52]

The Mexican Central again brought foreign workers to Tampico. They were a group of black workers from the British and French Antilles, who would work at the Doña Cecilia facilities. The company justified their presence claiming that Mexican workers lacked interest in the performance of the tasks assigned, and could not do them correctly because they did not understand English, the language used by all administrative personnel and technicians. Workers were housed in miserable multi-room dwellings in Arbol Grande, thus creating serious social and health problems. This time, unlike with the previous Black immigration from the United States, Tampico authorities did not pay much attention to these workers nor to their problems unless they caused any difficulties or troubled the local population.[53]

In 1902, the American Consul aided over 100 Americans, and stated in his report to Washington, that "the great majority were tramps and as such received scant consideration. They were farmers, railroad men, clerks, etc., who had come to México to better their condition, but failing wished to return home, but were without funds." Yet, not all U.S. nationals were in such dire need. By 1905, close to 5,000 Americans lived in the area comprising Tampico and San Luis Potosí, many of them working for U.S. corporations headquartered in Tampico, or for the eighteen steamship companies represented at the port. Furthermore, ships regularly brought in numerous passengers en route to other Gulf ports or to visit Tampico and enjoy its hunting, fishing or prospective businesses. The growth of the American colony had an impact on local imports from the U.S. When combined with the apparent affluence of the city, the result was a steady rise in the price of food staples and commodities, not only for the foreign colony, but for all residents. Still, residents were used to this phenomenon because Tampico had always been an expensive city owing to its poor transportation facilities to the interior, and to the constancy of poor crops in the municipality which had always made food items more expensive than at other Mexican cities. This problem continued in the future albeit under new circumstances.[54]

Tampico's economic growth between 1890 and 1905 was sensational. It was spurred by the presence of two railroad lines, merged into one single company by 1902. Growth increased with new port facilities, and trade expansion followed the construction of the Pánuco's jetties and of new canals connecting Tampico to Tuxpam and to Pueblo

Viejo. The 2% customs' allowance received by the city, new taxes from new businesses and professionals, and the new financial resources that appeared in town, allowed city officials to improve into what they considered Tampico's modernity. Population increase, although essential for an industrial city, brought problems of health, law and order, immigration, and public services. Thus, Tampico began its twentieth century as a progressive city, amidst the many changes occurring within the stable Porfirian peace.

The Mexican Central Railroad Company played a major role in Tampico's success story since 1890, and was a precursor for the its next phase of growth. The interest shown by the Central's president in the oil seepages of the Huasteca led to the discovery of great wells near Tampico, thus changing the city's economic climate and its national and international status.[55]

NOTES

1.Robert V. Kemper and Any Royce, "Mexican Urbanization Since 1821: A Macro-Historical Approach, " *Urban Anthropology* 8, (1979), 271; "Mexican National Railroad, " *USRCCM*, 36, 129, June 1891, 219.

2.Fernando Rosenzweig, "El desarrollo económico de México de 1877 a 1911," *El Trimestre Económico*, 32, 127, (julio/septiembre 1965), 426-430. Consuls advised U.S. businessmen to change their traditional practices, to adapt themselves to the Mexican commercial environment revising their marketing techniques. "Mexican Trade and How to Secure It," *USCR* 40, 146, November 1892, 385-412; Walter V. Scholes, "Mexico in 1896 as Viewed by an American Consul," *HAHR*, 2, (May 1950), 250-257. In 1890, there were $844,025,000 dollars invested in México: "Mexican Development and Commerce," *USCR* 39, 140, May 1892, 120. Also see "American versus European Trade in Mexico," *USCR*, 36, 131, August 1891, 582-584.

3."The State of Tamaulipas," *USRCCM* 35, 127, April 1891, 606; Rosenzweig, 433.

4."Imports of Mexico," *USCR* 36, 128, May 1891, 74; "Mexican Maritime Movements," *USCR* 40, 147, December 1892, 542-543; "Mexican Exports," *USCR* 40, 144, September 1892, 46.

5.*USCR*, 35, 127, (April 1891), "The State of Tamaulipas," 607.

6.In 1895, Mexican exports amounted to $90,854,953 pesos or $45,427,476 dollars. Imports reached only $34.002,749 pesos or $17,001,374 dollars. See "Economic Situation of Mexico in 1895," *USCR* 55, 206, November 1897, 354; *The Mexican Herald* (México, D.F.), 18 October 1895, 2; *POET* (Ciudad Victoria), 21, 46, 16 abril 1896,1.

7.Kemper and Royce, 271.

8.In 1894, the engineering firm of Pearson and Son won the contract to improve the harbor at Veracruz. The works started in the spring of 1895. *RUCFR 1895 and 1896*, I, (Washington, D.C., 1897), 413-414. Also see Tischendorf, 60. Harbor works at Tampico were already finished when port works were starting at Coatzacoalcos and Salina Cruz, Ernest Gruening, *Mexico and Its Heritage* (New York, 1928), 62.

9.Charles E. Hodson, "San Luis Potosí," *Catholic World*, 51, 303, (June 1890), 295.

10."Tampico," *USCR*, 33, 118, (1890), 492; NA, DCT, 84, 304, 96, 28 February 1890, Consul Greathouse to Assistant Secretary of State.

11.*The Mexican Herald* (Mexico, D.F.), 3 December 1897, 7; "The State of Tamaulipas," *USRCCM* 36, 127 (April 1891), 604. The Monterey and Gulf Railroad was the new name for the Belgian line, partly owned by Mexican investors.

12.*The Mexican Herald* (México,D.F.), 5 December 1895, 7.

13.National lands are all those along Mexican coasts, under lagoons, and on river shores, and it is up to the federal government to grant contracts for any works in them. "Constitución Mexicana de 1857," Título II, Artículo 42 in Felipe Tena Ramírez (ed.) *Leyes fundamentales de México (1808-1964)* (México, D.F., 1964), 613.

14.*The Daily Picayune* (New Orleans) 45, 46, 11 March 1881, 3:4; George P. Hammond and Edgar F. Good (eds.) *A Scientist on the Trail, Travel Letters of A. Bandelier, 1880-1881*(Berkeley, 1949), 60. Sources indicate that the harbor study was part of a U.S. Navy project of the Mexican coastal lands on the Gulf.

15.NA, DCT, 84, 304, 77, 1 August 1882, Consul Cassard to Assistant Secretary of State; *El Faro de Tampico* (Tampico) I, 18, 30 julio 1882, 2; AMT, *Actas*, 15 abril 1885.

16.*The Two Republics* (México, D.F.), 44, 53, 3 March 1897, 4. James B. Eads and Elmer L. Corthell were internationally famous American engineers, who built the Mississippi River jetties. E.L. Corthell, *A History of the Jetties at the Mouth of the Mississippi River*, Second edition (New York, 1881); *RDRIAM*, 274, Letter from E.L. Corthell to Secretary of War, 22 November 1915; NA, DCT, 84, 304, 25, 24 March 1891, Consul Lieberknecht to Assistant Secretary of State.

17.The north jetty was 6750 feet long stretching out on the Gulf on the Tamaulipas and Tampico's side of the river. The southern jetty extended 7000 feet, and was located on the Veracruz side of the Pánuco. Tropical storms and high tides damaged the jetties on numerous occasions, thereby creating a constant need for repairs and enlargements over the next decades. See "Tampico," *USCR*, 118, 313, 1890.

18.See chapter 2, note 29; also *The Mexican Herald* (México, D.F.) 30 October 1895, 6; Adalberto Arguelles, *Reseña del Estado de Tamaulipas* (Ciudad Victoria, 1910), 21; Leif Adleson, *Historia social de los obreros industriales de Tampico, 1906-1919* (Ph.D. diss., El Colegio de México, 1982), 6; NA, DCT, 84, 304, 9, 11 June 1894, Consul Maguire to Assistant Secretary of State; 304, 31, 9 October 1896, Consul Maguire to Assistant Secretary of State.

19.*The Mexican Herald* (México, D.F.) 30 October 1895, 6; NA, DCT, 84, 304, 7, 21 January 1892, Consul Lieberknecht to Assistant Secretary of State. The Central's plan was financed by Tampico investors well into the first decade of the twentieth century. The city has remained a popular resort for the region up to the 1960s, and Miramar beach is still as popular as ever.

20."Tampico," *USCR*, 489. Also see Emilio Coello Salazar, "El comercio interior, " in *HMM. El Porfiriato*, VI, 776.

21.*El Municipio Libre* (México, D.F.) 22, 289, 10 diciembre 1891, 3.

22.The silver crisis deepened in 1893. On 26 June, India ended its free coinage of silver, and 30 June, U.S. President Cleveland issued a call for an extra session of Congress to solve the silver problem. In México, Díaz became aware of the consequences of these events on the national economy. See Tischendorf, 52-54; George Malone, C. Dumas and Basil Rauch, *The New Nation, 1865-1917* (New York, 1960), 164-166; Guadalupe Nava Otero, "La minería bajo el Porfiriato," in Ciro Cardoso (ed) *México en el siglo XIX. 1821-1910* (México, D.F., nd.), 370-375; José A. Batiz y Enrique Canudas Sandoval, "Aspectos financieros y monetarios, 1880-1910," *Ibid*, 424-428.

23.Guadalupe Hernández Sotomayor, 39; *CRUSE* 2 vols., (Washington, D.C., 1902), I, 451; Friedrich Katz, *The Secret War in Mexico, Europe, the United States and the Mexican Revolution* (Chicago, 1981), 25.

24.*Diario Oficial del Superior Gobierno de los Estados Unidos Mexicanos* (México, D.F.), 32, 138, lunes 10 junio 1895, 3. The pooling continued until 1902; see Tischendorf, 55.

25.*The Mexican Herald*, (México, D.F.) 23 October 1895, 5.

26.*The Mexican Herald* (México, D.F.) 2 November 1895, 6.

27.*The Mexican Herald* (México, D.F.) 23 December 1895, 7. The Ward SS Lines made arrangements with the Monterey and Gulf RR. To take goods twice a week directly to the U. S. from Tampico. The Mexican Central had its own line of ships. At Veracruz, the Mexican Railway brought British ships via U.S. ports. Thus, the late nineteenth century rivalry between England and the United States was rather visible in this simple instance of cargo shipping out of Mexican Gulf ports.

28. *Manifiesto a la Nación de los documentos en que constan los compromisos contraídos y no cumplidos hasta hoy por la Compañía del Ferrocarril Central Mexicano con esta Ciudad y que se publican por acuerdo de este R. Ayuntamiento en Cabildo Ordinario de 21 de diciembre de 1893* (Tampico, 1894). Also see NA, DCT, 84, 304, 5, 16 March 1894, Consul Maguire to Assistant Secretary of State; *The Two Republics* (México, D.F.) 44, 53, 3 March 1897, 4; Covián Martínez, 122.

29.*POET*, 21, 44, 11 abril 1896, 2. The granting of the contract was related to the problem that the Mexican Free Zone created for U.S. border towns. President Cleveland had signed a bill placing partial restrictions on the shipment of foreign goods sent in bond via American routes to México's Free Zone. President Díaz retaliated with a decree, signed on April 1895, allowing the importation of foreign merchandise duty-free into the northern frontier from the ports of Tampico, Veracruz and Guaymas. Thus, it was imperative for México and for the Central to have the port at its best, not only for the volume of trade expected, but also to keep the city's elite in a happier, supportive and united mood. See Oscar Martínez Jáquez, *Ciudad Juárez. A Boom Town on the Frontier* (Austin/London, 1975), 27.

30.*The Mexican Herald* (México, D.F.) 7 December 1895, 2.

31. *USCR 1894-1895* I, (1896), 341-342.

32. The Mexican "ejidos" were lands held traditionally by Indian communities before the Spanish conquest. During the colonial period, Spain allowed this institution continue, but also let municipalities to keep some lands under their control for communal purposes. For many towns, these "municipal" lands were considered "ejidos." After Independence, liberals wanted to integrate the whole nation into the spirit of capitalism, that is, of private property. The mid-century Lerdo Law destroyed the ejidos and municipal lands, which taken from its historic owners was either granted or sold to private individuals. In Tampico's case, the documents always speak of "ejidos," yet there were no Indian communities within its jurisdiction, nor any Indian ejidos. It must be understood, therefore, that they refer to the municipal lands seized after the Juárez government took power in 1867.

33. "Contiene lo relativo a la instalación de este Ayuntamiento que ha de regir el presente año," AMT, Expediente 1, Enero 1896; *POET*, 21, 5, 11 enero 1896, 3; AMT, *Actas* 1 enero 1887, 1 enero 1888, 22 agosto 1888; AMT, Expediente 107, 29 octubre 1887; AMT, Expediente 16, febrero 1888. Also see *Indice general de los terrenos ubicados en el Ejido de esta Ciudad* (Tampico, 1894-1900). This document found in the Archivo Municipal de Tampico describes all the ejido lands with the names of those who had possession of them in 1894.

34. *POET*, 21, 62, 13 mayo, 1896, 3-4.

35. *POET*, 21, 66, 30 mayo 1896, 4; also 29 junio 1896, 3.

36. *The Two Republics* (México, D.F.) 44, 53, 3 March 1897, 4; *POET* 21, 5, 11 enero 1896, 3; *POET* 21, 62, 12 mayo 1896, 3-4.

37. Cortina Basadre's contract allowed him to collect the market tax known as "piso," which was paid daily or weekly for rent of stalls or floor space in the market area. In lieu of this benefit he paid a regular fee to the municipal treasury. He also got the contract for the city's garbage disposal services. AMT, Expediente 87, bis, 1897; *The Two Republics* (México, D.F.) 44, 53, 3 March 1897, 4.

38. AMT, *Borrador de la Memoria No. 2. Mensaje del Presidente Municipal* (Tampico, 1 enero 1898); *POET*, 21, 68, 6 junio 1896, 2; AMT, Expediente 87, 1897 and Expediente 10 junio 1898.

39. AMT, Expediente 713, "Carta del Gobernador Mainero al Republicano Ayuntamiento de Tampico," 27 julio 1898.

40. Covián Martínez, 40, 94. The Mexican Central built a sewerage system to serve its installations throughout the city. See Estado de Tamaulipas, *Informe del C. Gobernador del Estado Pedro Arguelles al abrirse el primer período de sesiones ordinarias del Honorable XVIII Congreso del día 1 de abril de 1906* (Ciudad Victoria, 1906), 27. Also

AMT, Documento suelto mecanografiado, "Memoria del 1904. 1 enero de 1905," numeros 982/986. **El Alto de los Americanos** was located to the north of the city, and the colonia (housing development) Campbell was built on and around it. Carlos González Salas believes that the builder of the colonia was Edward Campbell. Sources, however, indicate that his name was Donald H. Campbell, an American engineer, who remained in Tampico after completing the aqueduct project. See Carlos González Salas, *Tampico*, 198-200.

41.*POET*, 21, 10, 23 enero 1896, 6; 21, 55, 7 marzo 1896, 3; AMT, Expediente 81, "Reglamento de coches de servicio público," 24 mayo 1897; Covián Martínez, 10; González Salas, *Tampico* ..., 94.

42.AMT, Expediente 128, "Juez Registro Civil propone construir nuevo cementerio y pide usar el llamado Protestante por estar abandonado," 1 noviembre 1897; Expediente (unnumbered) 15 marzo 1899; Expediente 134, "Contiene todo lo relativo al acuerdo designando terrenos para Cementerio del Paso de Doña Cecilia, 1897; *POET*, 21, 2, 2 enero 1896, 4; Charles C. Cumberland, *Mexico...*, 191.

43.NA, DCT, 84, 304, 20, 25 April 1896, Consul Magill to Assistant Secretary of State; "Cuestionario sobre la luz eléctrica," AMT, Expediente 40, 25 febrero 1897; "Borrador de la Memoria 2. Memoria del Presidente Municipal," 1 enero 1898. The concession was granted for 15 years, AMT, Expediente 15, "Contiene secretos públicos," 30 enero 1898.

44."Memoria de 1904," AMT, (typewritten) nos. 982/986, 1 enero 1905; González Salas, *Tampico...*, 80.

45.*POET*, 21, 43, 9 abril 1896, 2. The Tampico agent for the Mexican Telephone Company was Mr. J.E. Torbet. *The Mexican Herald* (México, D.F) 22 October 1895, 6; 5 December 1895, 7; NA, DCT, 84, 304, 20, 25 April 1896, Consul Maguire to Assistant Secretary of State.

46.Lief Adleson, 11.

47.NA, DCT, 84, 304, 66, 2 November 1899, Consul Magill to Assistant Secretary of State.

48.AMT, "Oficio del Gobierno Federal solicitando datos sobre establecimientos industriales," 13 julio 1894; Expediente 189, "Apertura de establecimientos," 1896. *The Mexican Herald* (México, D.F.) 30 October 1896, 6; *POET*, 21, 12, 28 enero 1896, 4; *POET* 21, 143, 26 noviembre 1896, 3 and 21, 145, 1 diciembre 1896, 1. Tampico foundries did not compete with the giant American Smelting and Refining Company (ASERCO) owned by Standard Oil Company. ASERCO sent its mineral production to Tampico via the Monterey and Gulf to be shipped to Perth Amboy, New Jersey, in vessels of the American Smelters Steamship Company, also a Standard Oil. See Mira Wilkins, *The Emergence...*, 118; Jesús González Serrano, *Aguascalientes: Imperio de los Guggenheim* (México, D.F., 1982), 59; González Salas, *Tampico...*, 79-80. In 1901,

Enrique Camargo Bretón and G.F. Goestch opened a food preserve factory in Tampico; Covián Martínez, 63.

49.*POET* 21, 5, 5 enero 1896,2 and 21, 12, 28 enero 1896, 4; Covián Martínez, 102; AMT, Expediente 19, "Documentos relativos a la fábrica..." 30 septiembre 1903.

50.Fritz L. Hoffman, "E.L. Doheny and the Beginnings of Petroleum Development in Mexico," *Mid-America*, 24, (n.s.13), April 1942, 101-102; AMT, Expediente 39, "Contiene dictamen y aviso pericial del Salón Teatro Apolo," 7 marzo 1898; *Memoria del Ayuntamiento Constitucional del Puerto de Tampico. Correspondiente al Año de 1901* (Tampico, 1902), 12; Torrea y Fuentes, 281-282; González Salas, *Del Reloj en Vela*, 8; Covián Martínez, 68; AMT, "Memoria del 1904," 8.

51.Tischendorf, 60; Covián Martínez, 95, 102; AMT, "Memoria de 1904," 8.

52.*POET*, 21, 107, 3 septiembre 1896, 3; AMT, Expediente 14 julio 1898. A large number of "rurales" (rural police) patrolled the rail lines and outlying businesses of the municipality.

53.Adleson, 13-14.

54.NA, DCT, 84, 304, 27, 4 September 1896, Consul Maguire to Assistant Secretary of State; 304, 159, 18 February 1903, Consul Magill to Assistant Secretary of State; 304, 221, 31 October 1905, Consul Magill to Assistant Secretary of State; Torrea y Fuentes, 282; Mira Wilkins, *The Emergence...*, 124. According to Wilkins, the increase in prices wherever there is an American colony is a phenomenon called "the cluster complex," that is, when Americans live abroad in groups they remain consumers of U.S. products.

55.Hoffman, 99,101; Wallace Thompson, *Trading in Mexico* (New York, 1921), 201; *Review of Reviews*, 30 (September 1904), 372-373, also see its note 39.

4

OIL AND TAMPICO

> Tampico has been converted into one of the most important, and best known shopping and distributing ports in Latin America.
>
> U.S. Consul Griffith, 1908.

The twentieth century began for Tampico amidst an atmosphere of great promise. The railroad lines, the jetties, a modern port, a burgeoning international sea trade, and an excellent communications organization gave it an infrastructure that few Mexican cities could surpass. Tampico was rapidly overtaking Veracruz, a long-cherished dream among Tampiqueños. The seemingly unheard news given by the American Consul, David H. Strother, in 1883 that "almost inexhaustible beds of asphaltum exist on both banks of the river Tamesín about 60 miles above Tampico" finally became a reality in 1900, when oil was discovered, thus adding to the city's identity an international status held by few Mexican or Latin American cities.[1] This chapter analyzes the discovery of petroleum in Tampico's hinterland, and some of the factors which made it México's oil center during the first three decades of the twentieth century, and the first oil city in the world.

Petroleum has been known to humans since antiquity. Archaeological research indicates that oil was often used by the ancients as a bonding material instead of a mortar. It also served as setting for jewels, to caulk vessels and for road construction. Herodotus mentions how petroleum was procured in his time. Ancient Greeks called it **asphaltos**, meaning pitch. It was found in considerable quantities in the Dead Sea, and Assyrians, Phoenicians, and Romans, who called the Dead Sea **Lacus Asphalites**, made use of it to pave their roads. Lighter forms of this black liquid were included in the Latin word "bitumen." Persians and Arabs named the liquid **naphtha**, and also used it for paving, and lighting, for medicines and weaponry. Arabic Spain introduced to Western Europe the oil distillation process and this knowledge, taken to the New World by the earliest conquerors, was of little value until petroleum sources were found. The Aztecs and Huastecans of Mesoamerica called it **chapapotli**, but it was never an important economic item in their societies. Neither was it during the colonial period.[2]

The 1859 discovery of oil by Edwin L. Drake, at Titusville, Pennsylvania, U.S., created a whole new industry that changed world economy. Oil and its secondary products, its supply industries, and its effect on transportation systems altered human and industrial energy needs. First it affected most industrial societies, but eventually reached all nations in the world. Ever since Drake's first well was activated, there was a constant increase in oil production. Only two thousand barrels of oil were produced at Titusville in the first year after the discovery, but by 1874, the total oil production for the United States alone surpassed ten million barrels, an indication of the product's growing demand. One source indicates that "between 1860 and 1900 petroleum was used mainly for illumination and for lubrication."[3] By the turn of the century, gas and electricity competed with oil in all urban areas of the world, yet, in rural areas - hamlets, villages, and sparsely inhabited regions - demand increased rapidly as kerosene (an oil by-product) became a traditional necessity.

Bold entrepreneurs searched for the sources of this new wealth in the United States and around the globe. By 1900, explorations carried out by North Americans and Europeans resulted in the discovery and development of oil fields in Russia, Rumania, Persia, the Dutch Indies, and Burma. Surveys made along the coast of the Mexican Gulf led to the formation of two major oil centers: Houston in Texas, and Tampico in Tamaulipas.[4] Thus, while Tampico was beginning to benefit from the new port facilities and integration into the Mexican national market with a stronger presence through trade and commerce, unbeknownst to anyone, these new facilities and infrastructure would become the main attraction for the region's oil entrepreneurs, who, once oil was discovered, wanted to produce and export it.

"Chapapoteras" and the Mexican oil market

The Aztecs sold **chapapotli** in their open markets for a variety of uses. Fray Bernardino de Sahagún, in his *Historia Universal de la Nueva España*, describes how the chapapotli was found seeping from the ground in the northeast area of the central plateau known as the Huasteca.[5] For almost two hundred years after the conquest of México, Spaniards did not pay much attention to this **bitumen** or **jugo de la tierra** (juice of the earth), however, on 23 May 1783, King Charles III issued a Royal Ordinance for Mines which asserted the Crown's control and rights over oil. The decree established that the subsoil and its wealth belonged to the Spanish Crown.[6] This economic principle was adopted by the Mexican republican government after independence in 1822, and accepted as a national prerogative both in the 1824 and 1857 constitutions.

On 22 November 1884, President Porfirio Díaz promulgated México's first Law of Mines which eliminated government's control of the subsoil. The new law followed a concept traceable to France's legal system that land ownership included both the surface and its subsoil, thus depriving the nation of any claim over its mineral wealth. The new law was hailed by all foreign investors in Mexican minerals, but nationalists saw it as a treason to the nation. It brought on a debate that was only partially resolved by the 1917 Constitution, but which continued long after between the large oil companies and the Mexican government. It was in 1938 that it ended after President Lázaro Cárdenas nationalized the oil industry.[7]

Attempts to discover petroleum in great quantities in México started soon after Drake's discovery in Pennsylvania. It might have influenced Mexican engineer Antonio del Castillo, who began drilling near México City in 1860. Two years later, a small amount of oil was found and he used it to lit some lamps. Others also looked for the precious liquid, with limited success.

During the French Intervention period, specifically between 14 November 1864 and 6 November 1865, Emperor Maximilian granted thirty one concessions to oil prospectors.[8] One grant went to Ildefonso López, who searched and exploited asphalt and oil substances on his hacienda at San José de las Rusias, an area north of Tampico in Tamaulipas. Other concessions were for exploration along the Tamesín River, which had no success. Some oil was found and exploited in northern Veracruz State, near the town of Tuxpám, a river port about 150 kilometers south of Tampico.[9]

In 1870, Mr. A.G. Autrey, an Irish-American and reputed inventor of the Angostura Bitters, bought a property at Papantla, northern Veracruz, where he set up several stills. He registered the **Compañía Explotadora del Golfo Mexicano** (Mexican Gulf Oil Exploration Company), and built a small refinery to produce kerosene that was easily sold in the region's local rural markets. Another oil venture was made by a U.S. company, the Boston-Mexican Oil. It held an area covering over two thousand acres of lands where oil was suspected. Its lands were bought from four different haciendas named Gil, Tampamachoco, Chapapote, and Juan Felipe. Eventually oil was found in large quantities in all four haciendas, yet, the Boston-Mexican's exploration failed without ever finding the slightest trace of petroleum.[10]

While individual and corporate explorations were underway in the Mexican Gulf region, new industrial or technical applications for oil were devised in Europe and the United States reaching México's major cities soon after. Street lighting systems began to use kerosene for combustion, after 1861. The new method extended to Tampico, where a contract to provide gas, lamps, and kerosene was granted to Angel Saínz Trápaga, a wealthy Spanish merchant, a recent newcomer. Not long after, he was named President of the Tampico Board of Commerce, and Spanish Consul at the Port. A keen observer of his times, Saínz realized the profitable potential of petroleum, and started to import it from the United States. Eventually, he became a crucial figure for Tampico's entrance in the oil world.[11]

Another Spanish resident and businessman who also imported oil was Benito Zorrilla. He tried to provide the local market with home made kerosene, and started a distillation process system in the backyard of his Tampico residence, located almost in the center of the city. However, neighbors and "other concerned" citizens, such as Mr. Saínz and Mr. Claussen (a third oil importer), as well as other local oil importers, denounced him to the municipal authorities alleging that a fire could be started and destroy the city. Of course, their major fear was that Zorrilla's success in his endeavor would destroy their advantage in the oil import business. The council forbade Mr. Zorrilla's enterprise, thus keeping the Tampico oil business in the hands of importers, none of whom knew of the regional potential wealth in the rich black liquid. These "concerned citizens" preferred to make money importing kerosene rather than using the rich available sources that were so close to them, and of which they were ignorant.[12]

Meanwhile, the few oil discoveries made in México, done mostly by foreigners, brought a debate in México City about the amount and location of the sources, a dispute that began in the late 1870s and continued into the first decade of the twentieth century. In 1878, Edward Johnson, U.S. Consul in Tampico, stated that oil exploration and exploitation in his district was a losing proposition, but in 1880, U.S. engineers Samuel Fairbank and George Dikson discovered some oil in northern Veracruz, not far from Tampico, and began the construction of a small refinery nearby, that was completed in 1886. In 1883, U.S. Consul General David H. Strother, in response to a Department of State inquiry, sent Washington a report on Mexican asphaltum. He insisted that no efforts had been made to ship petroleum products from the México's ports, notwithstanding the large amounts of oil that could be found in the area of the Huastecas.[13]

Some people in Tampico knew of the oil deposits, seepages or chapapoteras that could be seen within a few miles to the northwest and south of the city. These, however, were found in the jungles, and to reach them or to transport the oil from them was a very difficult task. Only one Tampico merchant, Gerardo Claussen, consul of the German Empire, was exporting asphaltum to Hamburg from seepages found south of Tampico. Besides Strother, other American consuls also realized the existence of oil in the area. By 1890, U.S. Consul General Warren P. Sutton asserted that large oil fields could be found south of Tampico. Some of them were "developed and an extensive plant put in, but for some cause the enterprise has not yet been successful." He also questioned the sale of that oil plant or refinery because the high demand for "coal-oil" in México, and the excessive import duty on the refined product, made logical the profitable production of the regional crude oil.[14] He was amazed that no company had taken any interest in these large oil deposits.

On the other hand, some American companies and individuals became interested in supplying México's oil market, without taking into consideration the debate over the country's petroleum sources. Consul Sutton's advice was heeded when in 1890, a new refinery - connected to the Standard Oil Company - opened in México City "to which crude petroleum (was) shipped from the United States."[15] Between 1890-91, 260 railroad cars, carrying nearly one million gallons of crude oil, passed through the border town of Paso del Norte (Ciudad Juárez) for the refinery in México City. Some of the refined oil was marketed throughout México, and the rest was sent to the United States, but freight charges were prohibitive. However, the growth in demand for oil forced refinery owners to realize that Mexican production had to be increased, and that a new refinery was needed somewhere along the border or at some Gulf coast port.[16]

Agents went to México looking for a good site to build the refinery. One of them worked for the J. Findlay and Company, but the record is not clear on his whereabouts or actions in the country. Another belonged to the Waters Pierce Corporation, a two-thirds owned subsidiary of the Standard Oil Company of New Jersey, which had acquired the Fairbank & Dikson refinery in Veracruz, expanding its imported oil production to 500 barrels a day. By 1892, Waters Pierce had agents in all major Mexican cities, and had gained a virtual monopoly over the kerosene, lubricating oils, and gasoline markets of the nation.[17]

John R. Davis, Waters Pierce agent, visited San Luis Potosí in late 1895 or early 1896, in search of lands and government support, that is, tax breaks and investments, to build a refinery. Davis was coolly received by Governor Pedro Díez Gutiérrez, his officials, and the city council. Disappointed, he left the state heading for the United States via Tampico.[18] Angel Saínz Trápaga, aware of the Davis mission in San Luis, enlisted Tampico's business and official community to give the Waters Pierce agent a grand welcome as part of a plan to convince him of the benefits his company would enjoy if the refinery was built at the port. Saínz arranged interviews with governor Alejandro R. Prieto, and other Tamaulipas State officials. He persuaded the city's councilmen to grant a large municipal plot of land, on the right bank of the Pánuco and near the Doña Cecilia village, for the refinery grounds. Finally, he used his influence to win tax exemptions for the company from both state and city governments. For his intervention on behalf of the Waters Pierce, Saínz benefitted becoming the company's agent for the Huastecas, and helped himself selling some of the lands he had started hoarding in both Arbol Grande and Doña Cecilia. His convincing skills were well served.[19]

By March 1896, John Davis officially requested the state government for a seven year tax exemption on an oil refinery that Waters Pierce wanted to build at the Arbol Grande borough. Juan Zubiaga, secretary of the State Congress and a long-time Tampico representative in Ciudad Victoria, gave his full support and political skills to company's request. He believed that the large capital investment required for the refinery would benefit both city and state. It would bring hundreds of jobs to Tampico, trade would increase, and the tax base for both city and state would expand. Zubiaga's intervention was most favorable, and on 20 April 1896, the State Congress granted Davis's request.[20]

Construction began immediately, and by September 1897, the refinery began its operations at a rate of 2,000 barrels a day with crude oil imported from the United States. The company's total value in assets at the start of operations was of $150,000 dollars, including deposit tanks, warehouses, machinery, and offices at Arbol Grande and Tampico.[21]

American oil interests in México were challenged by British oil prospectors, who had searched for black gold in early 1890s, both in southern and northern Veracruz State. General Sir Richard Sarkey, head of a group of investors, acquired several large land concessions from both federal and state governments, including tax exemptions and permits to lay equipment "where the existence of petroleum has been conclusively established." Also, the Mexican Petroleum and Liquid Fuel Company Limited, another British firm whose investors included Sir Cecil Rhodes, began drilling operations in an area close to Tuxpám under the company name of London Oil Trust, with great hopes but little success, and by 1898, a Mr. George Jeffrey leased some oil lands in northern Veracruz.[22]

These British operations were viewed with concern and mistrust by A.B. Jones, U.S. Consul in Tuxpám. He feared that the British were plotting with the Mexican federal authorities to control Mexican oil lands in detriment of American interests, especially those of the New Jersey Mexican Asphaltum Company, another Standard subsidiary, that had started exporting asphaltum in 1899, and could be forced out of the market if the British were successful in their explorations. The consul's analysis was one more signal of the rivalry that began between British and American interests over Mexican oil lands - rivalry maintained and encouraged by successive Mexican governments seeking to gain more national control over its resources - while Anglo-Saxon capitalists fought over lands, or over benefits. At the turn of the century, however, these British oil enterprises in México at the turn of the century were still small compared to the growing power of the Standard Oil Company.[23]

By 1900, the Mexican energy market was controlled by Standard Oil of New Jersey with its refineries in Tampico, Veracruz, and México City, which were supplied with oil imported from the United States. The company was not involved in exploration or exploitation of any Mexican crude, but at this time oil prospectors in México had not yet been successful in their searches. Furthermore, Standard Oil had increased its control of the Mexican economy after it took an interest in the consolidation of the great mining complex known as ASERCO, and its subsidiary the American Smelters' Steamship Company, which sent lead, copper, and other minerals for refining from Tampico's port to Perth Amboy, New Jersey.[24]

Minerals reached Tampico from Monterey via the Monterey and Gulf Railroad, since 1898 also controlled by the Mexican Central Railroad. In 1900, Henry Clay Pierce, president of the Waters Pierce Company, was named president of the Mexican Central Railroad because he was Standard Oil's highest official in México. This action placed

Standard in an almost total monopoly of Tampico's external trade, (exports and transportation), and jobs, while monopolozing México's oil needs. The port's economic importance, now second to Veracruz, forced federal officials to consider this monopoly as harmful to the nation. México's powerful Finance Minister, José Ives Limantour, became apprehensive of the Standard's activities, and sought to thwart them through support of rival North American and British challengers to this monopoly.[25]

An American entrepreneur

Oil exploration and exploitation in México was carried out mostly by foreigners, and not very successfully until 1900. Two bold, daring and lucky men, one American and another British, conquered the difficulties that terrain, men, and laws presented to their quest finding and securing some of the world's richest oil lands available at the beginning of the twentieth century.

Edward L. Doheny, born in Fond du Lac, Wisconsin, had been a roving entrepreneur since adolescence. First, he prospected for gold in Colorado and Arizona making some small profits. These in turn, allowed him to search for oil in California, where he discovered important deposits near Los Angeles during the 1890s. Doheny realized that oil without a demand was useless, and became rather interested in finding new ways for its use that would create a broader market for it. He experimented using petroleum to move locomotive engines instead of coal. The tests employed machines provided by the Atchison, Topeka and Santa Fe Railroad Company, owner of the Mexican Central Company. Mr. A.A. Robinson, then president of the Mexican Central and one of Atchison's vicepresidents, called on Doheny after the success of his experiments. He wanted to use the newly-found techniques on his Mexican locomotives. However, aware of the oil seepages in the Tampico route that might provide the oil for the engines, he invited Doheny to visit the Huasteca in a fact-finding tour. Robinson promised Doheny a railroad supply contract, if the oil in the Huasteca route between San Luis and Tampico proved exploitable.[26]

E. L. Doheny and his partner Charles A. Canfield travelled from El Paso to the Hacienda "El Tulillo" in a private car placed at their disposal by the Mexican Central. This hacienda of 283,000 acres, located about thirty five miles west of Tampico, was remarkable for its numerous "chapapotes." Its owner, Mr. A. Arguinzonis, was selling it owing to the numerous oil seepages that did not allow for good agricultural use of the land, and to problems with the neighbors and their wandering cattle. The two men toured the place, and realizing its potential wealth immediately decided to invest in these lands. They bought "El Tulillo" as well as a neighboring hacienda called "Chapacao," of approximately 165,000 acres. The risk paid off handsomely.

Upon his return to the U.S., Doheny ordered prospecting equipment to be sent rapidly via Tampico. It included materials for stills, and enough barbed wire to fence the property. The partners also began hiring men from the neighborhood, and word spread across the Huastecas that jobs and good salaries were available at the Haciendas. Soon hundreds arrived and the first oil camp was established near the hill known as "El Ebano" (Ebony).[27] By March 1901, with enough equipment and men, drilling began in an area of "El Tulillo" called **La Dicha** (Happiness). The first well surged forth the 14 of May breaking all the machinery, yet, a few days after, its output slowed down to a meager fifty-barrel-a-day. Nineteen more wells were opened that year, but all had similar results.[28]

Doheny hired Pablo Martínez del Río, a prominent Mexican lawyer, to deal with the legal aspects of the company, and to win from the Mexican government total control over the prospecting and drilling in the three adjoining states where his properties were located, that is, Veracruz, San Luis Potosí, and Tamaulipas. Martínez del Río secured a monopoly for a ten-year period, probably by playing on the Díaz's regime dislike for Standard Oil's presence in México, but especially in the Huastecas. Officials in México City understood this federal concession as a safeguard against Standard's acquisition or control over a possibly rich oil area, and at the same time it was a threat to its Mexican monopoly.[29]

Doheny sold his California holdings to devote all his energies to the Mexican venture. He sought some other American investors, and then incorporated in California his first, and most important, Mexican oil company: the Mexican Petroleum Company of California, with a capital of ten million dollars. Later on he incorporated other companies such as Huasteca Petroleum, Tamiahua Petroleum and Tuxpam Petroleum. By the 1920s, all his companies were integrated into the Mexican Petroleum Company of Delaware. However, this corporate growth took time and efforts.[30]

Despite the sums invested drilling, the enterprise suffered serious setbacks. At first, oil production was very small at all the wells, which made investors apprehensive, with some of them pulling out of the venture. Furthermore, Doheny's contract with the Mexican Central to supply oil for its locomotives was cancelled in 1901 by the new company president, Henry Clay Pierce, who wanted to supply "his" engines with oil from his own refineries in México.[31] In the same year, Doheny's profits were threatened when the international oil market was flooded after the discovery of the Spindletop or Beaumont oil fields in Texas, which forced the world price of a barrel down to only 3 U.S. cents. Yet, Doheny was not a man who would give up easily on anything, especially when so much money was at stake. He continued to develop his lands, and the construction of new facilities continued unabated,

> sawmills, machine shops, warehouses, waterworks, and other essentials to the business were established. A short railway line was built, and fifteen tank cars purchased ...an asphaltum plant set up to take care of the company's heavy oil.[32]

Moreover, Doheny's perseverance received help from some unexpected quarters, giving him a trump card in this play of circumstances.

Two Mexican geologists, Ezequiel Ordóñez and Juan Villarello, arrived at Tampico in December 1901. They were sent by Minister José Ives Limantour, on a fact-finding trip on rumors that large quantities of petroleum existed in the Huastecas. It seems strange that until this date, the Mexican government had not been interested in the development of this mineral wealth, although it had granted concessions and permits for exploration. Limantour also wanted to know more of the activities of the Waters Pierce and Standard Oil companies, both in Tampico and its region. The two men set out on their assignment, but Ordóñez was injured in a train accident, and had to return to México City for proper care and recovery. Villarello continued alone, and in his report to Minister Limantour indicated that no large oil supplies existed in the Huasteca. México City officials accepted his report as the final truth on the oil issue. Yet, when Ordóñez recovered, he returned to the Huasteca and concluded his research. He requested Doheny's permission – granted with great interest – to visit "El Ebano" and his other neighboring haciendas, and found evidence of large oil quantities in the whole region. Upon his return to México City, Ordoñez filed his report at the Ministry which was greeted with incredulity and mockery because it contradicted the Villarello (now official) report. A story is told that one of the officers at the Ministry gave Ordóñez a flask which had some petroleum in it with these words – "this is all there is of México's oil."[33] Whether true or not, Ministry officials decided that destiny would favor the private enterprise over the government's interest in one of the nation's major natural resources.

Ordóñez, upset and ashamed by the treatment received, and by the attitudes and lack of foresight found in México City, resigned from his position at the Ministry. Doheny, hearing of Ordoñez plight and highly impressed by his work while in Tampico, hired him as the Mexican Petroleum Company's geologist. The American desperately needed to find some big oil source that would satisfy his investors and help check his company's growing deficit. Already 2.5 million dollars had been lost in their futile search, and new investments were not forthcoming. Gerardo Meade, Doheny's Mexican wealthy neighbor, was the only one who came to his assistance financially by securing additional credit from the Banco de San Luis Potosí, S.A. Therefore, Ordoñez' arrival to the company was most welcome.[34]

Not long after, and in a 1903 December night, Ordóñez convinced Doheny to drill at the **Cerro de la Pez** (Asphalt Hill), a section of "El Tulillo," where he was certain that oil would be found in large quantities. Crews started to work immediately, and on 3 April 1904, the **La Pez** No.1 well blew up flowing at a rate of 1,000 barrels-a-day, and growing to 1,700 barrels-a-day within a few days. It continued its flow for the next nine years with a total production of three and a half million barrels of oil. The discovery made international news giving México world-fame as an oil-producing country, and making Doheny a major player in the world oil market. He became "the most important oil entrepreneur after Rockefeller," and discoverer of the richest oil strip, "la Faja de Oro" (Gold Belt) yet found in the world until the 1920s.[35]

Investors raced to buy stock on Doheny's company as soon as news told of his success. Money poured in, yet it was advantageous for him because his previous losses had forced him to acquire a larger control of the company's stock. For Tampico, the No.1 well's success was also heaven sent, and benefitted heavily from it. First, the port and its infrastructure were now of utmost need by E. L. Doheny to receive more drilling equipment, and to export oil production. The rapidly flowing petroleum had to be stored rapidly, thus forcing the immediate construction of storage tanks and pipelines to carry the liquid to the port. Shipping and handling of materials needed for those facilities brought an increased activity to the port. Second, demand for refined oil led Doheny to plan the building of a refinery, of more storage tanks and other facilities, led to an immediate increase in land values along the Pánuco shores. Finally, agents for oil companies arrived at the port looking for office and home space in the city, thus increasing real estate values.

A British Wheeler-Dealer

While E. L. Doheny searched and drilled for oil west and southwest of Tampico, another oil explorer entered the scene. Weetman Pearson, an English engineer - later Viscount Cowdray - highly regarded by President Díaz owing to his successful projects in México, also began to search for oil, but in southern Veracruz and Tabasco. Díaz invited Pearson to visit México in 1889 after his engineering firm had successfully completed New York's Lincoln Tunnel. He was asked by the President to tackle the important project of a Grand Canal that would drain the valley of México in order to prevent the recurrent floods that the city endured every year after the rainy season, a centuries-needed project after Spaniards destroyed the dikes which held back the waters built on Lake Texcoco by the Aztecs. This colossal enterprise marked the beginning of an intimate friendship between the two men.[36]

By 1894, when the Grand Canal project was almost complete, Díaz gave Pearson another magnificent project: the improvement of the port facilities and harbor of Veracruz. It allowed Pearson and Son, Ltd, to become an important economic force at the port joining the already powerful British presence that used that city as their beachhead for penetration in the Mexican market. Not only did the Pearson firm fulfill its contract on the harbor works, inaugurated by President Díaz on 6 March 1902, but it also built a new railroad station for the Mexican Railway Company, and formed the Veracruz Electric Light, Power and Traction Company which controlled the city's electric supply as well as its tramway.[37]

In 1897, Pearson received another commission from President Díaz. The Isthmus of Tehuantepec had been a source of continued problems between American and Mexican railroad interests. The federal government had spent thirty eight million dollars in the construction of a rail line described as "so flimsily built that it could not carry the heavy traffic which alone could have made it profitable."[38] Díaz wanted Pearson to rebuild the railroad connecting the ports of Salina Cruz on the Pacific Ocean and Coatzacoalcos on the Gulf of México. He was also given the contract to build new harbor facilities at both ports. These projects allowed Pearson's company to exert a powerful economic influence over the Isthmus, especially after taking over the control of the electric and tramway systems of its cities. The railroad contract also made Pearson a partner with the Mexican government in the line's administration and in its profits. Accordingly, the most important causeway between the eastern and western coasts of the continent, before the inauguration of the Panama Canal, was placed indirectly under British control. Díaz' behavior also indicates how his policies favored the British as an alternative to imperialist Americans, especially in a route which had been one of their earliest railroad interests in México.[39]

When surveying the Tehuantepec road, Pearson became aware of the "chapapoteras" that also occurred in southern Veracruz, especially in the Isthmus area. He saw many of these oil seepages and was told of many others, and immediately began to buy some lands and lease others with chapapoteras in provision for further developments. During a trip to Laredo, Texas, in April 1901, Pearson was surprised with the excitement generated by the discovery of the Lucas gusher at Spindletop in Beaumont. A wild fever had taken hold of thousands. They came from everywhere to discover oil, to lease, and to buy oil lands in Texas. He returned to México caught up in the excitement, yet foreseeing what could be found in Veracruz State. Pearson hired the Spindletop explorer Anthony Lucas, to visit, inspect and report to him on the oil possibilities of the lands in the Tehuantepec route. Lucas' report was very promising, and Pearson decided to invest in the exploration. His locomotives used oil imported from Beaumont, and Pearson wanted to break down this dependence and high cost by finding local supplies of oil. He also built a huge reservoir tank that could accommodate any yield found. In his attempt to control as much of the oil lands as he could possibly obtain, he found strong resistance from the farmers and district's landowners. He then sought help from his friends in México City.[40]

On 26 December 1901, whether at Pearson's or Doheny's request, President Díaz signed a law that authorized oil exploration on vacant national lands, that is, on lands controlled by the federal government suitable for sale or lease, and on federal lands that were those under the sole and perpetual jurisdiction of the federal government such as the river beds of México or the coastal lands up to fifty miles from shores. The law also granted the right of way through private lands, and the circular protection zones of three kilometers around each oil well. *México's Oil*, a Mexican government source, states that this law "had no other limitation than the Dictator's desire to authorize expropriations."[41] Indeed, the law benefitted both Pearson and Doheny in their constant search and acquisition of oil lands, with a resulting monopolistic and competing control over this incipient industry. Both men needed the law because at this stage of their search for oil they had not been successful. Eventually, they would face one another in Tampico and join forces against their older, and powerful, external competition. Tampico benefitted from their discoveries and their competition, and was willing to accept their presence as it made the city world famous, and much more important port for the nation. The 1901 law was written on the assumption that México had almost no oil, and that the investments made by these entrepreneurs would be more beneficial to the nation than whatever they expected to profit from México, in a sort of supply-side economics. Moreover, and at the same time, the law closed the door to any other American investors (meaning Standard Oil), especially in southern Veracruz and Tabasco. The lawmaker's assumptions were ill-conceived, based more on traditional lore than on scientific proofs. The country was rich in oil reserves, and the world's greed for oil would bring an avalanche of investments in that industry, especially from the United States.

Pearson's efforts to find oil advanced rapidly. He built over one hundred wells, but similar to Doheny's experience at **El Ebano** not much oil was found. The Englishman then decided to move his exploration and exploitation efforts to the northern Veracruz district of Ozuluama, south of Tampico, where chapapoteras had been reported. By 1903, he had acquired a majority interest in an unsuccessful British enterprise called Oil Fields of México, which had searched the area for months without finding any worthy oil deposits. Pearson took control of "about 200 square miles of lands south of Tuxpám, known as the Furbero Field in honor of the company's earlier President, Percy Furbero."[42] But, these rich oil lands did not start yielding any oil until 1907.

By 1904, the Tehuantepec wells began producing more oil, and Pearson strengthened his monopoly over oil lands in the area. He won more lands in the neighboring states of Tabasco and Chiapas. Properties were bought or leased in Puebla, and finally, Pearson confronted Doheny when he began buying and leasing lands in San Luis Potosí and Tamaulipas. At the same time, he renewed requests for more concessions from federal, state, and municipal governments to seek and exploit oil.

In 1906, two related events gave Pearson's Mexican oil empire the support he needed. One was his construction of a large refinery at Minatitlán, a small town up the Coatzacoalcos River, on the Isthmus of Tehuantepec. The site was higher and cooler than nearer the Gulf coast, and less prone to tropical diseases, so that the work force was healthier and more productive. This refinery remains one of the largest ever built in México. The second event was his 18 January acceptance of another contract with the federal government granting him several new concessions. His company was allowed to explore federal lands, that is, the subsoil of lakes, lagoons, rivers, vacant national lands, and any other lands under federal jurisdiction in the State of Veracruz. He also won, from the governors of San Luis Potosí, Tamaulipas, Tabasco, Chiapas, Campeche and Puebla, similar rights over their state lands for a period of seven years. It was agreed that Pearson would build a refinery in Veracruz, with an initial investment of $800,000 pesos. In exchange for this obligation, he would enjoy, free of taxes, an export franchise of all petroleum products. He could import, duty-free, all materials and machinery necessary for the exploration and exploitation of oil. Moreover, and reinforcing the 1901 Law, his company was granted the right to expropriate lands for industrial purposes, and buy surveyed "national" lands at the price of vacant lands, that is, at a cheaper rate. Permission was also received to put pipelines across private properties whenever it was necessary for the company.[43]

Landowners from all the involved Gulf states complained against these monopolistic concessions to a foreign company, but little could be done against the combined forces of dictatorial polices, economic power, and social influence. In a memorandum dated 1 March 1906, Pearson stated that his company owned about 600,000 acres and had royalty leases of up to 300,000 acres in Veracruz state alone. His oil lands, spreading throughout all the states mentioned above, were among México's most productive. Notwithstanding, his company also took control over the sewerage, electric, and urban transportation systems of most major towns in México's eastern seaboard.[44]

The prospect for increased oil yields from his northern Veracruz fields led Pearson to open an agency in Tampico in 1906. He bought some nicely located urban property, and added to the port's activity by importing construction materials for his nearby wells, pipelines, and fields, and by exporting petroleum. In 1907, the Furbero field began to yield increasing quantities of oil, and Pearson decided to invest one million dollars in the creation of a fleet of tank steamers to ship it to his refinery at Minatitlán or send the crude to England or the United States. Pearson also signed a contract with the Waters Pierce company to supply its Tampico refinery with oil from his fields.

Despite all his successes, Pearson had not yet created an international organization of his own, and most of his crude or refined oil was sold to the United States with only a small portion remaining for the Mexican market. By 1909, the growth of his enterprises led him to organize the **Compañía Mexicana de Petróleo "El Aguila"** (Eagle Mexican Oil Company), incorporated under Mexican law which made it a national company that could obtain government protection versus "foreign" companies, such as Standard Oil, Waters Pierce or Doheny's oil companies. The **Eagle's** Board of Directors included President Díaz's son. It was a guarantee of political protection for the company, also representing the powerful hold that oil interests had started to create in the nation's political system by involving the presidential household as beneficiary of the national wealth.

Meanwhile, Pearson's wheeling and dealing, procured him another useful contract. This time it was the construction of a canal between his fields in Ozuluama and the port of Tampico. It was rapidly built. The canal measured ten meters wide and three meters deep, and was navigable by small crafts carrying oil. This contract increased Pearson's relationship with Tampico. By 1906, Pearson faced strong competition from both Doheny and Waters Pierce, who still controlled between 80 and 90 percent of the Mexican oil retail business, and from two newcomers, the International Petroleum Company and the Pennsylvania Petroleum Company (both associated to Standard Oil), but he slowly began to win the match. In 1911, he built his company's Gulf headquarters in Tampico. Then, he began seeking control of the city just as he had done at all other Gulf towns, including Veracruz. By 1912, the Pearson company owned the Tampico tram and electric systems, and had started the construction of a new refinery on the left margin of the Pánuco, controlling about 4 kilometers of river shores where piers were built to accommodate seven ships at the same time.[45] However, the presence of E. L. Doheny, Waters Pierce, and other American oil companies (Texaco, Gulf, and Standard Oil) inhibited his monopolistic activities at the port, allowing Mexicans - at the local and national levels - to play the rivals for the benefit of Tampico and México.[46]

Pearson's Tehuantepec wells produced only between two to three thousand barrels a day in 1906. Notwithstanding, he invested heavily in a refinery, and in a fleet of tank steamers. In 1908, in order to undermine the Tampico competition, he bought out the Pennsylvania Petroleum Company, an action that was successful because by August, one of the world's most productive fields ever, the San Diego, was discovered on lands received from the Pennsylvania. A few months later, the world was awed by news that the Dos Bocas well broke loose, caught fire, and gushed out about six million barrels of oil during the following six months. Over one million tons of petroleum burned for weeks with flames reaching over 500 feet high. The overflow formed a lake with a capacity for three million barrels of oil. This incident made Pearson extremely confident in the potential of his lands, supported Ordóñez's claims for México's oil wealth and Doheny's inspections, and proved to the world and to entrepreneurs that México was a fertile ground for oil riches. This also focused international greed and demands upon México, with the oil interests intervening in the nation's political and economic spheres.[47] Two years later, Doheny's fields had their turn to awe the world with the great gusher "Juan Casiano 7." Also Pearson's "Potrero del Llano 4" supported earlier conclusions, encouraging more international attention on México.[48]

Weetman Pearson and Edward L. Doheny were successful where others, national and foreign alike, had failed. Their tenacity, luck, and use of all available means to achieve their objectives brought both men great success. They invested heavily in their ventures, and luckily when productivity rose in their wells also did world demand for oil increase, allowing their profits to soar beyond their wildest fancy. Until 1908, Pearson had invested up to 5 million pounds sterling or close to $25 million dollars, and his profits were in the hundreds of millions by 1920. The British government made him a peer, gave him a seat in the House of Lords as a token of gratitude for his services, and during the First World War, he served as Minister of Transportation for the British Government. He served well his nation in the transportation and energy fields. E. L. Doheny became one of the richest men in the United States, and finally sold his Mexican interests to his competitor Standard Oil in 1921.[49]

Both men, their discoveries, and their companies were very significant for México and for Tampico. They won legal favoritism from Díaz, thus creating a trend that became difficult to eliminate from the national political panorama. They also intruded in the Tampico scene by moving their most important technical and administrative offices to the city. Within less than a decade, the wealth generated by oil and the presence of the companies took precedence in the economic life of the city affecting all aspects of its urban development, trade, and growth. Oil masters such as Pearson and Doheny, and companies such as Eagle, Standard, and Texaco significantly influence a whole set of social changes in the city: new wealth, new labor relations, new government-business relations, a stronger position of Tampico vis-a-vis the nation. A unique and new urban setting appeared after 1900 that characterized Tampico for the next three decades. A setting, however, that continued the same old city "spirit."

NOTES

1.U.S. Consul General David H. Strother in "Mexican Asphaltum," *Reports of the Consuls of the United States on Commerce* (Washington, D.C.), February 1883, 21, 141-42.

2.The word asphalt was later applied to the heaviest forms of petroleum found in nature. It can be softened by heat and used, among other things, to pave streets or as waterproof coating for concrete floors and roofs. Diodorus mentions that asphalt of the Dead Sea was bought by Egyptians to embalm corpses. Almost pure asphalt exists only in Trinidad, Cuba, the Dead Sea, and Perú. The word *bitumen* comes from Latin, and includes in its meaning all forms of petroleum such as gases, liquids, and solids. The Spanish language uses the following words to describe oil: bitumen, "jugo de la tierra," and nafta. See "asphalt" in *Encyclopedia Britannica, 1910-1911*; "bitumen" in *Enciclopedia Espasa-Calpe*, 1926; M. Jeep, *Der Asphalt und seine Anwendung in der Technik* (Wein, 1898); Victor Forbin, *Le petrole dans le Monde* (Paris, 1940), 7-8; Herodotus, *The Histories* (London, 1986), 405.

3.Scott Nearing, *Oil and the Germs of War* (Ridgewood, 1923), 3. The bulk of oil profits came from the sale of kerosene and gasoline.

4."Petroleum," *Encyclopedia Britannica* (1968); John M. Blair, *The Control of Oil* (New York, 1978), 29; Merrill Rippy, "The Mexican Oil Industry," in Carlos Castañeda and Thomas E. Cotner, eds., *Essays in Mexican History. The Charles Wilson Hackett Memorial Volume* (Austin, 1958), 249. An excellent study on Houston's development is Joseph Pratt, *The Growth of a Refining Region* (Greenwich, 1980); also see Craig Thompson, *Since Spindletop: A Human Story of the Gulf's First Half Century* (Pittsburgh, 1951); John McLean and Robert Haigh, *The Growth of Integrated Oil Companies* (Boston, 1954); James Marquis, *The Texaco Story, 1902-1952* (The Texas Co., 1953).

5.Fr. Bernardino de Sahagún, *Historia General de las cosas de la Nueva España* 4th ed. (México, D.F., 1979), 106, 569, 574, 696, 697. The Huasteca is a geographical region that includes the southern part of Tamaulipas, the eastern sections of San Luis Potosí, Querétaro and Hidalgo, and the northern part of Veracruz. It is a low-lying tropical region inhabited by Indian nations collectively known as Huastecans, who were under Aztec suzerainty when Hernán Cortés arrived in 1519. By mid-sixteenth century, Spaniards conquered and colonized the region. See Angel Bassols Batalla, *Las Huastecas en el desarrollo regional de México* (México, D.F., 1977), and Joaquin Meade, *La Huasteca Tamaulipeca*, 3 vols. (Ciudad Victoria, 1977-79); Robert G. Cleland (ed), *The Mexican Yearbook* (Los Angeles, 1922), 290.

6.*Ordenanzas de Aranjuez de 1783.* These laws were issued by Charles III. His first mining law, exclusively ordained for New Spain, remained in effect until 1884. His decree was based on the law numbered 13.1.3 set in the **Partidas del Rey Alfonso** (1215). See Guillermo Floris Margadant S., *An Introduction to the History of Mexican Law* (Dobbs Ferry, N.Y., 1983); H.W. Halleck (ed), A *Collection of Mining Laws of Spain and Mexico* (San Françisco, 1859); Merrill Rippy, *Oil and the Mexican Revolution* (Leyden, 1972), 5-7.

7.Lorenzo Meyer, *México y los Estados Unidos en el conflicto petrolero, 1917-1942* (México, D.F., 1981), 48-50; Gobierno de México, *México's Oil* (México, D.F., 1940).

8.Hoffman, 99; "El Petróleo," Capítulo III, Primera Parte in *Nosotros los Petroleros* (Pemex) (México, D.F.) 2, 12, 1980, 25; Antonio Rodríguez, *El rescate del petróleo. Epopeya de un pueblo* (México, D.F., 1975), 18-19.

9.Cleland, 291-292; "Commerce of Tuxpám," *USRCCM*, 35, August 1884, 617.

10.Cleland, *ibid*; "El Petróleo," 26; U.S. Senate Committee on Foreign Affairs, *American Petroleum Interests in Foreign Countries* 79th Congress, 1st. session, 15 October 1945, 332-333; Joaquín Meade, *La Huasteca Veracruzana*, (México, D.F., 1962-63), II, 131, 134, 135. Dr. Autrey was a chemist, who immigrated to México after the U.S. Civil War ended. In 1866, he bought two barrels of oil in Veracruz, and sent a sample to Boston for analysis. He became involved in the oil business when the results confirmed the sample was good oil. He married Emilia Dávila, and adopted Mexican citizenship. When his stills dried up in Veracruz, he moved to Tampico, setting up a pharmaceutical company that was well known in México.

11.Angel Saínz Trápaga had the street lighting system contract for several years. He introduced the use of kerosene in Tampico for both home and public use. By 1877, there were 241 kerosene street lamps supplied by kerosene imported by Gerardo Claussen, who also had an oil import business. Saínz knew the potential of oil for Tampico, and bought all the lands on the Veracruz's side of the Pánuco River for a length of almost 9 kilometers or 7 miles. Meade, *La Huasteca Tamaulipeca*, II, 194; AMT, Actas, 11 enero 1887, 41; "El Petróleo," 24-25; Alfonso Casados, "En mis archivos y viejos relatos," in *El Sol de Tampico* (Tampico), 24 febrero 1985, 15.

12.NA, DCT, 84, 304, 20 November 1877, Consul Edward Johnson to Assistant Secretary of State.

13.The Tampico U.S. Consulate opened in 1823 had a broader jurisdiction than the municipality's 45 square miles. It varied in time according to Washington's policies for the Gulf and for México. This diplomatic entity was usually referred to as the "Tampico district." Reports from the various city consulates began to refer to Tampico as a district, thus making more difficult to separate what these reports meant when using Tampico, which meant city, municipality or district. See AMT, Actas, Expediente 146, 5 agosto 1880; "Mexican Asphaltum," *USCR* 25, 28, February 1883, 141-142.

14."Tampico," *USCR* 33, 118, April 1890, 493, 495.

15."Crude and Refined Petroleum in Mexico," *USCR*, 38, 136, January 1892, 5.

16.One million gallons of oil amount to 23,809 barrels of 42 gallons each. The 42 gallon barrel was the United States standard measure in the oil business since the 1860s.

17.The J. Findlay Company was bought by the Waters Pierce Co., which built the México City refinery. "Mexican Trade and How to Secure It," *USCR* 40, 146, November 1892, 406; Lorenzo Meyer, *México...*, 54; Robert K. Midlemass, *The Master Builders* (London, 1963), 213. Standard Oil Company was the largest U.S. corporation at the turn of the century. By 1871, John D. Rockefeller had monopolized the refining and transportation of oil in the U.S. He mapped out the country into several divisions. The Southwest, that included Kansas, Missouri, Arkansas and Texas, was placed under the administrative control of one of its affiliates, the Waters Pierce Company of Missouri. By 1899, Standard controlled between 85% to 88% of crude oil supplies, 82% of the refining capacity , 85% of the kerosene market, and most of the pipelines and tanker-carrying capacity of the United States. The company moved abroad through subsidiaries building refineries in México, Cuba and Puerto Rico. Its affiliates entered the mining and transportation industries in México. In Texas, however, the state government barred Standard from having any business or activity in its lucrative oil development, owing to problems created by the Waters Pierce subsidiary. By 1906, the company entered the Mexican oil business. See Ida M. Tarbell, *History of the Standard Oil*, 2 vols. (New York, 1904), II, 32-33; Ralph and Muriel Hidy, *Pioneering in Big Business, 1882-1911*, (New York, 1955), I, 22, 128, 258, 310, 393, 514; "El Petróleo," 26; Kenneth J. Grieb, "Standard Oil and the Financing of the Mexican Revolution," *California Historical Quarterly*, 49, 49, 1, March 1971, 60.

18.*POET*, 21, 31, 12 marzo 1896, 4.

19.Joaquín Meade was the son of Gerardo Meade, former owner of the "Hacienda del Naranjo," a neighboring hacienda to "Hacienda El Tulillo," – bought by E. L. Doheny – which had large oil seepages, and covered the three neighboring state jurisdictions of Tamaulipas, Veracruz, and San Luis Potosí. Joaquín Meade was also grandson of Angel Saínz Trápaga. See Meade, *La Huasteca Tamaulipeca*, II, 194.

20.*POET*, 21, 50, 20 abril 1896, 2.

21.AMT, "Correspondencia varia. Ocurso del Sr. John R. Davis enviado a México," 25 abril 1896; Expediente 33, "Contiene minutas de remisiones al Gobierno del Estado de copias de simples escrituras inscritas en el Registro Público," 16 febrero 1896. The Waters Pierce Co. gave a different set of figures to Tampico and State officials. Those given the State legislature valued company's assets somewhere between $600,000 to $700,000 pesos. It is not clear whether these different figures were a maneuver to obtain higher tax exemptions faster or if the estimate given the state included properties or valuables located somewhere else in the state and not in Tampico. See AMT, "Carta de Manuel Perales (Secretary of the Tamaulipas governor) al Presidente Municipal de Tampico," 19 marzo 1898.

22."Petroleum in Mexico," *USCR* 58, 219, December 1898, 641; Tischendorf, 122; Francisco Colmenares, *Petróleo y lucha de clases en México, 1864-1982* (México, D.F., 1982), 19; Meade, *La Huasteca Veracruzana*, II, 134.

23.NA, Despatches from the Consul at Tuxpam, Record Group 59, 301, 12, Letter from A.B. Jones to Assistant Secretary of State, 14 April 1899. Some American consuls accused Díaz' advisers of favoring British concerns. Historian Ricardo García Granados, a contemporary observer of the Díaz-Taft meeting of 1909 at El Paso, stated that Taft was most worried about Mexican favoritism shown English oil companies, especially Pearson's. Moreover, he wanted México to cede its petroleum only to the United States. See Ricardo García Granados, *Historia de México desde la Restauración de la República en 1867 hasta la caída de Huerta* 2 vols. (México, D.F., 1956), II, 89. Also *The New York Times*, 6 July 1921, 10:3; 20 July 1921, 19:1; 24 February 1923, 5:1; and articles by John K. Barnes in *World's Works* for the months of May, June , July, August, and September 1920; U.S. Senate, *Congressional Record*, 67th Congress, 1st. session, April 1921, 161-167. The oil rivalry continued into the 1920s when England had secured an outstanding share of the world's known oil reserves, and the U.S. was secure and in control of various important South American and other world oil sites. See Scott nearing, *Oil and the Germs of War*; Louis Fischer, *Oil Imperialism*. International Struggle for Oil (New York, 1926); Anton Zischka, *Der Kampf und die Weltmacht Öl* (Leipzig, 1934); E. H. Davenport and Sydney Russell Cooke, *The Oil Trusts and the Anglo-American Relations* (New York, 1924).

24.See note 49, chapter III.

25.Wilkins, 123; Hoffman, 101; *CRUSE*, I, October 1901, 451; Cathryn Thorup, "La competencia económica británica y norteamericana en México, 1887-1910," *Historia Mexicana* 31 (4): 124, (Abril/junio 1982), 607-632. Pierce had problems with Standard officials in New York, and by 1910, Standard held less than half the shares of Waters Pierce. See "Standard Oil Company of New Jersey, et al. v. the United States," *US Reports* Vol.221, (New York, 1910), 1-106. Data on stocks for each company controlled by the Standard Oil can also be found in *Mexico's Oil*, 52.

26.Hoffman, 99; Wallace Thompson, *Trading with Mexico* (New York, 1921), 201.

27.Hoffman, 100; Meade, *La Huasteca Tamaulipeca*, II, 194; "Antecedentes del petróleo en México," *Nosotros los Petroleros*, III, 2nda parte, 2, 13, (1980), 8; Covián Martínez, 10. Mr. Arguinzoni's cattle was doing great damage to Gerardo Meade's lands because there were no fences between the two haciendas. Therefore, Meade offered Arguinzoni about $60,000 pesos for his hacienda's 90,000 hectares (283,000 acres approximately), but he wanted $90,000 pesos. Neither man knew the potential value of their lands, and when Doheny offered Arguinzoni $325,000 pesos for the hacienda, he immediately accepted. Doheny bought the Chapacao hacienda for $600,000 pesos. Eventually, Doheny's oil company owned 1,500.000 acres of oil lands mostly in the Huasteca region. See "El petróleo...", 26; Meyer, *México...*, 46.

28.Hoffman, 101; Covián Martínez, 33.

29.Hoffman, 103-104; Meyer, 47. On 24 December 1901, the Federal Congress passed its first oil law. Only the Executive could grant oil drilling concessions, and also imposed a 5 cent per hectare tax to be paid in government stamps. See "Antecendentes...," 8-9.

30.Hoffman, 106.

31.Wilkins, 123; Hoffman, 101; *CRUSE*, I, October 1901, 451.

32.Cleland, 294.

33."Antecedentes...," 10.

34.Primo Feliciano Vázquez, *Historia de San Luis Potosí* 4 vols. (San Luis Potosí, 1982), IV, 157-162.

35.Hoffman, 106; "Antecedentes...," 10; "Petroleum Interests in Foreign Countries...," 334; Meyer, 47.

36.Tischendorf, 122. The project began in 1890 and ended in 1896; see A. J. Spender, *Weetman Pearson; First Viscount Cowdray, 1856-1927* (London, 1930), 85.

37.A.J. Spender, 112. Pearson's engineering firm won the contract to provide Veracruz with a pure water and sewerage system, another contract to electrify its trolley and to install electric lamps in its downtown district. Once done, the company moved to other Mexican Gulf towns to carry out similar works. However, in Tampico, they had to compete with U.S. companies: Standard, Mexican Petroleum, Waters Pierce.

38.A. J. Spender, 123.

39.*CRUSE*, 1895-1896, I, 413-414; Tischendorf, 60, 118; A. J. Spender, 175, 205-207. The railway and ports were inaugurated with great splendor in 1907. The locomotives on this road used oil brought from Beaumont, Texas. Pearson had a huge storage tank constructed at Coatzacoalcos with a capacity for 1,500,000 gallons of oil. Filling this tank with U.S. oil was an expense he wanted to avoid. Notice, however, that the oil came from non-Standard Oil Company supplies.

40.A. J. Spender, 149; Gary W. Malamud, *Boomtown Communities* (New York, 1984), 37.

41.*México's Oil*, 12.

42."Nuestras raíces," II, *Nosotros los petroleros*, I, 5, Diciembre 1979, 23; Cleland, 294.

43.*Mexico's Oil*, Introduction, xxix-xxx; Spender, 151-152; Tischendorf, 122. A new law of 25 November 1905 decreed that subsoil ownership belonged to whoever owned the surface of any property. This law reversed the old Aranjuez Law and Mexican thesis on subsoil ownership, and became one of the most difficult issues of the post-revolutionary legal system.

44.Spender, 152; *Mexico's Oil*, 90.

45.*El Petróleo de México (México's Oil)*, 163.

46.NA, DCT, 84, 304, 221, 31 October 1905, Consul Magill to Secretary of State; Spender, 156, 159, 165; Desmond Young, 138.

47."La revolution industrielle provoquée à la fin du XIX[a] siecle, dans de nombreuses branches de production, et dans les transports, par l'invention du moteur à combustion interne; le developpement prodigée ont placé au premier plan des problémes le plus essentials pour toutes les Grandes Puissances la question de l'approvisionement en pétrole. D'une bonne solution de ce probléme dépend le developpement economique, militaire et politique de tout pays et par conséquent la place à lui reservée dans l'economie mondiale." Paul Apostel et Alexandre Michelson, *La lutte pour le pétrole et la Russie* (Paris: Payot et Co., 1922), 1.

48.Tischendorf, 125; "Petroleum Interests in Foreign Countries," 334; Russell G. Millward, "The Oil Treasure of Mexico," *National Geographic Magazine*, 19 (Nov. 1908), 893; Wilkins, 124; Spender, 159; Desmond Young, 432; Cleland, 295.

49.Robert K. Middlemas, 213; Federal Reserve System, *Banking and Monetary Statistics, 1914-1941* (Washington, D.C., 1943). The equivalency for that period fluctuated between 4.5 to 4.0 dollars to the pound.

5

RUMORS, BULLETS, AND OIL

> The Tampico district is at this moment a peculiarly interesting part of Mexico to the people of the United States.
>
> U.S. Consul C. Miller, 1911.

> Carranza's own political geography had four key points in Mexico: Tampico for its oil tax revenues...
>
> José López Portillo y Weber, 1975.

México was the world's second most productive oil country between 1910 and 1919. Meanwhile, the nation struggled to discard its colonial and early republican past. The 1910s witnessed three fierce and idealistic revolutions in China, México, and Russia as well as the First World War, all of which left deep imprints on humanity. Tampico was México's major oil export city in that period, and attained a most unusual position during the turmoil brought about by the Revolution and the Great War. The city held a different image for its observers. Mexican revolutionaries believed that if they could control Tampico its income from oil would provide them with money to buy weapons, to satisfy their needs or those of "their government." In a world at war, Tampico's oil was of paramount importance for the new motorized fleets of trucks, tanks, ships, and airplanes. Thus, its international stature grew rapidly when European and American allies protected the city and its oil fields from both internal and external foes. Foreign powers could have taken Tampico, and revolutionaries could have easily besieged and destroyed the city to keep it from falling in their enemies' hands; however, neither occurred. All groups of combatants needed Tampico. They preserved and protected it, while encouraging its growth when the rest of México was in turmoil, making it México's largest port, most expensive city - and for a few years, maybe its richest.

This chapter surveys Tampico's growth between 1910 and 1917. It describes the influence of the developing oil industry over the city as well as the impact it received from both the Revolution and the Great War. The economic and political power held by the Mexican Central Railroad Company was substituted by the growing power of the Doheny and Pearson companies, especially after General Díaz nationalized the railroad industry in 1907 with the excuse of saving it from bankruptcy. But, once the oil companies took power, the federal government realized the need to control them. The Revolution delayed the dispute, which was rapidly renewed after 1917. The period between 1909 and 1917 served the companies to consolidate their control over the city. They opened headquarters and offices in Tampico which were directly linked to their international centers in New York, Texas or London. They also found local collaborators willing to "aid" México's modernization process while enriching themselves. Moreover, a group of Tampiqueños expanded their views on international economic and social issues, both in business and labor, which in a way, alienated them from revolutionary México.

The city keeps growing

In 1910, Tampico presented visitors a most interesting urban profile. The city's architecture was "more American than most other Mexican towns display."[1] Houses were built of wood and stone with outer verandas and sloping roofs, and were painted in lively colors. Main streets were paved by the E. L. Doheny Mexican Asphalt Company using the bitumen found at his Ebano fields. Sidewalks and streets were kept clean under strict ordinances from the city council. At night, streets were brightly lit with electric lamps located at half-block intervals. Each one of the city's four plazas had several light posts, each one with five large bulbs. All this illumination not only increased people's sense of safety as they strolled through plazas and streets, but also gave the city a fantastic presence amid the waters and jungles that surround it. Already in 1910, Tampico was México's best lit town.

Growth in the number of visitors and tourists increased the demand for service industries. New hotels and guest-houses opened in the city. The seven kilometer trolley system - bought by a Pearson company in 1912 - provided a scheduled and efficient service within the municipality. Cable and telephone services connected Tampico with the nation and the world. Miramar beach was again a most popular resort as shown by the number of tickets sold by the Ferrocarriles Mexicanos Company, which had a line between Tampico and La Barra. The number of paid tickets for 1908 was 633,328, increasing to 800,000 by 1910. Consequently, new facilities were built to accommodate visitors. Fishing and sight–seeing trips along the rivers and lagoons surrounding Tampico became very popular among tourists, and were mentioned abroad as one of Tampico's major offerings to foreigners.[2]

Tampico's dynamic business community was responsible for the successful growth of the city. Its members continued to control local politics, and adhered to their ancestors's dreams of urban greatness. Municipal officers elected for 1910 included José María Maraboto as Presidente Municipal, the wealthy and staunch supporter of Tampico's development at the state and national levels of government since 1876. He helped oil industries move to Tampico. Other city council members were Joaquin Pazzi and Pablo Soules, local businessmen; Sabás Prom and Gustavo A. Populus, community leaders; Pedro Torres Grillo and Emilio Baldit, both members of the city's wealthier families. All were supportive of the Porfirian regime, maintaining reverence and respect for President Díaz as long as their personal interests were not threatened.[3]

Up to 1910, the city council continued to link Tampico's future with the export-import trade that had been important to the city for eighty seven years, and which had increased since the arrival of the railroad.

Together with the business community, they had seen an important industrial growth since the late 1890s, with North American and local investors participating, among other concerns, in a meat-packing factory, an asphalt plant, and a brewery. Not until 1906 did the discovery of oil - one hundred and fifty miles to the west and south of the city - had an impact on Tampico's economy. Until then, oil demand in México had remained partly satisfied by imports - Waters Pierce still controlling the greater share of the market - and world demand had remained within the productive capacity of the American and Russian (second world producer until 1917) fields. Demand for oil began to increase after 1908, partly due to the construction of newer and cheaper automobiles and to novel uses for petroleum. By 1910, great oil gushers began to appear in the Huastecan wells near Tampico. Area exploration for more petroleum brought about a huge shift in imports from manufactured and agricultural products to machinery, pipes for wells and for oilducts, and in exports from agricultural and mineral products to crude oil and its refined derivatives. Thus, by 1910, oil had altered Tampico more deeply than any other previously important trade product.[4]

1910 was a special year for México because of its Independence War Centennial. It also marked the beginning of the Mexican Revolution. The Minutes of the Tampico city council described 1910 as a normal year, except for only two political or economic issues. One dealing with oil, the other with the Centennial. The first dealt with the presence of Weetman Pearson and his company in the city. The "El Aguila" Mexican Oil Company decided to move its headquarters to Tampico, and asked the council for suitable municipal lots to build offices, warehouses, and a refinery. A great debate occurred in the council chamber during the last week of November 1910 over the location of the company's office building in downtown Tampico. To Tampiqueños, the Francisco Madero order for a November revolution was of no consequence.[5]

Of paramount importance, however, was the planning for Mexico's Independence Centennial celebrations that were held on September 16. The council wanted the celebrations to glorify Tampico's role in the national struggle for independence, while attracting tourists to participate in the festivities, and thus increase the city's national and international reputation, and its income.[6] New facilities for entertainment were planned and built. A new bullring opened on 1 January 1910 in the Llanos del Golfo borough, a lowland section east of the city. The ring owners, Alberto J. Ostos and Antonio López Márquez, contributed with the receipts of several bullfights to the Centennial Celebrations fund. A baseball park was also inaugurated in the same area. Every Sunday, teams of Tampiqueños, rich and poor, old and young, met to play against each other or with teams of American employees from the oil and service companies in town. A race-track opened north of the city at El Volantín, sponsored by the Tampico Jockey Club, whose members were Americans, British or members of the city's elite. Special games and races were also held to benefit the Centennial Fund, that was to be used for the construction of a new school building, and to commission a statue of Father Miguel Hidalgo, México's Father of Independence, to be placed atop a column in the Plaza Méndez, north of the city's center. The planning of these activities involved all social and economic sectors of the city.

The council also decreed that all downtown buildings and houses had to be painted and their surroundings were to be kept thoroughly cleaned. New central water fountains were built at the two major plazas, Libertad and Constitución. Moreover, the social clubs of the foreign community - the most relevant were the Chinese, American, British, and Spanish - raised money to install a clock in the spire of the Catholic Cathedral across Plaza de la Constitución. They also raised funds to commission statues of other Mexican patriots that were placed at various sites throughout the city. Amid the celebrations the nation was becoming restless over the political events at the border, but Tampico showed no signs of disturbances.

Madero and Pierce: Associates?

Francisco Madero's violent bid for power in México did not interfere with Tampico's dynamic life in 1910. He had visited the city in 1909 without receiving any strong support from the masses. Two of his most conspicuous advocates, Alberto Aragón and Manuel León, had founded the Anti-Reelectionist Club of Tampico. This was a national political organization that promoted Madero for president. The club invited Madero to speak at a city rally, but permission was denied by the city authorities, plainly showing their political position. Still, on 8 July 1909, Madero arrived by train at the Muelle Island station, but was coolly received by his supporters. Next day, "a few, bold citizens dared participate" in the rally held at the Apollo Theatre.[7]

Madero's political program - based on democratic rituals and on strict obedience to the 1857 Constitution and its rights for citizens - might have appealed to Tampico's workers, but they were not yet conscious of the conceptual and active propositions discussed in it. Tampico's wealth and its role as the legal center for southern Tamaulipas State had brought into town numerous lawyers, some having become active among workers and knowledgeable of the ideologies reaching the city from both Mexican and foreign socialists and free thinkers. A few supported Madero, but their power status was very limited in a city controlled by the business community. Madero's visit to Tampico did not endear him significantly among workers, but it did influence some powerful economic interests and city intellectuals, who saw him as an idealistic politician; a possible tool for their own benefit. Here was a simple minded unaware collaborator, who truly believed in helping his nation by turning it over to the others.

Henry Clay Pierce, the stubborn and cunning president of the Waters Pierce Oil Company and former president of the Mexican Central Railroad Company, deeply resented President Díaz for the support and favoritism he had shown the Pearson and Doheny interests in México. He believed that the government was persecuting his company, and that it would lose its monopoly over the Mexican kerosene market. Hawley Copeland, the company's private secretary, told President Woodrow Wilson that when the Mexican government seized the Mexican Central Railroad in 1907, Pierce's friends in the official board of the National Railroads were replaced by pro-Pearson partisans. Immediately, they introduced freight charges that favored Pearson's interests in southern Veracruz, and were discriminatory to the Waters Pierce Oil Company. In 1908, the two men met in new York, but Pearson did not accept Pierce's invitation to divide the Mexican oil market between them, probably because of his company's connection to President Díaz and to his government. Once the great Pearson and Doheny oil gushers came up - strengthening their companies - Pierce feared a greater competition, and worried about the future.[8]

The Waters Pierce Oil Company was affiliated to Standard Oil Company since 1878, yet it had never been completely under its control because Henry Clay Pierce fought fiercely to be his own boss. Standard's headquarters in New York described Pierce as a "most unsafe man...an aggressive individualist...who could never be persuaded to work as a member of a team."[9] It was Pierce's unsavory business practices in Texas that led to his company's eviction in 1908, and to a ban of any Standard Oil business in the state. This action was followed by several costly court cases. Furthermore, Pierce acted maliciously toward Standard Oil. He stopped payments on all dividends to stockholders on the excuse of financial losses from the fines imposed in the Texas cases. He also dismissed the Standard's representative from his Tampico offices, who supervised all Pierce's dealings in the name of the major stockholder. All these actions were highly resented in New York.[10]

Henry C. Pierce was not among the bold few who attended Madero's rally in Tampico; however, his actions during the early stage of the Revolution point towards an involvement in support of Madero and against the Díaz' regime. On 5 October 1910, Madero presented his "Plan de San Luis Potosí," stating the reasons to rebel against Díaz, and designated the 20th of November as the day "for all the towns in the republic to rise in arms after 6 o'clock P.M."[11] But the revolutionary call was not heeded by the masses. On 3 February 1911, Henry Pierce telegraphed U.S. President William H. Taft urging him to adopt a policy of strict neutrality in connection with the Mexican Revolution. This act was previous to that of any other American oil entrepreneur, and long before the Revolution was successful. On 15 February 1911, the U.S. State Department received news of a rumored Standard Oil involvement with the Madero movement.[12]

Ignorance of the exact relationship existing between Pierce and Standard Oil is probably accountable for the interpretation of the relationship existing between the Madero regime and the petroleum company. Originally, Standard Oil denied any wrongdoing or interference in México, but as Waters Pierce's major stockholder, any personal pro-Madero acts made by Henry Pierce or any of his associates which could have advanced his designs would have been beneficial to the company. Standard's strained relations with Pierce give credence to its official denials of involvement with Madero, yet it could be a shrewd move to further penetrate the Mexican market with presidential support versus the other oil companies. It is highly suspicious that by the end of 1911, Standard Oil Company appeared in the Tampico oil market separately from the Pierce Waters Company; and it is also strange to find a ten million barrel export contract signed with Pearson, Pierce's largest competitor. Furthermore, by 1914, Standard Oil built its own refinery in Tampico. These last actions were conducted through Standard's affiliates or subsidiaries such as the Standard Oil companies of New York, Ohio, Indiana, and California, the Penn Mexican Oil Co., the Magnolia Oil Co., and the International Petroleum Oil Company. An analysis of the Pierce-Standard-Madero relationship, and its consequences on the Mexican Revolution and on Tampico's economy is worth further inquiries and consideration.[13]

The relationship between Madero and Pierce can only be pursued indirectly. In May 1911, President Díaz resigned, and left the country. Madero assumed power as head of the revolutionary movement that toppled the old general, and was formally elected president in October 1911. While in power, some of his official actions benefitted Waters Pierce over the other oil companies in México. When in July 1911, close to 500 men went on strike at Pierce's Arbol Grande refinery, federal troops were immediately dispatched to break it up. In August 1911, the Tampico Municipal Council ordered the Waters Pierce Company to open the public roads - passing through its properties - it had appropriated both at Doña Cecilia and Arbol Grande, and the federal government overruled the order, allowing the company to keep the roads closed. One of Madero's earliest decrees as President imposed a twenty-cent tax on each barrel of crude oil, but the Waters Pierce Co. was unaffected because it was a refining and not an oil producing company. Furthermore, by late 1911, it was rumored all over Tampico that the Madero family was buying oil lands in order to organize a new exploration and exploitation company, and any oil found would be refined at Waters Pierce. In 1912, a great fire started by lightning, destroyed one of the largest oil reservoir tanks at the Arbol Grande refinery, but it also burned down most of the houses in the borough. Consequently, the Municipal Council ordered the company to stop building any more tanks in the area. Yet, Madero's

Minister of the Interior intervened in favor of the company; rescinded the order, and warned the council to stop harassing the Waters Pierce Company. To top these events, the oil enterprise stopped paying municipal taxes - the only ones it had paid - during Madero's incumbency and until his death in 1913. Although the above actions taken by the federal government on behalf of the Waters Pierce can be explained as residual activity of a pro-capitalist, positivist mentality among federal officials, the Madero-Pierce connection seems much more plausible at this time. Henry L. Pierce had not been at the Madero rally in Tampico, but his non-presence was well rewarded by the government.[14]

Pierce was Madero's strongest adherent among the commercial elite of Tampico. The city's oligarchy, entrepreneurial elite, and most workers did not like Madero. His supporters in town were mostly some lawyers, several physicians, and a few artisans and workers. As a whole, they did not constitute a threat to the city's establishment. Therefore, when the June 1910 elections were held in Tampico, Díaz was reelected with the support of all city groups. Rumors of a possible rebellion had little impact on city life, and the only public disorder had its origin in a local event unrelated to Madero.

Just before the Centennial celebrations, an incident occurred that might have marred them. On 14 September 1910, the Spanish Consul, Angel Saínz Trápaga, floated the Spanish flag atop the Mexican emblem on a pole placed above his house of business across Plaza de la Libertad. This building, now housing both the Spanish Consulate and Saínz offices, was the city's most historic site where Spanish General Isidro Barradas had signed Spain's surrender to General Antonio López de Santa Anna in 1829, thus securing Mexican independence. Some passers-by noticed the insult to the Mexican flag, and began to excite a growing crowd, which chanted with nationalistic fervor the old "**Muerte a los gachupines**" (Death to the Spaniards). As the crowd became menacing, hastily called police and federal troops were able to disperse the people. This was the only mob incident in the city during Madero's revolution; an indication of the lack of revolutionary support he had in the comparatively wealthy Tampico of 1910-1911.[15]

Although the Centennial Celebration was a huge success, not long after, the city was threatened by rumors of revolution. On 16 November, a political demonstration marched through the streets led by workers from Doña Cecilia. On 20 November - Madero's date for the revolution - all was quiet in Tampico while two nearby towns in the Huasteca, San Martín and Tancanhuitz, were engulfed in fighting. By the end of the month, however, ammunition and arms shipments began to arrive at the port to supply the federal army, and like in 1876, war became a real threat to Tampico. But, few people realized that Tampico's new position as an oil city - exporter of a highly demanded item - would give it an important international status, making the port more stable than most other Mexican urban and regional centers.[16]

In 1906, Edward L. Doheny began to develop the Juan Casiano field located about seventy miles south of Tampico, following geologist Ordoñez's advice. Luckily, he had prepared the site before attempting any drilling. A sixty five mile pipeline was placed between the field and Tampico after permission was received from President Díaz to lay the line traversing any properties in the way. Tanks for storage were built at Doheny's Huasteca Oil Company's terminal located in the Mata Redonda jurisdiction, across from Tampico. On 20 September 1910, the Juan Casiano #7 well began to flow at the extraordinary rate of 60,000 to 70,000 barrels-a-day, thus becoming México's first gusher. The event capped the Tampico Centennial events by making the city famous all over the world as synonymous with great oil production. It would now be the terminus for all the oil from the great gushers. Immediately after, numerous international oil companies and entrepreneurs reached Tampico with exploration and exploitation plans. Their presence helped to increase the port's tonnage, trade, and businesses. Supply materials intended for oil search, production, and transportation started arriving at Tampico in a continuous stream mostly from Atlantic and Gulf ports of the United States. Oil from Well #7 rapidly filled up the storage space at the Huasteca terminal, and Doheny, who had no contracts for this unexpected production rushed to build more storage tanks in Mata Redonda, in Tampico, and at the field. Yet, the Juan Casiano success was followed by an even larger one.[17]

Pearson's "El Aguila" Mexican Oil Company had been drilling at the Potrero del Llano field located twenty five miles south of the Juan Casiano field. In December 1910, oil surged in huge quantities. The first well was a gusher so powerful that it destroyed all the installations above it, and began to flow at a fantastic rate. After several months, it was determined that its flow-rate was an average 120,000 barrels-a-day. The company's temporary headquarters in Tampico were kept very busy by this well and its large production. More equipment and storage facilities had to be provided immediately. An oil duct was built from the Potrero field to the Tamiahua Lagoon shore, from where **chalanes** (flat river barges) took the oil for storage at twenty new tanks rapidly built at Doña Cecilia.[18]

The gushers generated a more violent reaction in Tampico than Madero's revolution. Fighting occurred in the neighboring towns of the Huasteca, but not in Tampico. Rumors of anti-Americanism, constantly denounced by the U.S. Consul, were based on isolated cases. Fear of military assaults brought constant demands from business leaders for more federal troops, yet no rebel attacks, looting or any form of popular misbehavior occured in the city. Still, the official elite decided to protect Tampico through several methods. One was to decorate their oratory with anti-Díaz rhetoric. Another was to have foreign investors, many of them

Americans, protest against any U.S. invasion because such action would harm their interests, and engender anti-Americanism. Moreover, the local business community and the city council formulated a plan to satisfy any possible loan demands made by rebels - in the event they took the city - through the creation of a special fund that would deter any violent actions in or near the petroleum production and storage areas. Despite these actions, rumors continued to frighten the populace after Díaz resignation of 25 May 1911, which was immediately followed by the defection of half the federal forces in Tampico.[19]

The city's social environment was not favorable to the revolutionaries, and it is not strange to find that only one pro-Madero incident followed General Díaz' resignation. Supporters of Madero, members of a workers's political club located in Doña Cecilia, decided on 28 May to have a march through Tampico's streets. A large crowd reached the Plaza de la Constitución, where about 100 men attacked and disarmed the police protecting City Hall. Afterwards, the crowd marched through the city's main streets chanting pro-Madero slogans on their way to free the prisoners at the municipal jail. However, arriving federal troops positioned themselves in front of the jail and shot at the crowd as it neared the building. The mob fled back to Doña Cecilia leaving six workers dead on the street. This flare-up of workers versus the Tampico authorities prompted by Madero supporters, who believed in his rhetoric to satisfy workers's demands, brought fear to the business community both for the show of workers's violence and of Madero's possible presidential program. Federal troops patrolled the city, and the commander of the Mexican gunboat **Morelos** - stationed in the river - ordered the lowering of the ship's movable cannons in order to have larger weapons to face a possible attack from Doña Cecilia. Soldiers and police were assigned to guard banks, federal and municipal buildings, and also the "hot" boroughs of Doña Cecilia, Arbol Grande, and Llanos del

Golfo, where most workers and their families lived. These actions and the lack of support from the Madero headquarters in México City "cooled off" workers' actions, and no further marches or attacks occurred at this time.[20]

A statement made by Tampico's mayor confirms that the Revolution had not been very important in the city. The Ministry of Interior, requested information on the effects of the Revolution and the Presidente Municipal, Dr. Antonio Matienzo replied that

> there is absolutely no Rebel leader in this city, who might have participated in the great passionate movement just finished in the Republic nor is there any Army Commander that has been part of any battle in the insurgency. Moreover, there are no Chiefs nor soldiers worthy of any reward, nor is there any family or business harmed by this triumphant Revolution.[21]

Initially, at least, no revolutionary event changed the basic structure of Tampico's politics. The January 1911 pro-Díaz elected officials were challenged in June by a group of Madero's supporters. They were accused of ordering the killing of the six workers during the 28 May riot. The challengers asked the newly appointed State governor, General Espiridión Lara, to either dismiss the city council, or name a **Visitador Político** (political manager) - an official with political and legal power over municipal and police officers across the state - to take over Tampico. Workers, led by Maderistas, held a huge and peaceful march against the municipal officials, who then decided to resign. However, they clearly stated that the people of Tampico had elected them with the support of major business and workers' organizations such as the Chamber of Commerce, the City Market Owners's Association, the trade guilds, and the the mutualist workers's movement. They also claimed having being Anti-Reelectionists against President Díaz, asserting their innocence, and explaining how the accusations against them affected their reputations and businesses, especially when their political objective had been to serve their fellow citizens and their city. More than 5,000 souls gathered in Tampico's Plaza de la Constitución to oppose their resignation thus forcing Governor Lara to refuse their resignations for the good of the "democratic system."[22] In this manner, the Porfirian-elected council continued in power until the end of that "revolutionary year," and a local precedent was re-enforced when national political views were subordinated to local interests.

Municipal officers in Tampico had always belonged to the city's wealthy and business elite. One of the reasons behind this class control was the unsalaried nature of these positions; these men had time, money, and usually, great pride and personal interest in working for their city. Those who served in the 1911 Council had a reserved attitude towards Francisco Madero. They feared the rebels and workers supporting the revolution; and also the bandits who roamed the countryside after Madero's election. Moreover, they did not like his policies. On 2 August 1911, Councilman Ernesto López resigned because

> the present national political situation supports the harmful elements which have introduced disorders and provoked conflicts, calling on the popular classes, already ignorant, to rebel and to disobey the proper authorities. All these events are tolerated by officials willing to accept them.[23]

His position was shared by many among Tampico's elite.[24]

An analysis of the composition of Tampico's municipal council between 1910-1915 reveals a certain continuity of individuals who shared ideas about national politics and Tampico. Their main concerns had nothing to do with "national" events taking place in the country. They were basically interested in Tampico's continued development and growth under the capitalist structure that had served them so well.

Table 8 (see Appendix) offers the names of Tampico city officials for the period 1910-1914. Most 1910 officers were strongly pro-Díaz, but his support dwindled as the months went by. The 1911 slate included two men from the previous council, who remained in office until their term was over, except for Ernesto López, mentioned above. Officials for 1912 and 1913 represented a more radical position, still within the liberal mentality that had engendered them; however, after the federal forces of Victoriano Huerta took the city, they were forced to resign in October 1913 and were replaced by strong pro-Díaz men, who had served in 1910 or previously. In 1915, and after Venustiano Carranza forces took the city, Tomas R. Morales - a carpenter - was named mayor for two consecutive years. It was during his tenure in office, that all council members began to receive salaries; a change apparently designed to wrest municipal government control from the hands of the powerful local elite. Morales represented the new Carranza-Obregón approach to labor that placed workers in a more prominent position for political purposes. Yet, the municipal government's actions were not basically changed in their policies toward the big oil and other foreign-owned companies in Tampico. Therefore, salaries do not seem to have changed the fundamental urban spirit of municipal officers. This first revolutionary period was characterized by a sort of political continuity, notwithstanding the new Revolutionary events.[25]

Labor in Tampico

Madero's campaign throughout México apparently supported workers in their struggle for better salaries and working conditions. In a speech at an Orizaba rally in May 1910, Madero told workers: "You want freedom, you want rights to be respected; you want to be allowed to form powerful societies that united will help you defend your rights."[26] Workers understood this rhetoric useful for their objectives and principles; however, Madero's political actions were far different from what could have been expected from his orations. The first approach gave him workers's recognition, especially after his election in 1912. In Tampico, US Consul Miller observed that the common people supported Madero at first. Yet, their endorsement was conditioned by the economic changes that occurred in the city between 1910 and 1913, and by the actions of the federal, state, and municipal governments during that period.

The true nature of Madero's labor policy became clear to workers after they held two strikes in Tampico. The waterfront was served since the late 1890s by thousands of stevedores, working directly on the piers or from lighterage boats. The work contracts for the whole harbor had been monopolized by a company created and owned by three U.S. partners, Edwin M. Rowley, George W. Clynes and Harry Dalin. The **alijadores** (stevedores) were banned from doing any independent work and were forced to operate only through the E. M. Rowley Company. By mid-July 1911, the alijadores decided to strike, and form a union that would represent them. The strike was a success as more than 3,000 men remained idle paralyzing the port at the crucial moment when supplies and materials for the oil fields were arriving in large quantities. Orders received from the **Ministerio de Relaciones Exteriores** (Foreign Relations Ministry) told both state and municipal authorities to protect the E. M. Rowley Company and to stop the political agitators behind the strike. The municipal government offered the company a number of "scabs" to take care of the port work; however, one of the partners, George Clynes, refused the proposal. He preferred to settle the strike by recognizing the union and to give workers a 33% increase in salaries. Two factors were taken in consideration: first, that management knew that there were not enough "scabs" in Tampico to replace the lost hands; and second, because the alijadores had developed an efficient and structured organization that could not be replaced easily, and its loss would greatly hinder the port's trade at this historic moment. The strike was settled on 28 July 1911. The workers, now free to organize, formed the **Gremio**

Unido de Alijadores (Stevedores's United Guild), which has remained one of México's most powerful labor unions.[27] Conditions at the port determined the outcome of this situation, yet, it also showed the ambivalent nature of the Madero regime toward labor. Workers were somewhat confused on the President's position.

The second strike of that year occurred at the Waters Pierce refinery where more than 500 men stopped all work in November 1911. The strike was settled violently by federal troops ordered to guard and protect the plant from radicals. Workers lost the battle, but gained understanding of Madero's labor policy. The President did not support them.[28]

Tampico's economic growth, now linked to oil, brought a higher standard of living, thereby forcing a natural increase in salaries that were higher than elsewhere in the nation at that moment. Raises, and government's anti-labor actions, sustained a relative labor peace until 1914. In 1910, a non-classified worker earned between 75 cents to one peso daily, and by 1914, it was up to $2.25 pesos per day. Meanwhile, skilled workers (mostly foreigners) earned from five to ten dollars a day (or the equivalency of ten to twenty pesos a day).[29] The need for an easily available work force led companies to increase salaries; a trend that continued until the 1920s. This inflationary tendency affected all other productive and service industries. By 1913, the city council had to raise the salary of municipal employees from $1.25 to $2.00 per day. These salaries also lured workers to Tampico, especially as conditions in the rest of the nation deteriorated during the revolutionary period. Thus, the city's salary structure helped it move into better economic times, yet created the ambiance for inflation.

On 13 May 1914, Tampico was occupied by Constitutionalist troops loyal to Venustiano Carranza. The city was one of his main trophies. It controlled most of México's oil, and its Customs house was one of the few receiving any income from abroad. World demand for oil increased after the beginning of the First World War, and income from oil similarly increased. Once in town, the Constitutionalist Commander, General Jacinto B. Treviño, worried about keeping his men from deserting to work in the oil fields or refineries, then in full production. Soldiers were paid one peso a day in depreciated government printed money, whereas Tampico workers could get as much as 17 to 20 pesos a day paid either in dollars (with an equivalency of two pesos per dollar) or in gold. These conditions lured men to Tampico, but also made life in the city very expensive. Interestingly, conditions also made workers become aware of their power in a capitalist society.

Workers' struggles for better salaries and working conditions led them to understand that it was their own militancy the ultimate source of their power, rather than the government's interference or the patronizing attitudes of the companies. They also realized how intimately connected were their lives and the presence in Tampico of the foreign capitalist community.[30] As long as Tampico was somewhat isolated from the rest of México, its labor force would be at the forefront of the nation's labor movement. The knowledge of their power, encouraged by theories and foreign workers' previous experiences, led Tampico workers to seek eventually a larger share of control over municipal and industrial affairs, but conditions had to mature for such actions.

Huerta's interlude

Rumors of war alarmed Tampico in 1912. At first, there was only political turmoil in the Huasteca after Madero's gubernatorial candidates lost their bid for election. In March, new unrest developed after the two unsuccessful rebellions of Pascual Orozco and Apolinio Treviño occurred in northern México. Hundreds fled from nearby Huastecan towns to Tampico seeking refuge from the accompanying disorders. Several American colonists whose farms were attacked by the rebels were among the refugees. Several told stories of a rising anti-Americanism in the whole region. In Tampico, the U.S. Consul charged the city council of being anti-American based on their refusal to let Mr. A. Hudson, of the Santa Fe News Co., import arms and ammunition through the port - to sell to the rebels. Oil companies' officials used all these stories to accuse Madero's government of anti-Americanism. They alleged that Madero had imposed a 20 cent tax on petroleum, and petitioned the American ambassador, who called on the government to say that the tax was "discriminatory and confiscatory" and was imposed "out of anti-American sentiment." The rhetoric attached to "anti-Americanism" was only the camouflage for other designs, not yet clearly understood, but, there was some truth to the allegations. An anti-American rally was scheduled for 16 March in Tampico, and the mayor received an anonymous letter accusing him of inciting an American invasion of the city, and threatening to kill him and the municipal secretary. Both the mayor and the U.S. Consul asked the Mexican federal authorities for protection against any disorders. On the night of 15 March, the Mexican gunboat **Bravo**, stationed in the Pánuco, kept its search lights constantly over the town while the streets were combed by armed patrols of federal soldiers. Next day, all was quiet.[31] Whoever scheduled the demonstration realized that participation would be greatly hindered by the presence of the soldiers.

Félix Díaz' revolt - Porfirio's nephew - was more popular in Tampico than most other rebellions of the period. Consul Miller believed that it represented a general approval of the old President's political actions. This rebellion began in October 1912 at Veracruz, and spread rapidly to the Huastecas. Some daring rebels "pillaged a warehouse in Tampico and tried to patrol the harbor with a small motorboat."[32] General Manuel Peláez, a Díaz supporter, whose family owned Huastecan oil lands leased to the Pearson company, mustered a few hundred men and seized the oil fields of northern Veracruz. On 16 October, Comsul Miller immediately recommended a joint intervention by the United States, Great Britain, Germany and other countriess to prevent rebel fighting that would endanger oil properties in the region. He suggested the neutralization of Tampico, meaning the internationalization of the city owing to oil's growing demand.[33] Although the advise was not heeded, soon after, warships of many nations assembled off-shore Tampico.

Our earlier contention that Madero's popularity in Tampico was relatively limited is supported by the fact that his assassination on 22 February 1913 did not create any public disorders or rebellions in the city. Conditions were normal and the display of foreign warships, especially those from the U S., played a significant role reassuring the "economically correct people" that order would be preserved in the city and its environs. Already on 3 November 1912, the mayor and the city's military commander had told Consul Miller that the arrival of the warship **USS Tacoma** was a welcome sight that would help to keep order in town.[34] Yet, a popular event indicates that, although the President was not very popular, the masses were affected by his death.

Historian Ricardo García Granados tells how he arrived by train from San Luis Potosí as member of a commission sent by Victoriano Huerta seeking to win Tampico masses' allegiance to the new regime. The arrival occurred on 24 February 1913 (two days after Madero's death in México City), and as the train entered the station, a large and threatening crowd surrounded it. Men climbed to the windows peering into all the cars as if searching for someone or something. The commissioners, frightened and surprised, asked the reason for this strange behavior. People answered that they were looking for the body of the slain president because a telegram had reached Tampico advising of the arrival of Madero's body to the port. The crowd wanted to pay homage to the man. Once the people realized that the corpse was not aboard the train, they withdrew and dispersed quickly and peacefully. The commissioners, afterwards, were received by all local authorities, who immediately accepted the Huerta government. Thus, the murder of the man who had initiated the Mexican Revolution elicited respectful curiosity, but hardly fervent opposition in Tampico.[35]

On the other hand, Madero's death forced the oil companies into greater cooperation. Some U.S. analysts believe that México's political problems were created by the U.S.-British rivalry over oil, but facts indicate a different interpretation. By 1913, Pierce's fight with Pearson had dwindled considerably after both had agreed to an equal share of the Mexican market on all refined products. Pearson and E. L. Doheny, on the other hand, mutually agreed to build a pipeline from their Huastecan fields to the Doheny refinery in Arbol Grande. Furthermore, Standard Oil Company began to compete directly in the Tampico oil district when its subsidiary, Magnolia Oil Company - headed jointly by the presidents of Standard New York and Standard New Jersey - bought four hundred acres of land in the municipality, and started making advantageous arrangements with the municipality. It also attempted to buy Pearson's oil interests in México, yet deemed it more promising to negotiate a large oil contract with him and with Doheny, to sell their products abroad. Those actions brought together British and American interests in Tampico's oil industry between 1911 and 1913. It was a worthwhile union with all companies involved profitting as world demand increased. Therefore, it was important to join forces as the Revolution threatened their Mexican oil properties, and their profitability.[36]

An example of this cooperation was present in the interview held in Washington on July 1913, between President Wilson and the British Primer Minister's private secretary, Sir William Tyrell. The British "recognized the predominant character of the American interest (in

México) and were willing to accept any policy in which Washington would take the lead." Their only request was "that British property and British lives be protected," and Great Britain was to "stand aside and let the United States deal with Mexico in its own way."[37]

Civil war engulfed México after Madero's death, bringing with it a steadily rising toll of death, hunger, disease, destruction, and migration. In Tampico, Huerta's rule was mainly symbolic and short-lived. Yet, diverse groups of bandits and rebels roamed the Huastecas' countryside, robbing or extorting money from the companies as loans for the "Revolution." Residents feared that these brigands would enter the city. On 13 May 1913, the municipal government called for a meeting to prepare for any possible attack from the rebels who wanted to oust General Huerta from power and destroy all the others who had risen in rebellion for specific personal reasons. Those invited to the meeting decided to create an armed guard of 100 men, who would protect the shops, plants and warehouses, and would assist the police and federal forces. The Huasteca Oil Co., soon followed by other oil companies, also created an armed corps to defend its properties. These armed men, later called **guardias blancas** (white guards), were kept on their jobs well into the 1920s.

Moreover, a major effort was made to control the "masses" from certain "excesses." The plan created great animosity against Tampico's government in the masses. For some observers, it helped create a pro-Carranza attitude in the poorest neighborhoods and boroughs. The city also had to deal with destitute and desperate Americans seeking refuge and a ticket to return home. Their presence in Tampico and México was used by Huerta in an anti-American campaign used to resolve its differences with the Wilson administration. It was a diversion of public attention from the revolution that engulfed México.[38]

Fear took hold of the city as rebel and government troops moved into the Huasteca, but also by the actions taken by the governments of México and the United States. Most oil companies' executives reacted strongly against Wilson's recall of their friend, Ambassador Henry Lane Wilson, on July 1913, and protested to Washington. In that same month, the Huerta government dropped the gold standard and depreciated the currency, leading the nation into an growing financial stress. Tampico's response was to use U.S. dollars as the common currency for international and local commercial exchange. Numerous Americans left México after Wilson ordered their evacuation in October 1913. However, since early May, Tampico was their major port of departure with more than eight hundred Americans leaving for Galveston and New Orleans. Meanwhile, a new local political crisis occurred.

On October 7, General Antonio Rábago, took over the Tamaulipas State government, jailed deputies and senators and dismissed the Tampico mayor, naming instead someone who "legally" select Huerta as president in the coming elections. For the rest of the month, a tight rein was kept by the Huerta forces in the city. In early November, Rábago was forced out of the capital, Ciudad Victoria, by the victorious forces of the Constitutionalists. The General moved south to establish his headquarters in Tampico, making it the state capital, and setting up office at the Gabino Barreda school located right across the Plaza de la Constitución.[39]

Venustiano Carranza's Army had increased its efforts to conquer this invaluable city. However, the presence of General Rábago and his men in Tampico raised the possibility of an armed confrontation in the city's center. The population was terrified, and foreigners and wealthy Mexicans were evacuated to the warships moored in the river and the Gulf. On 10 December, Constitutionalist Commander Jesús Agustín Castro attacked the city with his Twenty First Brigade. The men moved rapidly to less than a mile east from the downtown area, in the neighborhood of the Cortadura Canal, which connects the Carpintero

Lagoon with the Pánuco River; and about three miles north of the cemetery, around the **Escuela del Monte** (Hill School). Two federal gunboats, moored in the Pánuco, the **Veracruz** and the **Bravo** shelled rebels' positions. Shots were hurled over city houses and buildings frightening the population. Three days later, more federal troops arrived forcing the Constitutionalists to abandon their positions, and withdraw to Altamira, but they vowed to return and burn the oil tanks and the Waters Pierce refinery. The threat brought four more gunboats into the river, but by the Christmas holidays all was calmed in the city. The threat had been a stratagem to scare federal authorities, and to soften the business community for possible loans, in case Constitutionalist forces took Tampico. This first attack left just a few burned oil tanks, and some wounded and dead on both sides.[40]

Tampico, however, was heavily protected from internal or external invasion by the foreign navies. This alien presence led eventually to Huerta's collapse. On 26 January 1914, the city's new federal commander, General Ignacio Morelos Zaragoza, was named governor of Tamaulipas with headquarters in the city. With over 2,000 men protecting oil properties and Tampico, and with numerous foreign warships lying in the river and the Gulf, the general could feel rather safe. Foreign ships included the German cruiser **Dresden**; French cruisers **Jeanne d'Arc**, **Condé** and **Descartes**; and the Spanish cruiser **Carlos V**. The British had their Fourth Cruiser Squadron commanded by Admiral Christopher Craddock, and the U.S. Navy had a large fleet made up of the gunboat and flagship **Dolphin**, moored in the river, and off-shore the battleships **Connecticut** and **Minnesota**, cruiser **Des Moines**, scat cruiser **Chester**, collier **Cyclops**, hospital ship **Solace**, and mine depot ship **San Francisco**, all under the command of Rear Admiral Henry T. Mayo.[41] Still, the protection afforded by the ships was illusory. Most towns in the Huasteca had sided with the Constitutionalists, and foreign warships would not intervene in any struggle, especially on behalf of the Huerta regime. In fact, General Morelos was in a very difficult situation.[42]

Constitutionalist General Luis Caballero, moved his army to Tampico's outskirts, and on 28 March 1914, Colonel Emilio P. Nafarrete took Doña Cecilia, and Colonel Silvano García retook the Escuela del Norte. Constitutionalists had a reputation for looting, murder, and forced extraction of loans, and their successes rekindled fears among the notables, empirically confirmed by the large number of refugees streaming into Tampico. Thus, foreign warships and other vessels - oil tankers and cargo ships - were asked and did take as many refugees as they could hold, but there was a limit to space. Tankers were idle because for the first time since petroleum's discovery in the Huasteca, oil companies shut down their operations completely. All field technicians were evacuated to Tampico by 2 April, and immediately the companies claimed great losses.

Admirals Craddock and Mayo, concerned for the safety of foreigners, joined the consuls visiting the contending commanders, Constitutionalist generals Caballero and the newly-arrived Chief Commander of the Northeastern Army, Pablo González, and Federalist Morelos Zaragoza. At first they asked for, and later demanded, protection for their nationals and their properties. The Spanish Consul, Angel Saínz Trápaga, and the German, Ricardo Everbusch, begged General González to postpone for forty-eight hours his attack on Tampico until they could get their nationals out of the city. Admiral Mayo threatened General González with the invasion of Tampico if any Constitutionalist attack harmed the city. But, he refused to accept their requests knowing that most consuls were pro-Huerta, and also that the German ship **Ypiranga** was expected with a cargo of arms and ammunition for the federal army. The Admiral's threat was rebuked as an imperialist bravado from a foreigner. Still, this foreign presence in

Tampico and the protective intervention of military and diplomatic forces created a very tense situation for the rebels, for the city, and for México.[43]

The Tampico Incident

The city's tense situation led to a U.S. intervention in México both to protect and secure the oil fields and to topple Huerta's government. Woodrow Wilson considered Huerta's regime as anti-democratic, pro-British and pro-German, but he also believed Latin Americans had to be taught lessons in democratic behavior. The events following a simple disagreement at Tampico's port show how they served the U.S. government to further Wilson's political agenda for the Americas using México as an example.

General Morelos gave strict orders to keep foreign military personnel out of Tampico unless permission was granted by federal officers. On the morning of 9 April 1914, Lieutenant Commander Ralph W. Earle (**USS Dolphin**) needed some gasoline for Admiral Mayo's boat. He contacted a Tampico German merchant, Max Tryon, who had some gasoline barrels for sale at his warehouse on the Cortadura Canal. The sale was made, and Commander Earle sent a detail of eight sailors led by twenty-three year old Assistant Paymaster Charles W. Copp to collect the gasoline. Their boat docked alongside Tryon's pier. As the men loaded the gasoline drums into the boat, a squad of federal soldiers came upon them. The Mexican lieutenant ordered the U.S. sailors to show their permit. The Americans did not understand Spanish nor did they have the permit asked for. Tryon tried to intercede in the dispute, but the Mexican officer stated that he had to follow his orders, and placed the detail under arrest. They were marched through town under an armed escort to General Morelos' headquarters. Once arrived, higher ranking officers, who spoke English, cleared up the misunderstanding, and excuses were given. Meanwhile, Tryon advised the **Dolphin's** commander of the incident. Once informed, Admiral Mayo was highly infuriated and demanded an apology from General Morelos that had to fit the international rules of military behavior. However, under these rules, the apology would have been an insult to México's sovereignty, and their proclamation exarcebated a strong nationalist response from the masses.

General Morelos stated that he was willing to salute the United States flag with five guns (instead of twenty one), but only if the American ships in the harbor would do the same for the Mexican flag. Mayo spurned this reply, and began to plan an American assault on Tampico. In Washington, President Wilson, informed of the situation, gave his immediate support to Admiral Mayo. However, by 13 April, Mayo began to have second thoughts about the invasion. The sandbar at the Pánuco's entrance had built up considerably after years of improper maintenance, and U.S. warships offshore would not be able to enter the river, thus making them useless for any attack. Without their big cannons to support landing, such action would have been reckless because the attack would have stopped the civil war, and unite Mexicans against an invader. Beyond Mayo's change of heart, however, other political and logistic reasons were behind the planning changes. Navy Secretary Josephus A. Daniels had sent a transport with a Marines' regiment to land in Tampico, but en route, orders were changed to disembark at Veracruz on 22 April. Meanwhile, Mayo remained with his ships and crews offshore Tampico to impress upon Mexican belligerents and populace alike that any attack on American citizens or their properties in the area would be retaliated by force.[44] Yet, his show of force was no longer a personal matter of national honor. It was taken out of his hands, and now Wilson was in charge.

Rumors of a possible attack on the city created a new panic among residents because it was known that the federal garrison had few weapons to resist any invasion. Wealthy Tampiqueños bought tickets for the various passenger ships that were due at the port. For days, any report that Americans had landed at La Barra was followed by a rush of wealthy people with tickets running to the piers, and with poor people racing back to the safety of their homes. Especially after the attack on Veracruz, stories were told of savage and brutal Americans burning, looting, and destroying all Mexican properties, including kitchen earthenware. Among many, a nationalist fervor took hold, mixed with a strong anti-American attitude, that favored General Morelos' order to induct all able-bodied men, and also led to street demonstrations against the United States.

Fear was not the exclusive property of the Mexicans. Mayo feared the worst could happen to Americans remaining in Tampico, and he sought the help of the British and German naval commanders at the port. Boats bedecked with flags of those nations went up river to evacuate any Americans willing to come to the ships on the Gulf. Thus, four months before the First World War began, the future warring rivals cooperated in a humanitarian action off the Gulf coast of México.[45] Oil executives were also afraid. After a New York meeting on 7 May 1914, they called on Wilson to send troops and neutralize the port and the oil region. Four days later, General Caballero attacked Tampico, and Wilson immediately issued a declaration of neutrality for the city, rapidly rejected by federalists and rebels alike as a violation of Mexican sovereignty. Yet, Tampico fell on 13 May, and the U.S.action became void.

General Morelos had expected reinforcements and ammunitions, but none arrived. At 7:00 A.M., 13 May, Huerta authorities and federal employees in Tampico boarded the Mexican gunboats **Zaragoza** and **Bravo**, which rapidly travelled down river under heavy rebel fire from the shores. Federal troops boarded the train for San Luis Potosí, a destination they never reached. The forty-seven day siege of Tampico was over, and the city would never again be in such danger for the duration of the

Revolution. The Constitutionalists now held the city and its revenues, but the Huasteca remained under the oil companies' control by the payment of fees to groups of "rebels," who "protected" the oil fields and their properties. After the Tampico incident, the city became more dependent both on oil and on the United States.[46]

Constitutionalists and oilmen

For Tampico, the Revolution was almost a foreign event. One city resident recalls how she and her family experienced it. They could hear shots in the distance, and the shelling from the gunboats in the river. At times many men rode through town on horseback, but her daily life as a young woman was hardly disturbed. Although her father was a member of the city council, and a labor leader, her family was never bothered. People living in the boroughs of Arbol Grande and Doña Cecilia were the most affected in town because of the skirmishes twice occurred there. American officials and employees of "El Aguila" Mexican Oil did not bother to leave the city. They took refuge at the company's headquarters, a five-story concrete building finished in 1913. Whenever shooting could be heard, many ran to the roof from where they could see the action taking place. Actual damage to the city itself was minimal, except for a few oil tanks set on fire.

After taking the city, Constitutionalists named a new municipal council. Lieutenant Colonel Marcelino M. Murieta was named to oversee the new municipal officials. In a matter of days, normal life returned to the city. Consuls opened their offices for business as usual, and most commercial life returned by 14 May. Residents returned from the ships, and safety was reassured by the new authorities. Refineries and field stations reopened, oil flowed again, and prosperity returned now definitely associated to the petroleum industry.[47] Tampico was now México's oil city, pehaps the first one in the modern world of the twentieth century.

However, Constitutionalist leaders faced a new situation where the oil companies had almost total control of the fields and of the wealth generated as it benefitted foreigners and not the nation in need of revenues. Generals Pablo González and Luis Caballero, new governor of Tamaulipas, issued various decrees - following the nationalist policies of Carranza - that tried to control foreigners by asserting Mexican authority over their actions and over the national territory. Among those decrees which had a local effect were the imposition of a loan for one million peso to be granted by the Tampico business community, and also a number of restrictions on the shipping of oil for tax-collection purposes. Colonel Francisco J. Múgica, in charge on all federal operations in Tampico and its regions - customs house, telegraph, post office - ordered the oil companies to pay their taxes in Mexican gold, while U.S. gold was to be accepted only at an exchange rate of two pesos for each dollar, while the true value of the peso was equal to 9 U.S. cents. This financial maneuver was aimed to bring in needed foreign reserves to support the war effort.[48]

Venustiano Carranza visited Tampico on 24 July 1914 to meet with an envoy of the provisional government of México - after Huerta's demise - who would deliver national power to him. He spoke to the city's commercial and diplomatic groups, and vowed to protect foreigners civil, economic, and political rights. Yet, his promises were not consistent with his official actions. He had decided that oil was México's property and wealth to be used for national welfare, but could not constitute a threat to national integrity or sovereignty. Thus, Tampico, center of the oil industry, of its distribution, and México's international port, became the legal battlefield for these revolutionary goals.[49]

At first, the American oil companies decided to play along with Carranza. The Great War required large quantities of oil, and worldwide demand was rising. The wells continued to surge despite the Revolution and the political issues, therefore, it was easier to pay the government than to have the wells blown up, as General Cándido Aguilar, Constitutionalist Governor of Veracruz, had threatened to do. Sir Weetman Pearson, however, was not happy with the American attitude. His company's policy was to join Americans as long as they protected British interests in México. However, after his officials in the Huasteca oil fields were able to secure the protection or assistance of General Manuel A. Peláez, the policy shifted to a less helpful position toward the Americans. Peláez had originally supported Félix Díaz, later favored Francisco (Pancho) Villa, and after the Battle of El Ebano decided to fight for "his" own brand of Revolution. He had a well trained and equipped army of 800 men, which allowed him to control the Huastecas until 1920, threatening the towns and cities of the whole region. At first, he received the economic support of the British, notwithstanding Pearson's aid to Huerta. Later on, his services were required by other oil companies. Their executives did not want government or rebel forces to reach and threaten their oil fields, and paid Peláez very well. They also felt that since Constitutionalists controlled the two major oil ports of Tampico and Tuxpám, they needed a port of their own without governmental restrictions; and created a new facility, lying half-way between both cities, and named Port Lobos. Through these exclusive facilities, the companies began to export large quantities of oil, unmeasured and untaxed by the government.[50]

Pearson's major concern in Tampico before 1912 was oil, but circumstances changed his interest. Some of his associates had built an urban monopoly of electric plants, sewerage and transportation systems throughout México, especially at the port cities of the Gulf. Tampico also offered great possibilities in this area, and Mr. A. Schonduke was charged with bringing the city's utilities into their control. Schonduke approached the city council in late 1911 seeking the concession for the tramway system which was to be auctioned. He also wanted to acquire the telephone system concession. B. Spielen, another Pearson man, asked the city council for the electric system concession that included two power plants, two river stations, and the city's tramway system. Pearson was bidding against himself to take over the utilities. Another one of his companies acquired the contract to provide fuel for the water pumping stations of the city's water supply and sewerage systems. Whether willingly or unwillingly, the city council consented to grant these concerns to the Pearson interests, and a new company was formed that included all of them, **Compañía de Luz, Fuerza y Tracción de Tampico, S.A.** (Tampico Light, Power, and Traction Co., Ltd.). All federal, state, and municipal permits were granted to Pearson, although the council had some strong reservations about this monopoly, especially as all services were now really out of their hands.

Pearson had now a direct control and influence over Tampico's basic services, kept until he sold them to workers' cooperatives in 1921, an action indicative of a change in the city's spirit. The trolley was completely modernized after 1912 with new large electric cars bought in New York that began service in 1914. New routes were opened, increasing the possibilities for urbanization; one of them to Miramar beach in open competition with the railroad line. Another route served the **colonias** or new urban developments springing up north of the city. A very modern electric plant replaced the original and less efficient older ones, providing Tampico with what to many observers was the best and most powerful system in the nation.[51] Pearson, aware of the city's population growth and its future possibilities, formed a real estate development company that built the colonia "El Aguila," a luxurious complex of residences on a high terrain to the north overlooking Tampico and the Tamesín River. Soon after, these elegant homes were occupied by the city's foreign and local elite.[52] Thus, while Tampico's surroundings were controlled by Peláez and the oil companies, the city was shared by Pearson and the Carranza government. The 1914 Tampico Incident radically changed the controlling historical urban forces, and new circumstances threatened the old spirit of enterprise and capitalism with both the international forces of imperialism and monopoly, and the nationalist ideals of the Revolution.

Carranza v. Villa

The great struggle between Francisco Villa and Carranza began after Huerta's collapse in the last weeks of 1914. Villa's forces held most of the country, but Carranza's armies held the important ports of Veracruz and Tampico. The *New York Times* reported that

> the possession of Tampico would not only vest the Villista government with control over the oil region but would provide it with its first port of entry on the Gulf of Mexico, enable it to collect customs, and to strengthen itself with the foreign industrial interests by taking a liberal attitude toward the operation of the oil wells.[53]

Carranza was aware of the danger to his men if Tampico fell in Villa's hands. The Constitutionalists' precarious situation led them to concentrate efforts to preserve the city under their control. Again, Tampiqueños were an audience, rather than actors in the conflict, because there was little they could do against the warring opponents' actions. Large numbers of Constitutionalist troops passed through Tampico to and from the battlefields, yet the city's daily life continued as usual throughout most of this tense confrontation between the two leaders. However, the specter of hunger closed on the city.[54]

Hunger was a real problem while Villa's troops controlled the Huasteca in their attempt to take over the oil fields. Some companies closed their field operations, and by 13 January 1915, over 1200 unemployed Americans streamed into Tampico seeking aid. Other companies sent the women living at the camp sites to Tampico for safety.

Hundreds of refugees from Huastecan towns also made their way to the city, and thousands of soldiers were moved from Carranza-held territory to protect Tampico. In March 1915, 4000 soldiers arrived by ship from Veracruz. These new arrivals created a sudden demand upon the available food supply, and with no roads open to the Huastecan agricultural areas, food prices went up, and Tampico became more dependent on foreign staples, mainly from the United States.[55]

Carranza's decree forcing the use of Constitutionalist paper money - called **infalsificables** - brought disapproval and non-compliance among Tampico's commercial and business groups. The infalsificables lost their value rapidly, falling from a rate of 5 to one dollar in 1914 to 100 per dollar by 1916. Thus, the city's dependency on U.S. currency increased, and caused the businessmen to steadily lose in the exchange rate. Attempting to force the local government to change its policies, and wanting to make some profits, some food merchants hoarded supplies and raised prices. The Constitutionalist Military Commander tried to avoid food riots, and allowed the city council, now led by Tomás R. Morales, a carpenter and pro-labor mayor, to buy food from the oil companies' warehouses and to sell it to the poor and unemployed in the city at low prices. After several outbreaks, Tampico's storekeepers realized that the situation was turning against them, and came to terms with the municipal and military authorities. The commander ordered the import of flour and other foodstuff from New Orleans, and soon after the difficult situation eased. The U.S. press accused Carranza for Tampico's situation, and when journalists asked him about it, he stated that there was no food shortage in the city and "no serious discomfiture there."[56]

The city endured seventy two days of constant military presence between February and April 1915, with troops arriving and leaving for the front. Among them were the famous "Red Battalions," made up of workers from México City, and sponsored by the **Casa del Obrero**

Mundial, an anarchist group supported by the Industrial Workers of the World (IWW). General Alvaro Obregón, Carranza's gifted right hand man, had approached the capital's workers seeking their help against Villa, and they had accepted his request.[57] These "Red Battalions" presence in Tampico encouraged pride in the local labor movement, already one of the strongest in the nation, but few local workers joined them. The Constitutionalist defense of Tampico was placed in the hands of staunch generals such as Luis Caballero, Maclovio Herrera, Antonio Villareal, Jacinto B. Treviño, and Pablo González. They had under their command between 18,000 to 25,000 men positioned in a semi-circle around Tampico. They also had airplanes at a makeshift airstrip located on Moralillo Island, from where - and for the first time in Mexican history - pilots flew to bomb enemy positions and to defend Tampico. Villa's threat to the city was thwarted by the massive presence of Carranza's troops and their weapons. The military confrontations at El Ebano - Doheny's oil field thirty five miles west of Tampico - and Celaya sealed Villa's fortune as a revolutionary leader, and left the Constitutionalists as the strongest faction of this civil war.[58] Once Villa was defeated, Tampico returned to its normal routine. The oil fields continued as productive as ever, and industrial growth continued on the upswing as Europe's war did not abate.[59]

This chronicle of rumors and threats of war epitomizes Tampico's growth within its critical role as a source of revenues for Mexico's governing authorities, and as a rich outpost for an international community of oil interests. The city's development became inextricably linked to oil, especially after 1910, but more so during the Revolution, when diversification was almost impossible owing to the local and international circumstances of the period. Huge oil gushers appeared in its hinterland, and the city, prepared with the most modern infrastructure for this black gold, became its exit to the world.

Although city politics were apparently determined by the victor of the national revolution, the real power remained in the hands of the old business and commercial elite, now enlarged by oil executives. This period also points toward a new political force, until then quiescent: labor. Workers's struggles for wages, better working conditions, and social reforms, inasmuch these affected them, became an important factor to be considered by politicians and businessmen alike. The inevitable foreign presence, both of capitalists and workers, affected Tampico's urbanization as well as its intellectual environment. Dependence on the U.S. slowly developed on food, currency, amenities and tourism. After 1915, Tampico could boast of having an English daily, *The Tampico Tribune*. The powerful foreign presence was negative inasmuch as it placed Mexicans in a discriminated working status in their own land, yet positive, by providing newer ideas and knowledge surging from similar struggles of North Atlantic communities. These ideas served México well.

Whereas most Mexican cities participated more fully in the Revolution, Tampico remained rather isolated from it. Tampiqueños were basically observers of the war, even when it happened in their backyard. With little damage suffered, the city was a haven for refugees. It became an oasis of peace, work, money, and fun in a nation victimized by war, hunger, and death. But the Revolution was not over yet, and Tampico's importance merited more national involvement.

NOTES

1.Marie E. Wright, *Mexico: A History of Its Progress and Development in the Hundred Years* (Philadelphia, 1911), 362.

2.Adalberto J. Arguelles. *Reseña del Estado de Tamaulipas*, 68, 176; Torrea y Fuentes, 320; Adleson, 90.

3.AMT, *Actas*, 1 enero 1910, 5 diciembre 1910.

4.AMT, *Actas*, 21 enero 1910.

5.AMT, *Actas*, 21 noviembre 1910; Arguelles, 286.

6.AMT, *Actas*, 21 enero; 21 junio 1910.

7.Covián Martínez, 72; Charles Cumberland, *Mexican Revolution: Genesis Under Madero* (Austin, 1952), 74.

8.Spender, 156, 159, 165; Cleland, 295; "Railroad Control in Mexico," *Review of Reviews* 36, (December 1907), 747-748; "Mexico's Experiment in Finance," *Review of Reviews* 39, (April 1909), 503-504; Tischendorf, 125; Ralph W. Hidy, *History of Standard Oil Company*, 2 vols. (New York, 1955), Vol. I, 463-464. Also see Ralph W. and Muriel E. Hidy, *Pioneering in Big Business, 1882-1921* (New York, 1955).

9.Hidy, I, 22, 64, 111; Ida M. Tarbell, *History of the Standard Oil*, (New York, 1904), II, 32-33.

10.Hidy, I, 195, 336, 393, 403, 448, 449, 451, 646; Tarbell, II, 46-48.

11.Translated from the Plan de San Luis Potosí, Manuel González Ramírez (ed.) *Fuentes para la historia de la Revolución Mexicana* 7 vols., (México, D.F., 1954), 37.

12.*RDRIAM* 1666, Tampico, Charles A. Canfield, Norman Bridge, and Edward L. Doheny to Secretary of State, 5 May 1911; *RDRIAM*, 846, 194, Tampico, Consul Miller to Secretary of State, 15 May 1911; Cosío Villegas, *HMM*, VI, 398-399; *CRUSE*, (Washington, 1911), 129; Hidy, I, 450.

13.Alfonso Uribe Rubalcava, *Ciudad Madero* (Tampico, 1980), 10; Spender, 171; Rodríguez, 88; Gobierno de México, *El petróleo de México* (México, D.F., 1940), 14; Adleson, 146.

14.AMT, *Actas*, 28 abril 1911, 23 agosto 1911, 6 septiembre 1911; *Boletín Municipal* (Tampico) 7, 12, 25 mayo 1912, 425-426; 7, 13, 8 junio 1912, 433-434; 7, 15, 15 junio 1912, 442; Meyer, 64; *RDRIAM*, 5045, 13, 347, Consul Miller to Assistant Secretary of State, Tampico, 31 June 1911.

15.*RDRIAM*, 343, n.n. Consul Miller to Secretary of State, Tampico, 15 September 1910; 346, 746, 17 September 1910; 347, 81, Tampico, 19 September 1910; Torrea y Fuentes, 293.

16.*RDRIAM*, 423, n.n., Tampico, 18 November 1910; 431, n.n., Tampico, 19 November 1910; 468, n.n., Tampico, 23 November 1910; 475, 132, n.n., 23 November 1910; AMT, *Actas* 20 septiembre 1910; Torrea y Fuentes, 293; Carlos Collins Rojas, *Estudio del puerto de Tampico y desarrollo futuro* (Tésis de ingeniería, Universidad de Veracruz, 1969), 5.

17.Well #7 produced about eighty million barrels of oil until November 1919. See, U.S. Senate, *Petroleum Interests in Foreign Countries*, 79th. Congress, 1st. Session, 15 October 1945 (Washington, D.C., 1946), 334-345; Cleland, 295; Adleson, 76; W. J. Archer (ed), *Mexican Petroleum* (New York, 1922), 29-33.

18.Rodríguez, *El rescate...*, 23; "Petroleum Interests...," 334; *CRUSE* (Washington, D.C., 1911), 562; Adleson, 76-77; Cleland, 295. The well at Potrero produced between 100,000 to 120,000 barrels-a-day before it was controlled.

19.*RDRIAM*, 719, 179, 29 January 1911; 846, 194, 15 February 1911; 1200, 236, 28 March 1911; 1845, Telegram 18 May 1911; 1666, Telegram 5 May 1911; 1716, Telegram 10 May 1911; 1728, Telegram 11 May 1911; 1906, 270, 15 May 1911; 1989, 274, 25 May 1911. Young men were recruited to fight in case of American intervention. Fear came as the city of Tula was sacked and plundered by rebels.

20.Covián Martínez, 64; *RDRIAM*, 1937, Telegram, Tampico, 29 May 1911; 2050, 283, Tampico, 30 may 1911; AMT, *Actas*, 28 mayo 1911.

21.AMT, *Actas*, 14 junio 1911.

22.AMT, *Actas*, 26 junio 1911; 5 julio 1911; Ciro B. De La Garza Treviño, *La Revolución Mexicana en el Estado de Tamaulipas* (México, D.F., 1973), 68, 71, 73.

23.AMT, *Actas*, 2 agosto 1911.

24.*RDRIAM*, 3366, 472, 15 March 1912; 3855, Telegram, 9 May 1912; 2995, 465, 23 March 1912.

25.See Table 8.

26.Federico González Garza, *La Revolución Mexicana. Mi contribución política-literaria* (México, D.F., 1936), 420.

27.Gabriel Saldívar, *Historia compendiada de Tamaulipas* (México, D.F., 1945), 280; also Adleson, 173-195.

28.*RDRIAM*, 812, 5045, 13, 347, Tampico, 31 July 1911.

29."The Foreigners in Mexico," *The Tampico Times* (Tampico), 3 May 1913, 4.

30.Adleson, 66; AMT, Expediente 17, "Informe del Presidente saliente, Carlos B. Sahagón, 11 de octubre de 1913."

31.*RDRIAM*, 2691, 442, Tampico, 8 January 1912; 2795, Telegram, Tampico, 14 February 1912; 2901, 463, Tampico, 17 February 1912; 3336, 472, Tampico, 15 March 1912; 3157, Telegram, Tampico, 16 March 1912; 3550, 475, Tampico, 17 March 1912; 3379, 476, Tampico, 20 March 1912; Gene Hanhara (ed), *Documents on the Mexican Revolution. Abajo el Gringo! Anti-American Sentiment During the Mexican Revolution* 6 vols, (Salisbury, N.C., 1982), I, 6, 73; *Boletín Municipal* (Tampico), 7, 18, 14 junio 1912, 467; Saldívar, 281-282; Gruening, 565. See Michael C. Meyer, *Mexican Rebel: Pascual Orozco and the Mexican Revolution, 1910-1915* (Lincoln, 1967).

32.Peter N.W. Henderson, *Felix Díaz. The Porfirians and the Mexican Revolution* (Lincoln, 1981), 56.

33.*RDRIAM*, 5262, Telegram, Tampico, 17 October 1912; 5318, Telegram, Tampico, 22 October 1912; 5363, 481, Tampico, 22 October 1912; 5365, 625, Tampico, 22 October 1912; 5376, Navy Department to Secretary of State, 28 October 1912; Joaquin Meade, *La Huasteca Veracruzana* 2 vols., (México, D.F., 1962-63), I, 161.

34.Hanrahan, 6, 167; *RDRIAM*, n.n., 654, 3 November 1912; 6882, 7114, Tampico, 19 March 1913.

35.Ricardo García Granados, II, 378-386.

36.*RDRIAM*, 6684, Stanley Copeland to Secretary of State, 1 March 1913; "Investigation of Petroleum Interests...," 132-133; Daniel Cronon (ed), *The Cabinet Diaries of Josephus Daniels, 1913-1921* 2 vols., (Lincoln, 1963), I, 43; Desmond Young, 138; Spender, 171, 202.

37.Desmond Young, 161.

38.AMT, "Carta del Presidente Municipal Carlos B. Sahagón a diversos ciudadanos," 13 mayo 1913; *RDRIAM*, 7563, Telegram, Tampico, 16 May 1913; 7600, Telegram, Consul to Secretary of State, Veracruz, 24 May 1913; 7422, Telegram, Tampico, 29 May 1913; 72, Telegram, Tampico, 15 June 1913; 48, 91, Telegram, Tampico, 21 June 1913; 48, 210, Telegram, Tampico, 6 August 1913.

39.Meyer, 77; Covián Martínez, 74-91; *RDRIAM*, 8185, Telegram, Tampico, 27 July 1913; 9316, Telegram, Tampico, 21 October 1913; 9429, Telegram, Tampico, 25 October 1913. See *The Literary Digest* (New York), 40, 7, 2, 13 September 1913, 405-406 and Charles Jenkinson, "Bringing 60,000 Americans out of Mexico," *World's Work* (New York), 27, February 1914, 460-466.

40.*RDRIAM*, 9615, Telegram, Tampico, 7 November 1913; 9740, Telegram, Tampico, 14 November 1913; 9852; Telegram, Tampico, 19 November 1913; 9926, Telegram, Tampico, 25 November 1913; 10038, Telegram, Tampico, 3 December 1913; 10171, Telegram, Lind to Department of State, 13 December 1913; Torrea y Fuentes, 235-237, 295-297, 329.

41.Covián Martínez, 18, 24; Charles C. Cumberland, *Mexican Revolution. The Constitutionalist Years* (Austin, 1974), 119; Jack Sweetman, *The Landing at Veracruz, 1914* (Annapolis, Md., 1968), 43.

42.*RDRIAM*, 10457, Telegram, Tampico, 6 January 1914; 11099, Telegram, Tampico, 8 March 1914; 11162, Telegram, Tampico, 11 March 1914; *POET* 39, 4, 14 enero 1914, 2-3; *POET*, 39, 14, 18 febrero 1914, 3; *POET*, 39, 15, 21 febrero 1914, 3.

43.Covián Martínez, 38; Meyer, 77-78; Ronald Atkin, *Revolution! Mexico, 1910-1920* (London, 1969), 186, 188; Cumberland, *Mexican Revolution*...y, 121; Torrea y Fuentes, 247, 250.

44.The Tampico Incident rates among the most famous events of the Mexican Revolution. Two valuable interpretations are those of Robert E. Quirk, *An Affair of Honor, Woodrow Wilson and the Occupation of Veracruz* (Lexington, 1962), 1-33, and Jack Sweetman, *Landing at Veracruz*. Also see "Tampico Incident," *Review of Reviews* (New York), 49, 5, May 1914, 517-525; *RDRIAM*, 11466, Telegram, U.S. Consul San Luis Potosí to Secretary of State, 9 March 1914; 11483, Telegram, President Wilson to Secretary of State, Washington, 10 April 1914; 11488, 748, Secretary of State to Mexico, 14 March 1914; Gruening, 579.

45.Atkin, 199; José Domingo Lavin, *Petróleo. Pasado, presente y futuro de una industria mexicana* (México, D.F., 1950), 101. Admiral Werner von Spee commanded the German fleet off Tampico. A few months after these events, von Spee and Craddock battled each other off the coast of Chile.

46.*POET* 39, 38, 13 mayo 1914, 1-2; *POET*, 39, 39, 16 mayo 1914, 1; *RDRIAM*, 11924, Telegram, Veracruz, 13 May 1914; 12025, Telegram, Tampico, 14 May 1914; Covián Martínez, 56, 58; Torrea y Fuentes, 244-276.

47.*RDRIAM*, Telegram, Tampico, 12 April 1914; 12030, Telegram, Tampico, 29 May 1914; AMT, *Actas*, 16 May 1914. Interview with Mrs. Milagros Prom, Tampico, 16 January 1983. Meyer, 92; Spender, 196; Charles W. Hamilton, *Early Days. Oil Tales of Mexico* (Houston, 1966), 115-124. Also María Antonia Alanís de Salazar, *En el Tampico aquel* (Tampico, 1981), 78-80.

48.*POET*, 39, 4, 14 enero 1914, 2-3; *POET*, 39, 62, 5 agosto 1914, 2; *POET*, 39, 46, 10 junio 1914, 2; *RDRIAM*, 512, 266, Telegram, Consul Tampico to Secretary of State, 3 June 1914; 512, 284, Telegram, Tampico, 17 June 1914; 512, 286, Telegram, Tampico 20 June 1914; 512, 295, Telegram, 25 June 1914; 512, 347, Telegram, Tampico, 15 July

1914. The rate of exchange was closer to 3.5 pesos per dollar. Withdrawal from the gold standard brought about a considerable depreciation of the peso. Its value was also affected by the Revolution and by the large amount of paper money printed. See Raúl Ortíz Mena, "Moneda y crédito," *México. 50 años de Revolución* (México, D.F., 1960-1962), 83-89; E.W. Kemmerer, *Inflation and Revolution: México's Experience of 1912-1917* (Princeton, 1940), 10.

49.*POET*, 39, 73, 12 septiembre 1914, 2-3; *RDRIAM*, 12643, Telegram, San Luis Potosí, 27 June 1914; 12648, Telegram, Saltillo, 28 June 1914; Lavin, 101-102.

50.*RDRIAM*, 12436, 1089, Tampico, 21 May 1914; Javier Santos Llorente, "Nuestras raíces. Capitulo VII. La intervención norteamericana de 1914," *Nosotros los Petroleros* (México, D.F.) 2, 10, (1980), 26; "Nuestras raíces. Capítulo XIII. Mundo sin ley," *Nosotros los Petroleros* 3, 16, (1981), 18; Covián Martínez, 11, 59; Meyer, 94-95; Mira Wilkins, *The Maturing of Multinational...*, 13; Atkin, 185; *El Petróleo en México*, xxxiii; Gabriel A. Menéndez, *Doheny el Cruel* (México, D.F., 1958); Jorge Basurto, *El conflicto internacional en torno al petróleo de México* (México, D.F., 1976), 21-22.

51.*Boletín Municipal* (Tampico), 6, 37, 6 diciembre 1911, 320-321; 7, 12, 25 mayo 1912, 2; 7, 15, 15 junio 1912, 440; 7, 17, 29 junio 1912, 457-459; AMT, *Actas*, 27 septiembre 1911; Archivo General de la Nación, Fondo Gobernadores, Secretaría de Comunicaciones, Obras Públicas y Marina, 385/61, "Contrato entre la Secretaría de Comunicaciones y Obras Públicas con la Compañía Eléctrica de Luz, Fuerza y Tracción de Tampico, S.A. para su construcción."

52.*Informe del gobernador César López de Lara del Estado a la XXVIII Legislatura de Tamaulipas* (Ciudad Victoria, 1923), 102-104.

53.*NYT*, 25 January 1915, 5:1.

54.*RDRIAM*, 14327, Telegram, Tampico, 19 January 1915; 14369, Telegram, Tampico, 9 February 1915; Friedrich Katz, *The Secret War in Mexico, Europe, the United States and the Mexican Revolution* (Chicago/London, 1981), 253-297.

55.*NYT*, 23 January 1915, 4:6; *RDRIAM*, 14203, Telegram, Tampico, 13 January 1915; 14593, Telegram, Tampico, 6 March 1915; 14595, 1368, Tampico, 6 March 1915; 14388, Telegram, Tampico, 13 February 1915; 14696, Telegram, Tampico, 24 March 1915.

56.*RDRIAM*, 1413, Thomas H. Bevan to Secretary of State from a letter by Captain M. Trejo, 30 March 1915; Kemmerer, 49, 118; Adleson, 249; *NYT*, 3 June 1915, 4:6.

57.Mira Wilkins, *The Maturing of...*, 35; *NYT*, 3 June 1915, 4:6; John M. Hart, "The Urban Working Class and the Mexican Revolution: the Case of the Casa del Obrero Mundial," *HAHR*, 58, February 1978, 1-20; Pablo González Casanova, *La clase obrera en la historia de México. En el primer gobierno constitucional, 1917-1920* (México, D.F., 1980); Douglas W. Richmond, "Carranza: The Authoritarian Populist as Nationalist

President," in Douglas W. Richmond and George Wolfskill (eds), *Essays on the Mexican Revolution. Revisionist Views of the Leaders* (Austin/London, 1979), 60-61.

58.*NYT*, 22 January 1915, 9:2; *NYT*, 4 February 1915, 4:5; *NYT*, 14 March 1915, 6:1; *NYT*, 13 April 1915, 4:5; Torrea y Fuentes, 289-290.

59.*NYT*, 9 June 1915, 4:5; Ray C. Gerhardt, "Inglaterra y el petróleo mexicano durante la Primera Guerra Mundial," *Historia Mexicana*, 25, 91, (1), jul/sept. 1975, 124.

6

A RICH NON-REVOLUTIONARY CITY

> Tampico is the second most active port in the New World after New York.
>
> New York Times, 6 July 1921.

> Practically all industrial growth and development, a large share of agricultural ownership and permits, and an important share of the mercantile and trading element is American in origin and management.
>
> U.S. Consul Dawson, 1921.

The eight years between 1916 and 1924 were momentous for Tampico's industry and economy. Large amounts of oil money entered the city's economy bringing immediate modernizing elements at a faster rate than expected by residents. This income affected all classes, but mainly workers and their families whose average rose within national levels. Labor attained a higher social plateau both by turning into a consumer society of items inaccessible to most other Mexican workers, and also becoming more aware of their importance in the economic life of the city and the region.

The impact on Tampico's growth occurred by the merger of various elements. Among them were the emergence of more productive wells in the Huasteca, the rising world demand for oil, and the stability achieved in the region after Villa's collapse in 1915 when the various warring factions made an agreement to protect the Huasteca and the city. In the words of Pearson, neither side would "kill the goose which laid the golden eggs."[1] Still, a new scenario of conflicts came about between the new "revolutionary national government" and the oil companies over control of the oil wealth; and also with labor activists, who wanted political and economic power. Thus, labor faced oil companies and a new nationalist and revolutionary government's policies.

The clash between the federal government and the companies began immediately after Carranza asserted México's legal control over its oil industry using the 1917 Constitution, but the need for revenues forced him to reach some understanding with the companies. The early stage of the dispute did not alter Tampico's life, which continued receiving the influence of external forces welcomed by the elite, the business community, and the workers. The city remained less Mexican and more international, and it can be suggested that until the 1930s, it represented what many revolutionaries had wanted: a México that was part of the "modern" North Atlantic world.

National disputes ocurring between 1916 and 1924 that were relevant to Tampico and its problems are the theme of this chapter. It will also describe those changes caused by the new wealth, and the problems that influenced the main actors in the city's economic life: government, oil companies, and workers.

Oil boom and its problems

México was in a deplorable condition by 1920. After ten years of war and disorders, of powerless central governments, of foreign intervention, and of weak political leaders such as Madero, Huerta, and Carranza, only one spot brightened the suffering nation: Tampico. The city reaped benefits that spread to the whole nation from the newest and richest oil wells ever unearthed in the world. Oil production increased rapidly after 1917 when the Russian Empire collapsed, and México became the second oil world producer after the United States.

The Huasteca and its main port, Tampico, were the source of a wealth that seemed never to stop. Oil reached its highest output in 1921 (See Table 9), but under President Obregón, the dispute with the oil companies reached its zenith. By 1920, the conflict grew stronger. Prophets of doom predicted the forthwith downfall of the oil fields. A prophesy based on the emergence of water in previously rich oil wells, and on the government's attitude hindering new investments. Pan American Petroleum s president E. L. Doheny attacked the oil oracles, who wrote from the comfort of their offices in London and New York, or from their luxurious quarters at the Imperial Hotel or their "El Aguila" residences in Tampico. He was confident in the wealth of his wells owing to the size of México's oil reserves, and stated that "their pessimistic conclusions are regarded with skepticism by men who have spent years in the country."[2] Certain oil interests wanted to wage a psychological war on the nation by forcing water in some wells using special pumps, even though a few were really exhausted, according to the investigation of a special agent of the US War Department. American journalist, John K. Barnes, accused the companies of wrongdoing at the wells in order to increase the price of light oil sold to the U.S. Shipping Board.[3] Another rebuttal came from the American Consul in Tampico, Claude G. Dawson, when he stated that

> It suffices to say that invested capital here as a whole is least of all concerned over the reputed exhaustion of the present Tampico fields; but it is rather apprehensive of a stagnant oil market in the face of surplus production and the depressing political and economic factors now confronting the Mexican oil industry.[4]

Fear of oil exhaustion was part of the new scenario imposed on Tampico by changes occurred after the end of the War.[5] A decreased oil demand created a market glut and reduced profits, and the problem of private v. national lands became components of what the industry and the city had to endure.

Tampico was affected as headquarters for many of the five hundred oil-producing, exporting or refining companies, in México and home for a large number of satellite industries associated to aspects of oil production. Besides, it was México's largest oil-export city with the nation's second largest financially powerful foreign community. Its customs provided the nation increasingly with its major source of hard currency. Its industrial growth and safety attracted thousands of Mexicans and foreigners, forcing a growing urbanization, and making it the nation's fifth largest city by 1921 (see table 10). Whomever controlled Tampico and its oil fields could monopolize a valuable international asset, and México's immediate financial future.[6] (See Table 11).

After 1916, Mexican exports of minerals and oil increased rapidly to fulfill the military needs of the Allies in the European War. México's revenues increased almost 50% in 1918, and 170% by 1921, but once the war ended, ore exports collapsed, and the treasury became more dependent on oil to pay for imports and for its foreign debt. Oil amounted to over 50% of exports for the 1921-1925 period as well as 25% of the national income. Although, government figures for the 1921-25 period are not very reliable owing to the prevalent accounting upheavals, still there was an unaccounted source of federal income received from a 25% participation of state and municipal taxes. Charles C. Cumberland accurately summed up this question stating that "the income from oil served as the mainstay of government finance to the end of Obregón's tenure."[7]

Frederick Starr, American scholar and Mexican observer, had negative comments in his analysis of the city and its national importance. He believed that its growth was of little benefit to the nation, and that foreigners took advantage of its wealth and were only creating corruption, and unrest. For him

> What real advantage was it to Mexico that the city of Tampico should grow, when the only railroads from that port led to El Paso and Eagle Pass and Laredo and not to the city of México....the great petroleum fields of Tamaulipas and Veracruz are of little real benefit to México. They increase the business of Tampico; they furnish labor to a certain number of hands; they produce a valuable material for world use; they make fortunes for a few American and English speculators; but they

> contribute little to México's upbuilding; they lead to political corruption, to local unrest and disturbance, to meddling and interference, to constant threat of intervention.[8]

However, Professor Starr never understood that Tampico's growth was not necessarily directed by outside forces, but by the combination of its "geist" and of national interests; he never predicted how important would Tampico's revenues become for México.

The Tampico "Great Oil Boom," begun around 1916, created a bonanza for the city, added to the national income, and became part of the national and international problems of the "revolutionary" governments, at least until the 1930s. The oil controversy for power and national sovereignty began to weaken around 1924, and even though the government seemed to have won most battles, they were Pyrrhic victories. The companies paid their taxes, hired rebel "protectors" and armed guards, but lost the protection of the United States government owing both to Obregón's effective public relations campaign that included a number of small American oil companies, and to the famous Tea Pot Dome Scandal of 1923. The companies retaliated by slowing down production, firing thousands of employees from their jobs, and foremost, by abstaining from further investments and explorations in Mexican oil lands. Their actions coincided with the sale of Doheny's and Pearson's oil interests to Standard Oil and Shell Dutch Oil respectively, and also with the growing productivity of those companies' oil fields in Venezuela, Peru, Bolivia, and the Middle East. The companies' international and financial power was used to threaten México with their total withdrawal from the country – carried out partially – and to coerce the government from enforcing laws that would have nationalized the mineral industry. Notwithstanding, the government regained eventual control over the oil fields and the companies slowly began to abandon them, thus hurting Tampico's development in the 1930s and later.

The national scene

Venustiano Carranza won political power over most of México after Villa's armies were defeated by Alvaro Obregón at the Battle of Celaya in 1915. This power, however, was jeopardized throughout his incumbency by local caudillos and by the numerous bandits that roamed over the countryside. He was the first revolutionary leader to attain national control, but he needed more than military victories to hold it.

Carranza's immediate political goals were to solve México's national and international problems. An immediate task was to acquire international recognition for his "de facto" regime, especially from the United States. Once recognized diplomatically, his administration could ask for economic and military assistance from foreign nations, and could also try to resolve some of the international issues affecting the Revolutionary regime. Carranza's next step was to impress upon the nation his views on the pacification process, and the need to return to normality.

President Woodrow Wilson decided to recognize Carranza, yet two conditions were met. Carranza wanted the U.S. to stop supplying arms and ammunition to Pancho Villa; and the U.S. asked México to grant American citizens certain advantages over the Europeans, which had been given by Díaz, Madero, and Huerta. Wilson wanted a preferred–nation status from México. It was easy for the U.S. to stop supplying Villa; he was no longer a statesman, but a rebel and bandit. Yet, it was not easy for Carranza to give Americans the concessions asked because it was a violation of the Constitution. Besides, Carranza's own personal pro-European stance and his belief in one of the basic tenets of the Revolution – elimination of foreign control – could not bring him to allow those concessions. All foreigners in México had to abide to the laws without any special preference; their actions and conduct had to be useful and not detrimental for México. In this matter, Carranza was forced to act openly as an ultra-nationalist, but whether or not some type of agreement was secretly made, his views were persuasive enough and U.S. recognition was granted on 19 October 1915.

Other countries immediately recognized México's government. Villa's supplies were stopped, and Obregón's victories in the north increased Carranza's territory. Still, the sad experiences of Mexican–American relations, and Carranza's obstinate attitude and vanity, "from what he considered the triumphs of his rationalist diplomacy," resulted in a complex international situation.[9] His apparent anti-American position led the German government to believe that México could become an agreeable ally against the United States, which probably lead to the 1917 Zimmerman Telegram Crisis. Moreover, it happened because Washington believed similarly. American views on Carranza were obscured by their confusion with the nationalist revolutionary goals of some Mexican leaders, the influence that radical ideologies exerted among others, and the growing concern of Bolshevism and Communism at their doorstep after the 1917 Russian Revolution. Many wealthy Mexicans as well as most of the major foreign corporations with interests in México, including the oil companies, became enemies of the Revolution and promoted the fear - of a Carranza Socialist Bolshevik government - in Washington and elsewhere, terrified by the possibility of social and economic changes that would eliminate them as privileged political or economic entities.[10]

Carranza grew out of the old Porfirian elite and, although of a more modern breed, was still immersed in nineteenth century Mexican liberalism.[11] The 1857 Liberal Constitution had served Díaz well for his rituals on democratic behavior. It had also inspired Madero's rise to power, and fueled Carranza's revolutionary factions, but, by 1916, the nation was ready for a new political system that would bring social justice and real democracy to all Mexicans. Douglas V. Richmond has called

Carranza "an authoritarian populist," a most fitting title. The First Chief, as he liked to be addressed, knew the people and their hopes, and attempted to satisfy them despite his rather meager resources. The nation was still in the throes of war: disorder, hunger, unemployment, graft, corruption, inefficiency in government, a general financial chaos, and its north invaded by an American Army. For Carranza it was of paramount importance to satisfy the nation's needs and, at the same time, to prop up his regime. A new constitution would institutionalize his regime, strengthen nationalism, and stabilize the nation through the embodiment of all Mexicans' aspirations. As his Constitutionalist movement grew, he called on all those unjustly treated, who made up the rebel forces such as workers, farmers, indians, but especially middle class "democrats" to assist in the creation of a "new" México and of a new law of the land that would protect it from "domestic conservatives and external economic interests."[12]

Carranza, like Díaz, wanted to have a legal instrument on which to support his political control of the nation. Luis Cabrera, Treasury Secretary under Carranza and foremost ideologue of the Revolution, stated that the mere re–establishment of legal order without any changes, would be tantamount to the simple reconstruction of the old regime. To avoid this, any revolution has a second stage, always known as the period of revolutionary government. During this period, force is employed in the form of a dictatorial government, to establish the required reforms, which is, to lay the foundations of the new social, economic and political structure.[13] Thus he justified Carranza's political behavior before and after the constitution was written and ratified.[14]

On 2 February 1916, Carranza ordered the assembly of a Constitutional Convention at Querétaro, whose members were to be elected freely in October. He had already decided that the new Constitution would be a revised 1857 Charter, and sent a draft of it to all the delegates; but, according to Andrés Molina Henríquez, who was one of the nation's keenest observers, Carranza's draft did not include any social reforms. Furthermore, it displayed Carranza's desire to betray revolutionary ideals. Convention delegates thought likewise, and only 30% of them approved the plan. Meanwhile, other delegates led by generals Francisco Múgica and Alvaro Obregón, labored during the Convention to incorporate a several radical measures that were opposite those of Carranza.[15]

Even though most of the Constitutionalist military leaders elected were not amicable to the Carranza's views on México, they did agree with him on having a strong presidency, and on the support of nationals versus foreigners, a long-time held problem. Diplomat Juan B. Rojo states that

> written law existed in México merely as a matter of form and only in texts. Its guarantees and its sanctions were never applied for the benefit of the common people. Only foreigners, and especially those in such high positions that they could bring their influence to bear upon their diplomatic representatives, could secure the application of the law through diplomatic channels, provided such law was favorable to them. It is now the purpose of the revolution that all may equally enjoy such benefits.[16]

The delegates also tried to protect Mexicans through the preservation of the nation's natural wealth. México's mineral and land resources were placed under the control of the federal government, yet with measures to protect property rights and equal protection under the law incorporated in the text.

This protection of specific items became a highly debatable and irritant issue. The radical measures of Articles 27, 123 and 130 included land grants to millions of Mexicans whether in individual or communal lots (ejidos), and guarantees to workers and peasants' rights. They also reaffirmed the State's control over the Catholic Church, and asserted national domain over the mineral resources of the country.

Conservatives, Carrancistas, the Catholic Church, the oil and mining companies as well as the land corporations rallied to attack the social reforms promoted by the Constitution, that was finally ratified on 1 May 1917.[17]

Carranza's regime was soon after legalized. On 6 February 1917, presidential and congressional elections were announced for March. Carranza won the presidency and, on 1 May, he was sworn in assuming "all the limitations implied in a constitutional regime."[18] Once having the legal sanction to rule, he ignored the Constitution, and decided it was necessary to "stabilize" the country before its Articles could be effected. He did not ask Congress for laws to implement the constitutional provisions, and instead ruled by decrees. His attitude revealed an ambivalent political position that not only benefitted the enemies of the Revolution and its social and economic reforms, but also alienated forces that had originally supported his regime.

By setting up his governing plans, Carranza's views defined the Revolution. In several states, where radical municipal and state officials were elected, **campesinos** (farmers) beneffited from local agrarian reforms. Carranza, however, force the return of many seignorial lands to their former owners. Organized labor – especially those associated to the Casa del Obrero Mundial – whom Carranza had courted through General Obregón in 1915 to defeat Villa, was now too radical for his taste, and workers were harassed and persecuted. Their organizations were outlawed and their headquarters closed. The government also began to organize a state-controlled labor movement that would manage workers under the assumption of new revolutionary rules. Workers' independent movements were opposed by the federal bureaucracy, and foreign labor organizers were deported. These actions led many of Carranza's former supporters and friends to withdraw their governmental support, leaving the First Chief in the hands of his most conservative associates.

Corruption reappeared in most states governed by Constitutionalist generals whose most important task was to enrich themselves. "Their" Revolution was a replacement of power rather than a vital social upheaval. Bandits roamed the countryside, and federal forces could not control or defeat them easily. Many Constitutionalist officers were more interested in joining the old - still wealthy - elite, rather than in fighting any more. Pancho Villa continued to ravage the northern countryside, and Emiliano Zapata's forces kept most of the southern states in turmoil; two other Revolutions that represented a serious threat to Carranza's regime. Nevertheless, and until 1920, the First Chief was able to control most of the nation with his dictatorial imposition rather than through presidential persuasion; but his collapse was in the making owing to the nature of his regime.

The American embargo on weapons, and its recognition of Carranza's "de facto" government, deeply hurt and disappointed Pancho Villa, who had considered Americans as his "friends." In order to punish them, he crossed the border into New Mexico on 9 March 1916 with an army of 400 men. They attacked the city of Columbus killing three U.S. soldiers and wounding twelve, both civilians and military. An immediate national outcry to invade México was heard in Washington and response from the government was rapidly expected. Woodrow Wilson directed his anger toward Villa and his "bandits" by sending a special military body or "Punitive Expedition" to enter Mexican territory, seek Villa, and bring him to the United States for trial. For Carranza, and for most Mexicans, such action violated the nation's sovereignty. At first, he attempted to stop the incursion through diplomacy citing previous nineteenth century precedents whereby México had captured and turned over to the U.S. criminal offenders such as the Apache chief Geronimo and his staff. For Wilson, however, national honor was at stake, and did not accept Carranza's request.[19]

In late March, General John J. (Black) Pershing led the American army into México. All over the country, groups of patriots called for the defense of the Fatherland, and a surge of anti-Americanism appeared everywhere. In Tampico, Consul Dawson asked for a larger American warship to protect U.S. residents, and oil companies ordered the evacuation to Tampico of all American women and children living in the fields, and the city was awash again with evacuees and rumors of invasion. Meanwhile, Carranza had to play a difficult game. He publicly opposed the American invasion, and strictly limited the territory over which troops could search for Villa. He also ordered his federal Army not to give any assistance to the invading troops. Yet, secretly he welcomed the American's aid to eliminate one of his most powerful rivals. Some tense moments occurred on 26 June 1916 when troops from both nations had a gun fight at "El Chamizal," and war seemed unavoidable. All diplomatic efforts to avoid a conflict were rebuffed by Carranza. But the unsuccessful search for Villa, and the imminence of an American intervention in the Great War, forced Wilson to recall his troops by January 1917. Carranza's public position was acclaimed as heroic throughout the country, and some even believed that the United States had been defeated.[20]

German war aims led to an unlimited U-boat warfare in early 1917, which led to a strong possibility of war with the U.S. However, the German Foreign Office saw México as a potential ally to win the war, and a plan was made to lure México into a military pact with the Kaiser. If México attacked the U.S., Germany would help it regain the lost territories of Texas, New Mexico, Arizona, and California. Alfred Zimmerman, Germany's Foreign Minister, sent this offer in a coded message to Carranza, without knowing that the British Secret Service had received and deciphered it. The message was immediately sent to the White House. To Germany, it was an embarrassing episode during the war, but for Carranza, it became a useful tool in his confrontation with the U.S. and its corporate leaders. Still, he feared that German spies would attempt to blow up the oil fields and the Tampico installations. He reasoned that such an action would lead to an American–British invasion, in which case, it had to be resisted with the possible assistance of the good German "friends." Friedrich Katz states that "all these considerations make it understandable that the Mexican government did not dismiss the Zimmerman note out of hand as a phantasm."[21] Thus, Carranza became a threat for the allies owing to his eagerness to control the oil fields, to make them profitable for the nation, and by not repudiating the Zimmerman telegram; but he also forced oil to become a significant issue in México's international relations.[22]

Carranza, however, did make oil an important element of his national policies. On 31 August 1916, he placed all petroleum issues under federal jurisdiction, and by 22 September, the oil companies were ordered to register at specific government offices in the oil district. Several federal commissions were created to study the oil industry, and some of their conclusions were integrated into Article 27 of the future Constitution. A Petroleum Department was created in 1917, under the Ministry of Industries; and a special section was formed at the Treasury Ministry dealing only with oil revenues, and with branches at Tampico, Tuxpám, and Minatitlán.[23]

On 13 April 1917, a special Stamp Tax on oil was decreed, which had to be paid in national gold. The oil companies complained immediately to their governments, and to Carranza. The government stated that the decree was supported by Article 27 which allowed for the revision of any previous oil concessions. It also claimed that the companies had betrayed the concessions' terms, and when these were revised, both Doheny (Huasteca) and Standard Oil (Transcontinental) were found legally at fault. Pearson (Aguila), holder of the largest concessions, had complied with the original terms, and was not found guilty.[24]

Carranza, in his efforts to implement strong codes to stop the oil companies' abuses, and to increase profits for the nation, made a series of decrees after April 1917 that included safety regulation at the wells and refineries, productivity controls, and enforcement of Article 27. These decrees became the main source of conflict between the Mexican government and the companies until 1923.

Nevertheless, Carranza's policies failed thoroughly. First, the companies' protests were accompanied by their resistance to the decrees. Second, the United States, Great Britain and other countries pressured México diplomatically, and kept a constant presence of warships in the Gulf outside Tampico and the oil region. Third, Carranza did not have the power to enforce his decrees nor the political maneuverability to force the companies into compliance. Since 1915, the oil region was protected by companies's well paid strongman, General Manuel Peláez. His army - varying between three to eight thousand men - was well trained, better equipped, and was powerful enough to defeat all federal attempts to destroy or dislodge them from the Huasteca. It was not until 1920, after Peláez was lured by Obregón to join his government, that the Huasteca returned to national control.[25]

Finally, Carranza's oil policies were morally defeated. One decree allowed Mexicans to claim lands not registered officially or controlled by the oil companies. It was intended to force these corporations to register all their land holdings, thus forcing them to accept the government's right over the land. However, many of these claimants had no money, and accepted the companies' cash offers to withdraw their claims, or fell victims to the companies' "white guards" or to Peláez' army. Carranza had sent to the U.S. his Minister of Finance, Luis Cabrera, with assurances of México's respect for all just concessions given to foreigners in its territory. A few months after his return, the decrees violated Cabrera's assertions. Both events gave little moral support to Carranza's trustworthiness.[26]

One unexpected consequence of Carranza's policies was the renewed alliance between the American and British oil companies. Their directors and officials in New York, London, México, and Tampico, drew up a temporary "entente cordiale" for the defense of their "capitalist rights against the common menace of nationalization. President Carranza's pro-German tendency completed the damnation so far as the Anglo-Americans were concerned."[27] An Association of Producers of Petroleum in México (APPM), with offices in New York and México City, was born. In Tampico, meanwhile, the companies' managers also formed a "Local Managers Association" (LMA). Both organizations rapidly and successfully sought financial, legal, and diplomatic assistance to prevent Carranza's plans.[28]

The First Chief, however, had some critical political problems. In his desire to perpetuate his regime and personal power, he had selected his successor for the 1920 national elections. The man selected, Ignacio Bonillas, was considered as Carranza's puppet and a strong opposition developed even among the President's closest supporters. General Alvaro Obregón, the best military leader of the Revolution and probably the most politically talented, decided to oppose his former friend and superior. Obregón, never defeated in battle, had toyed dangerously with all the socialist and revolutionary ideals without ever involving himself too deeply in any of them. As a middle class capitalist farmer and educator, and aware of the needs and desires of both his social group and those of the populace - not necessarily defined during the Revolution - he decided to seek the presidency; and created a solid popular and military support for his candidacy.[29]

Carranza's reaction was to persecute Obregón and his supporters.

After failing to arrest him, Obregón's friends, the "sonorenses" Plutarco E. Calles and Adolfo de la Huerta, revolted against Carranza on 11 April 1920. Immediately a Plan - **Agua Prieta** - was prepared which accused Carranza of betraying the constitution, thus making him incompetent to rule. The plan was supported by most of the generals and Army troops, and the country was again on fire. Carranza realized his regime's collapse and fled to Veracruz, but he was ambushed and killed on 21 May 1920 in the town of Tlaxcalantongo by orders of Colonel Rodolfo Herrero, who had recently left the Manuel Peláez army, and who thought that his action would be useful to Obregón. Fear gripped the nation, and the U.S. withdrew its diplomatic recognition of México's government.[30]

In the capital, Congress appointed Sonora's Governor Adolfo de la Huerta as provisional president until elections were held later on that year. De la Huerta was in office between June and December 1920, and opened the way for a new political style of government. The change was announced when his inaugural parade was presided by generals Alvaro Obregón, Benjamin Hill, and Manuel A. Peláez with a retinue of 25,000 men. Especially for the oil companies, the public appearance of Peláez next to Obregón was already a signal that they had lost a major ally, and that something was brewing against them.[31]

A new international situation was arising. The new Washington administration was predisposed toward big business. Oil bigwigs and bankers with Mexican debts, now had many friends in the new Congress and at President Harding's White House. México's international creditors and foreign governments pressured De la Huerta to deviate from Carranza's strict and resented economic and constitutional policies. He, then, allowed exploration and exploitation of oil lands to any company that could present contracts previously made. Moreover, Americans were told that the Mexican Supreme Court would reverse itself in several oil cases dealing with the retroactivity of Article 27. But, De la Huerta allowed only the exploration and exploitation of federal lands near the oil fields, and appeared to favor the Atlantic, Gulf and West Indies Company (AGWI) which accepted México's policies unquestionably. Thus, his actions did not convince the oil executives, who asked Washington and London to deny recognition to the Mexican government; request that was heeded.[32]

World recession was over by 1920, and oil was back in demand. Meanwhile, México's Golden Lane, between Tampico and Tuxpam, continued to produce even larger amounts of oil with higly productive wells. The great oil boom occured which affected deeply both Tampico and the Huasteca. At least 38% of México's oil production was being refined at Tampico, and ships could be seen waiting in moving lines on the Gulf to enter the port to load and leave immediately. Yet, this Mexican major export commodity continued to enrich foreign companies and individuals, and not the nation. Madero and Carranza had tried, De la Huerta's period had been too short, and in 1921, it was up to Alvaro Obregón to make oil profitable for the nation.[33]

General Obregón won the 1920 elections and was inaugurated in December. He was a keen politician, who understood his government's need for diplomatic recognition. He also realized that too many problems plagued the nation's stability. The Revolution had been an explosion of dreams, wishes, and needs that had to be developed into some kind of organization if it was to succeed. Carranza had failed, but had left several useful directives to follow or avoid. Obregón was a different player with the same deck of cards, and his game had to be better or the nation would collapse.

Obregón was a popular hero, and his strong will and political acumen saved him from great failures. He continued to disband the Army, coopting and destroying the caudillos, attacking the Church by devious measures, and starting a large agrarian reform program.

Although supportive of independent labor movements, he continued Carranza's formation of a national workers' organization thus attacking the former. He was very successful convincing Peláez to leave the oil companies, and accept the government's control of the Huasteca. U.S. Consul Dawson complained to Washington on 27 May 1920 on how Peláez had left the city: "reluctantly and against a general protest, but feeling that a refusal to obey Obregón would force a rupture" that he was anxious to avoid.[34] Dawson also demanded to "require from Obregón et al. the retention of Peláez's control here, where he commands the confidence, respect and good will of all classes."[35] Thus, removing Peláez from the Huasteca was a masterful political stroke that weakened the powerful entrenchment of the oil companies in the region, before he had to confront them.

In February 1921, the President enforced the Carranza decree of 18 August 1918, whereby companies that could show documents of sale or lease would be granted permits for drilling. However, the companies had to request these at the branch offices of the government, and by doing so they had to acknowledge national domain over the underground wealth. Company managers were not fooled, and few permits were requested. By March 1921, the companies decided to show their resistance, and to force the withdrawal of the decree fired hundreds of workers from the fields and the refineries, and lowered wages twenty percent. It was alleged that their action was the result of a stock market oil slump, but the *New York Evening Post* accused oil interests of creating adverse conditions for the Obregón administration. On 11 April, he decreed that any company daring to drill without a permit was to be fined from 5,000 to 20,000 pesos, and if found without permits it would be stopped by force. The companies retaliated by spreading rumors that salt water was appearing in many of the large wells, but even the U.S. government was skeptical of these assertions. A U.S. Army intelligence report told Washington that the major companies had acquired special types of pumps that allowed underground water to flow up the wells, without destroying their oil capacity. But the rumors hurt the companies more than the government because their stocks suffered a sudden drop in the financial markets that soon forced them to deny the charges.

Then, Obregón adopted a much harder line. In three consecutive decrees, between 23 May and 7 June, he declared all contracts for oil lands previously made to 1 May 1917 to be null and void, raised the tax on production, and doubled the existing export tax. He reasoned that these taxes would protect oil reserves from excessive exploitation, and would partly help pay México's foreign debt; a payment that would please both foreign bankers and the U.S. government.

Major companies' response was to export all stored oil - close to 40 million barrels - by 1 July, date when the new tax had to be paid. After that date, they stopped exporting any oil. They also decided to fire thousands of workers from the fields and the refineries, and supported another revolution headed by General Daniel Martínez Herrera. But, the government did no budge to these pressures.[36]

The oil boycott imposed by the companies hurt them more than it did the government. For two months, their revenues dropped. Furthermore, 35% of the world's tankerage went idle because it was used to service Mexican oil exports. Thus, the embargo placed a heavy burden on those companies owning the fleets. On the other hand, Pearson's interests and small American and other foreign-owned companies continued to export their oil, and paid the required taxes. Even the boycotting companies could not impose a total cut of their exports because they had contracts on delivery for those two months that had to be fulfilled. The revolutionary attempt of Martínez Herrera was suppressed in three days by the army, and immediately oil companies' headquarters in New York and Tampico denied having supported the movement.[37]

Two American warships, the **USS Sacramento** and **USS Cleveland**, sent to protect American lives and properties, arrived in Tampico on the 6th and 7th of July respectively. The Obregón authorities, however, were in complete control of the city and of the region, and the only battle fought was on the baseball field where the ships' sailors played against a Tampico local team. On 8 July, the vessels were ordered back to the U.S. when Washington realized that there was no need to worry.

The conflict with the companies continued. Close to twenty five thousand workers had been fired, and Obregón ordered the companies to pay indemnities according to Article 123 of the Constitution that protects workers. He also ordered the Tamaulipas State government to provide workers with free transportation anywhere in México they needed to go. Furthermore, the President ordered one of his staunchest supporters, General Manuel A. Peláez, to head the federal army in the oil region so it would be protected against any disturbances.[38]

On 15 July, Obregón opened negotiations with the companies, but no agreement was reached until 20 August, when the Mexican rules were accepted. The 7 June tax was delayed for payment until 25 December 1921; the other taxes on oil were lowered, and the companies were asssured that Article 27 would not be retroactive. Besides, a secret agreement was prepared on 3 September designed to lower México's external debt with the companies' help. These would join into a New York financial group to buy Mexican bonds in the Stock Exchange at their market value. These bonds would, then, be returned to México in lieu of taxes, but at their original stock value. The plan allowed México to regain its bonds, forced the companies to pay the new taxes, and freed México from directly paying its external debt to the creditor banks. On the other hand, oil companies which resolved their dispute with the government were able to restart production and exports, and could make a profit from the difference in the value of the bonds, which had lost 40% of their original value by September 1921. The plan was excellent. It did not violate Mexican laws, nor did it hurt government revenues from the 1 June 1921 extra tax imposed. Obregón also guaranteed the companies that no more concessions for drilling permits on federal lands would be granted. He also had the Mexican Supreme Court decide a case in favor of The Texas Company which set a precedent for the protection of companies' rights.[39]

The plan was never carried out. After a visit to México on 19 October 1921, Thomas W. Lamont, chairman of the Banker's Committee on the Mexican Debt, declared that no new foreign loans could be floated to the country prior to recognition by world powers. A plea was made by the bankers to the U.S. government not to recognize México because they had uncovered the plan between Obregón and the companies, and realized how badly it would have hurt their interests. Moreover, the companies had not kept their part of the deal because as stability returned to México after September, its market securities began to grow in value, and their expected profits disappeared.

Thus, by December, the problem was still unsolved. Obregón ordered the companies to pay back the taxes due since July, now amounting to twenty two million pesos. Instead, Standard Oil and the other companies threatened to stop their oil investments and leave México. The president attacked by bankers, with no prospects for loans, and threatened by the companies, postponed the payment and set new talks on both the foreign debt and the oil taxes.

A new plan was needed to bring about a successful outcome for México. A "modus vivendi" was reached with the companies by 22 January 1922, but was never fully established. The June tax was lowered 40%; then postponed indefinitely. Bankers were appeased with a first, and only, payment on the debt on 2 January 1923, after talks between

Adolfo de la Huerta, new Minister of Finance, and Mr. Lamont. Meanwhile, Obregón managed to receive U.S. support for his political ability and efficient public relations. With the aid of the British oil companies and of a large number of U.S. independent oil producers, he set up a large public relations campaign against those opposed to his government's recognition.[40]

Some foreign events also aided him. One was the decreasing influence of the oil lobby in Washington owing to three main reasons. First, the collapse of their spokesman senator Albert B. Fall, after his involvement in the Tea Pot Dome Scandal of 1923. Second, Washington was less apprehensive about its oil reserves depletion, and American companies were allowed to enter other international oil fields. Washington had heeded complaints against México fearing geological studies' predictions that U.S. oil reserves would be depleted by 1919. Moreover, immediately after the war, Great Britain and France had started hoarding all possible sources of petroleum around the world, and excluded American companies. Thus, México's rich wells became very important as a U.S. reserve between 1919 and 1923. The situation was eased when in 1923 large oil deposits were found in California, increasing U.S. reserves; and when the British-American rivalry over oil entered a smoother relationship. The third event was that U.S. companies were very successful in exploring, finding and developing large deposits of oil in Venezuela, Colombia, Argentina, and Perú with the support of regimes willing to collaborate in order to assist their countries, to exchange their natural resources for some needed revenue. Thus, the oil cartel reduced its political power in Washington. Now Obregón, aware of the new setting, realized that the coveted recognition was closer than ever.[41] The President had to act rapidly on behalf of his country, his revolution and his political plans. The *New York Times* reported that

> Mexicans in authority now believe that Wall Street, which means the oil interests, have a back seat. Harding being more concerned in restoring friendly relations which will benefit thousands of manufacturers and investors who never heard of oil in Mexico.[42]

Obregón could now make his political maneuver to attain international recognition. Furthermore, he was aware of a growing rebel movement against him, and his successor General Plutarco E. Calles.

The Bucareli Conferences, held between March and August 1923 at the Ministry of Foreign Affairs in México City, were the prelude to the 1 September 1923 recognition of Mexico's government by Washington. These meetings have been the source of an abundant historiography and of numerous debates owing to their secretiveness and results. For Obregón, recognition at this moment was of paramount importance. Thus, it is reasonable that he agreed to "informal" assurances of Mexican behavior toward U.S. interests.

Events proved Obregón correct. On 5 December, his former friend, Minister of the Treasury Adolfo De La Huerta, rebelled against him with the support of a large number of generals and state governors. Rebels took Veracruz and attempted to take Tampico, but failed. This revolution was rapidly crushed, and was almost over by February 1924, thanks to the American aid received by President Obregón that included military supplies and logistic information about rebels' movements and activities. This victory allowed Obregón to insure the stability and tranquility of his last months in office, after which he transferred the presidential sash to General Plutarco E. Calles that started the Mexican precedent of orderly political succession, almost unique in Latin America for the most of the twentieth century. Thus, the Revolution was institutionalized within the parameters delineated by Obregón and his successors.[43]

Alvaro Obregón led México in the aftermath of the Revolution's bloody period. He instituted a firm commitment to the principles of the

Constitution, but his mandate was founded on the power he exercised as president using revolutionary rhetoric rather than by a democratic operation of the system. He and Calles, were instrumental in the creation of techniques for post-revolutionary Mexican "democracy," a style of government more faithful to the political realities of the nation than to the ideals of political philosophy.

These national problems of the 1916-1924 period were reflected in Tampico's political, economic and social life more intensely than previous ones. The city became the center of the oil dispute. Although, it was under federal control, the companies, the local oligarchy, and workers retained the economic and local political power until 1920. It was also a period of great progress and rapid modernization for the city, one that made many of its citizens believe that they were no longer part of a México that was so poor and backward.

Tampico, the new city

The city grew rapidly after 1914 when war raged around it. The presence of the Constitutionalists in Tampico, and the continued visits of American warships gave internal stability to the municipality's daily life. Moreover, immigrants continuously arrived seeking jobs and the high salaries paid in the city. Hundreds fleeing the turmoil and ravages of war, and looking a better future, found their way into Tampico and its boroughs.

Mexicans reaching Tampico joined local residents - already a minority in their town - but also foreign men and women. The largest group of foreigners were Americans, whose presence had increased considerably since 1910 when there were 2,000 of them. Many of these outsiders were technicians and experts in handling of machinery and tools for the industry. Others provided services to workers and the urban population. When American author Jack London visited Tampico in 1914, and described the atmosphere he saw as

> that of the West, of the frontier, of the mining camp. It was more nearly reminded of the Klondike than of any where else. In truth, within an hour, I encountered a dozen sourdoughs.[44]

The city was enthusiastically alive and full of vigor. It also had an international environment difficult to find elsewhere in México at that moment. Another author not only saw this interaction among men whose single purpose was wealth based on oil. He describes some of them:

> The fellow at your elbow at a lunch counter, blond stubble in his hard jaws, blue eyes narrowed against you and against the sun, might be a hobo from the States or an escaped convict, a younger son of a titled British family or a youth tired of Kansas haystacks. Coated with chapapote, they all looked alike.[45]

One interesting group of foreigners were the Chinese. According to Consul Dawson, by 1921 there were as many Chinese as Americans. They began to arrive after a group of rioters killed 303 Chinese in Coahuila in June 1911, in what has been called the "Torreón Massacre." Most Chinese came to México attempting to cross the border into the United States, after their legal entry was barred by an 1882 immigration law; yet few made it across and remained in México. There they looked for jobs and safety, and Tampico attracted many of them for the various opportunities available in service industries such as restaurants, clothing, and laundry stores. Besides, Tampico was a port where the constant and cheap transportation to the U.S. might allow some a chance to enter the country by sea. Yet, most of them remained in the city, and became hard-working Mexican citizens. They formed strong social and cultural movements and organizations, still present today. Two examples were the Chinese Club or Casino founded in 1912, and the Chinese Chamber of Commerce.[46]

In Tampico, a new social atmosphere appeared that combined the national idiosyncracy of the Mexican majority with a constant external world culture, all within the limited confines of the municipality. News from all over the world could be found in the various Spanish and English newspapers published in the city. According to Charles W. Hamilton, manager of the Gulf Oil Company in Tampico, the *Tampico Tribune*, published continually from 1912 to the late 1930s, was México's best English daily. Foreign workers brought with them not only their former experiences, but also newer ideas on social and political issues. The availability of money allowed even the poorest workers and their families, goods that elsewhere in the nation could only be obtained by the wealthy. Thus, this social group was able to become more sophisticated as to the requirements of the modern world. It also made them more aware of those requirements and of their special relation to capitalism. National leaders wanted to make México a modern nation; however, Tampico was already a modern city. Although local residents had resented all immigrants, eventually they mixed to create a cosmopolitan veneer and a new world vision.[47]

People came to Tampico by foot, on horseback, carts, trains, autos, trucks, and on a diverse array of boats and ships. The demand for sleeping quarters, increased rates, rents, and leases; and also created a boom for land developers as well as the problem of land squatters. The poorest people, who could not pay the high rents, invaded the few available empty lots near the city which were mostly under lease to the National Railways of México. These lands were located in the boroughs of Llanos del Golfo, Arbol Grande, Doña Cecilia and La Barra. Most squatters also built flimsy huts in the marshy lands along the Pánuco and Tamesín Rivers, and all around the foul-smelling Carpintero Lagoon. The size of this migration forced many others to sleep out in parks and under the arcades of Rivera Street and around the Plaza de la Libertad.

After 1916, work was available for thousands daily, although some jobs were only termporary. An observer relates the way used to hire many of these men. Early every morning, foremen from the various oil fields in the Huasteca walked through the city streets, hiring men on the spot to work for the day. Then, they were marched to the Pánuco from where boats and barges would either cross them to Mata Redonda and to a train line - built after 1910 - that connected to most of the Huastecan fields, or take them directly up river or through the lagoons to other inaccessible fields. Most men hired returned to Tampico that night, unless the field was too far for a round trip; yet, thousands returned for weekends. Men not hired for the fields had several other working options within the city, such as the refineries, topping and other industrial plants, local commercial warehouses and stores, bars and restaurants, as messengers or carriers for the numerous businesses and offices in town, as construction workers and as stevedores at the piers (now extending for over 12 miles on both sides of the Pánuco). Both the National Railways and the Electric Company had daily jobs available for over 2,000 men. Still, the supply was higher than the demand, and some unemployed had to use their wits to make a living.

A story is told of a man, who upon reaching Tampico too late for the daily morning induction, and with no money in his pockets, was able to make a small fortune for himself in a few hours. He asked for help from a lady at a house in town, and she lend him a bucket of water, some sugar and two lemons, and told him to go to the piers and sell lemonade to the stevedores. The man did as told, and by mid-afternoon his business was booming, thanks to a boiling sun! The first bucket had provided him with enough cash to buy two more buckets, water, sugar and lemons. That night, he returned the bucket to the good lady, and spent the night at a good hotel with over 300 dollars in his pockets. Anecdotes of this nature were common in Tampico's daily life.[48]

Entertainment also boomed in Tampico. Thousands of men

looked for all sorts of amusements, but mainly those associated to sex and booze, and these were easily provided also by many immigrants. Thrilling haunts appeared everywhere, and also elegant and fashionable locales that catered to all the social needs of the residents. The city's elite and foreigners had their Casinos or Clubs. The most exclusive Club in town was the Casino Tampiqueño, where only members of the city's affluent oligarchy and their families were admitted. Americans had their Colonial Club; Englishmen had their British Club, and the Spanish and Chinese had their own Casinos. The wealthier groups mixed at the golf and tennis courts of the two Country Clubs in the city. One of these, located north of the downtown, also had a Regatta and Swimming Club on the Tamesín River. The other, called "Los Mangos" Country Club, was located near Doña Cecilia. Workers fraternized in mutual societies since the 1880s, with a membership made up mostly of higher paid employees and craftsmen. These mutual societies had game and meeting rooms, libraries, and other facilities for its members and their families. Conferences on a variety of subjects were offered continually as well as dances and other social activities.

By 1920 Tampico had ten movie houses, and there was also one theater, **Teatro Principal**, with weekly presentations of plays, musicals, and operas performed by troupes from México City or from abroad. Pleasure trips were sold to New Orleans or Galveston in passenger or tanker ships that continuously left the port for those cities. Also New York, Havana, and Europe could easily be reached from Tampico. New Orleans was an inexpensive destination, only about seventy dollars for the round–trip; and short, only two days at sea. Thus, its pleasures were also available to those with cash in Tampico.[49]

Excellent hotels were built in Tampico with the most modern conveniences, among them, the Imperial, Inglaterra, Bristol and Southern. Their services were considered as good as those of the best hotels in New

York. There were also hundreds of restaurants and bars all over the municipality. Two of the restaurants gained world-wide reputation for their excellent food and service. One was the Cafe Luisian, housed in the corner of an attractive New Orleans-styled building across the Plaza de la Libertad. It offered food and spirits twenty-four hours a day. The other was "El Suizo" with a chef known to have worked for several European royal households.

Entertainment was unending. Bars such as "Pennsylvania," "Chicago," and the "Palace" were opened twenty four hours a day. Two tea houses and some illegal opium parlors opened in 1920. There were daily and weekly newspapers, that by 1920 included *El Popular, La Prensa, El Diario, La Reforma, El Mundo, El Correo, El Bolchevique, Vida Libre, La Opinión, and The Tampico Tribune.*[50]

Since 1910, saloons for all budgets opened throughout the city. Many with dancing platforms and live music played by Mexican or American orchestras, favorites being black jazz groups from New Orleans. Some night clubs had excellent shows performed by women of all races, who, especially after the oil boom started, were nightly showered with gold coins, flowers, diamond bracelets or whatever the fancy of the customers wanted. "El Foco Rojo" (Red Lantern) acquired international reputation, and also the "Montparnasse," a club with an entrance simulating a devil's mouth. Gambling houses and casinos were also permitted, and were most profitable.[51]

Prostitutes were part of the urban scene since its origin, and the city council passed a regulatory code in the 1880s to control their presence. The code forced women to undergo weekly compulsory medical examinations, and also taxed them for their services as professionals. However, the number of prostitutes in Tampico was low up until 1911, when the oil gushers brought a large masculine migration into the city. To the 98 legally known prostitutes of 1912, 172 appeared in 1913, and 333 were counted in 1914. This accounting seems to stop in city's records after the revolution, but it is logical that the number of prostitutes increased between 1916 and 1924. Proof of their presence were the complaints brought to City Hall from the city's elite.

The conspicuous solicitation of services in streets and plazas was prohibited, and removed to a special location. On 18 June 1912, a plan was approved, whereby the area around the Plaza de la Unión, north of the downtown, was designated as a "red light district." All entertainment and sex-related businesses were given 30 days to move to some location within the designated area, "for the good of public morality," or they would be fined. Moreover, the sanitary rules were more stringently applied, owing to a rise in venereal diseases - after 63 prostitutes treated at the Municipal Hospital were found infected - in late 1911. The "Union" attained worldwide fame, and became a hotbed for social problems until its elimination several decades after.[52]

Population growth and urbanization

For some visitors, Tampico was "the most American city in the world outside the United States," owing to its architectural resemblance to New Orleans and other American cities. There were many modern buildings, but housing facilities grew scarce as demographic growth increased. The downtown area could not accommodate more people in homes and rental places. Also few new structures could be built unless they fitted the city's decree specifying construction materials - cement or adobe - for the downtown.[53] Rents were raised, and many began to look elsewhere for cheaper housing. Those who had some money could move into the new colonias constructed by American engineers Donald Campbell, Alex Smith and Joseph Martin, which were very comfortable houses of two, three, or four bedrooms, several baths, and with electrical and sewerage installations. They were also served by the tramway and telephone systems. Mansions were built on a slope overlooking the Tamesín River, which commanded an excellent view of the downtown area, the harbor on the Pánuco, and the lagoons. The wealthiest of the new colonias were "El Aguila," "Guadalupe," "Altavista," and "Las Flores." Residents were wealthy Mexicans, both businessmen and country elite, and high officials of the oil and service industries in Tampico and the Huasteca. Middle class colonias were located towards the Carpintero Lagoon with names such as "Tolteca," "Colonia Americana," and "Campbell." By 1921, Tampico had, especially near its downtown, about twenty colonias with over 9,000 residents, mostly in the higher and upper middle class economic brackets. Urbanization increased revenues for the city as urban property taxes were raised almost yearly since 1913, an increase needed to cover the expenses that the same growth was causing.[54]

The city's downtown and the new colonias had paved streets with new sewerage and sanitation works. But the boroughs – inhabited by the poorest workers and their families, and by a floating population of drifters – had few or none of the municipal services except for a police station and public baths. Three types of dwellings could be found in these neighborhoods. Shacks for workers, owned by the railroad or oil companies, built with highly flammable materials, and found perilously close to the railroad depot, the oil tanks or the refineries. There were skilled workers' houses built by the refineries inside their property, and independent housing, mostly owned by workers themselves, who built these single unit dwellings on lands leased or owned by the railroad, the municipality, the federal government or the oil companies. The borough residents did not have paved streets nor sidewalks, sewerage, electricity, health facilities, telephone service or even a cemetery. Pigs and dogs roamed freely among the widely scattered houses of these areas. No planning was developed for this natural and haphazard urbanization. The only electric bulbs to be found ran along the railroad and tramway tracks, and few stores could provide the daily needs or entertainment for the residents. Most trade was done from stalls on wheels, and some small entrepreneurs used their homes for businesses. These living conditions, however, sheltered a most unique group of people. Men who earned very good salaries - compared nationally - were poor owing to Tampico's high cost of living, thus making them and their families peripheral to the modernity enjoyed by other social sectors of Tampico's society.

This economic and class division was a major determinant for the political division occurred to Tampico's municipality in 1924. Leif Adleson, who has studied Tampico's labor scene for the 1919-1924 period states that

> Doña Cecilia and Arbol Grande were proletarian boroughs away from Tampico that owing to their physical and social characteristics looked more like rural and interior towns rather than boroughs of a great modern city. However, many of its residents, in due time, developed a labor identity to the...industrial corporations that... fused them into a regional labor community which eventually transcended the peculiarities of their local environment.[55]

After 1916, labor representatives in the city council tried to modernize these boroughs. A plan to urbanize Doña Cecilia was prepared in 1917. Another plan to aid those living along river and lagoon shores was also prepared, but the city had no revenues for these projects. Large sums of money had to be invested in non-taxable lands, requiring a shift in the priorities and income of the city. Also lengthy court cases had to be carried out against the companies owning or leasing these lands and were profiting from them.

One of Tampico's major problems was its need for lands near the downtown that could be developed for more industries or for colonias. Plans to drain or fill the Carpintero Lagoon had been made since mid-nineteenth century. Its stagnant waters and foul odors had ill effects over the city's population, and had been the reason for the earliest plans. In 1856, the state governor asked French engineer M. Bouneville to make a channel connecting the Tamesín River to the Lagoon, so that its flow would clear the stagnant waters into the Pánuco River. Work began, but was stopped by a revolution, and later by the French invasion. Smallpox and yellow fever epidemics were a constant threat, and in late 1879 and early 1880 became a scourge for the city. Dr. Emilio Robert, Civil Hospital's director, called upon the authorities to drain the Lagoon because it was a major breeding ground for disease-carrying mosquitoes. A plan to drain the Lagooon was submitted to the council on 21 October 1880 by engineer Enrique Aldama, but it was prevented by economic limitations. Similar reasons were given for the rejection of the 1896 project presented by engineer Alejandro Prieto.[56] The Lagoon's drainage was also promoted by Carranza in 1917, when he tried to help Tampico's landless workers acquire lots. Once concluded, he would have exchanged lands owned or leased by the National Railways in Doña Cecilia for similar lots on the new landfill. It was never carried out.

By 1920, however, the lack of urban space gave the project a great priority. If the Carpintero Lagoon was dredged it would create 215 acres of land next to the city's downtown. On 18 October 1920, the México's *Diario Oficial*, (government register), called for proposals to fill in and urbanize the Lagoon. It was a federal government concern because constitutionally all bodies of water and their beds in the Republic were part of the national domain. Rules for urbanization were also provided in the ad, but again the project was never accomplished. The Carpintero Lagoon continues to be one of Tampico's landmarks.[57]

The plan was not successful because a new land development occurred within the city's core. The Tamesín River runs west of Tampico into the Pánuco River, and the flow accumulated silt at their meeting point. It was recorded, by 1866, that two islands had formed right across from Tampico forming a channel that allowed the Tamesín to run parallel to the Pánuco for more than a mile before their waters met at a spot called **Paso de las lanchas** (Ferries' Crossing). These islands were named **Moralillo** and **Zapotal (Muelle)**; the latter being the longest of the two. Considered as ejidos until 1880, they were divided in lots and granted to various families for cultivation. However, federal, state and municipal officials ignored these grants and transferred their possession to the Mexican Central Railroad Company in 1880. **Muelle** island served as the site for a new federal pier, and for a new Custom House inagurated in 1902. A wooden bridge connecting the island to the mainland - dedicated to Porfirio Díaz - was built in 1876. In 1902 was replaced by an iron structure called "Romero Rubio," and rebaptized "Francisco Madero" in 1912. The bridge was moved upstream in 1918 to connect the western tip of **Moralillo** island to its opposite shore over the Tamesín river; an indication that it was no longer needed in Tampico.

Plans to drain the channel between the islands and the shore were made in 1916. Presidential approval was given in 1917, and work began immediately. At the same time, a long-awaited dredging of the Pánuco began which provided the silt to close the channel. The filling required more than 1,000,000 cubic meters of silt for an area measuring 2300 meters (7544 feet) long by 60 meters (262.4 feet) wide. This project was finished by mid-1920, and Tampico won 27 hectares (675 acres) of new lands. Now its shore was no longer along the Tamesín but on the Pánuco. The new lands were divided into 51 blocks along several streets, and plans were made to accommodate 6,000 people, many businesses and plants. However, the unstable economic situation in the city between 1921 and 1924 discouraged the urbanization plans, but people, businesses and warehouses moved rapidly to the new area, with the city market and a new railroad station built on the lands.[58] Especially foreigners saw the advantages of the new quarter for their businesses, and were partly responsible for its fast and confusing development.

A small section of the marshes between the Carpintero Channel and the landfill - **La Isleta** (Islet) - attracted businessmen's attention. Located at the eastern tip of Tampico, it comprises an area of 601 hectares or 1,324 acres. American lawyer and Tampico resident, William F. Buckley, acquired it from the federal government to install his corporation **La Compañía Terminal La Isleta, S.A.** The city council also granted his request to tax this area as one single unit in order to have him develop it. The land was divided in lots with sewerage and electricity, that were sold or leased for lumberyards, factories, warehouses, foundries, and other enterprises (see Table 12). By August 1920, the place was fully under development without any political or planning control by local or federal authorities.[59]

Between 1916 and 1924, Tampico searched for lands. Workers and businesses were fully supportive of this interest The city's geographical situation forced urbanization north and east along the Pánuco shore. Since most people, especially workers, wanted to remain close to the downtown area the plans to desiccate the Carpintero Lagoon and the Tamesín channel held great interest for the citizenry. The success of the second plan changed the city's landscape, especially with the input of resident Americans, who took over the new development. American journalist L. J. De Bekker, visited Tampico in 1919 and stated that "seeing only Tampico, the visitor to México would be impressed by the extent to which American influence has grown."[60]

City views

Jack London visited Tampico in 1914, a year of rapid growth for the city. He described its landscape as his ship traversed the Pánuco from the Gulf upward. It was an awesome sight as more and more terminals and tank forms lined lined both banks of the river.

> I remarked – `There's the city at last' – indicating great masses of buildings on the north bank. But I was informed it was the boiler stacks, warehouses, paraffin plant, and agitators of the refinery... The Canal teemed with dugout canoes and chalanes (flat bottomed boats)... Everywhere boat building and repairing was going on. There were paint shops, machine shops, and shipways, and there were liners, steamers, barges and launches, not by the score, but by the many hundred.[61]

This constant activity in Tampico's harbor increased rapidly until 1922, afterwards it began to slow down because of the oil issue between the companies and the federal government. Oil's importance for the local economy superseded all other components. There were three refineries in its jurisdiction, and three more in Mata Redonda, but also controlled from Tampico. Every piece of land on both shores of the Pánuco between the city and the Gulf, and for several miles upstream from Tampico, was lined up with piers and docks, mostly leased to the oil companies. For example, in one single 1920 day, Tampico's port received 105 ships that were immediately loaded with oil and left the same day. The year after, 3,230 ships entered Tampico, notwithstanding the July-August stoppage ordered by the companies, when the port was partly closed. Petroleum brought a continued flow of people that made Tampico a twenty-four hour city – probably the most glamorous and expensive city in México between 1918 and 1924.

Like Jack London, visitors received a surprising view of the city. Travel books called it the "New York of México, the Sultana of the South, the Queen City of the Mexican Gulf, and the Capital of the Oil World."[62] It was considered an example of what American energy coupled with brains and purpose could accomplish in the `languid South.' For many entrepreneurs Tampico had stopped being a Mexican city and now was supposed to be the display of American initiative in many diverse ways.

> Tampico is predominantly American. The Mexican whimsically refer to it as Gringoland, and say it is **muy americanizado** since they observe American reminders on every hand...The tolerant and helpful Mexicans may not realize it, but they too are **algo americanizado**, for they hustle with an alacrity and a purpose usually surprising to the southern brethren.[63]

What outsiders could not understand was that Tampico's development was not ruled by whatever outside forces (mainly American) had wanted it to be. The city's capitalist `geist' had accompanied it since its foundation, and the successful commercial and trading enterprises started in the 1880s had renewed business ideals. Tampico struggled to complement its spirit against the forces of nationalism and internationalism, and Tampiqueños seemed Americanized because it was for many an equivalent to being modernized, yet, this apparent outlook brought them problems of a different nature.

The world's best and most expensive items could be found in Tampico's stores, which served a highly diverse group of shoppers. Before 1914, most luxury items came from Europe, afterwards the United States supplied most of them. Workers and their families were able, if they wanted, to afford luxuries unavailable to their peers elsewhere in México. Women could wear French silk stockings, Italian and English nightgowns, and Irish linen handkerchiefs. Their houses could boast of Persian or Chinese rugs, Irish tablecloths, and English silverware in their dining rooms. Yet, in order to afford such luxuries sacrifices had to be made because the basic food basket items were very expensive.[64]

The Revolution disrupted the flow of supplies from the Huasteca into Tampico, and the municipality did not have enough rural lands to produce the necessary provisions for its growing population. Supplies were, therefore, sought from foreign sources. From 1916 to 1924, Tampico was highly dependent on food from New Orleans, New York, Galveston, and Havana. By 1921, practically 90% of the imports came from the United States. This dependency was also due to the city's American colony, which numbered over 6,000, and who wanted to consume home products. Furthermore, this dependency increased the use of U.S. currency in Tampico, which although contrary to Mexican federal regulations, helped people protect themselves from the instability of the Mexican peso. By 1921, the exchange rate between the two currencies was two pesos per dollar. Even children in Tampico knew this rate of exchange. They bought ice cream cones for either a U.S. dime or a `veinte' (20 cents Mexican). Other basic articles were as expensive as the ice cream cone. Some of these items in U.S. dollars were as follows: one pound of butter, $1.25; a loaf of bread, 25 cents; a pound of lard, 50 cents; a pound of cheese, 75 cents; dozen eggs, $1.00; quart of milk, 50 cents; a pound of coffee or tea was 75 cents and $1.25 respectively. Thus, both the oil boom and the revolution had created a high inflation in the city.[65]

Of a different nature were the social changes that had appeared by 1923, now more visible by a geographical urban division. Two social and powerful groups lived within the municipal perimeter. One was made up of a business elite and white collar employees of the city's industries. The other group was formed by workers and the unemployed. They had increased their demands and gained a certain amount of power through the success of their labor movement and the ideological support received from the Constitution and pro-labor government officials.

The division showed a city of workers and their families living amid or near the great refineries and oil plants, by the railroad tracks and the river shores. An unplanned city of the poorest, with few social and public services, unpaved and dark roads, and an economy almost totally controlled by outside capital. A city of people striving to be heard and to participate in the decisions that affected them. That city began at Arbol Grande and continued east towards the Gulf.

The other city included Tampico's downtown with its commercial, financial, and industrial headquarters, with its nearby residential areas for the affluent - management, federal, state, and municipal officials, and professionals - with hospitals, and the cemetery. It included a small and poor area for a labor force mainly related to the service industries: food, shops, hotels, bars, entertainment, maids, servants, and prostitutes. It was the cultural, religious, medical, financial and commercial center of the municipality and of the Huasteca, and the State's richest spot, with a broad political power supported by federal and state courts; with political appointees to oversee the Tamaulipas Huasteca, and with high standing worldwide. This was a happy, carefree, and modern city, with paved streets, some petty crime, strolling plazas, theaters, and other less than usual entertainment. A good police force kept things well under control. The first city worked to make oil lucrative, the second profited from it. In the one, oil was worthless and people got paid to handle it, in the other, oil was given its market value, and wealth derived from its possession and its use.

As México moved into the modern 1920s, oil became its most important natural and financial resource. However, the Revolution promoted nationalistic, democratic, agrarian and pro-labor measures and attitudes that threatened the capitalist-oriented Porfirian society that had survived and the foreign interests that had taken advantage of the previous circumstances. Tampico's growth was related to its capitalist pre-oil society, but suddenly - and after the end of the Revolution - it became a battleground for the struggle between oil and national power, and between labor, national power, and the oil interests. Many Tampico workers were affected by the conflict between the federal government and the companies, but workers also became aware that a struggle for power and independence had started since 1916 between them and the federal government. Labor's independence was a threat to the Carranza-

Obregón's policies, to the municipal oligarchy of pro-revolutionary businessmen, and to the oil companies themselves. Tampico's growth, therefore, had to be limited.

NOTES

1.Alan W. Knight, *The Mexican Revolution* 2 vols., (Cambridge, U.K., 1986), I, 131.

2.John K. Barnes, "The Crisis in Our Oil Policy: The Race Between Production and Consumption of Oil," *World's Work*, May 1920, 30. See AGNPPM, Legajo 104, Doc. P1-P9, 15 agosto 1921, Joseph F. Cheston, War Department's Special Agent, "Investigation of the Oil Men."

3.John K. Barnes, "The Crisis...," 29-34.

4.Archer, 75.

5.*CRUSE*, III, Report 190, August 1921, 817; Robert E. Quirk, *Mexico* (Englewood Cliffs, 1971), 95; John E. Kelly, "Mexico's Industrial Progress Since Diaz," *Engineering and Mining Journal*, 110, 20, 13 November 1920, 942; CACT, 18, 442, (1921), Claude I. Dawson, "Report on Prospective Oil Output in México."

6.Manuel López Gallo, *Economía y política en la historia de México* (México, D.F., 1965), 439; Merril Rippy, "The Mexican Oil Industry," Thomas E. Cottner and Carlos Castañeda (eds) *Essays in Mexican History: The Charles Wilson Hackett Memorial Volume* (Austin, 1958), 253; Gobierno de México, Departamento de la Estadística Nacional, *Censo general de habitantes. 30 de noviembre de 1921* (México, D.F., 1925-1928).

7.Cumberland, *Mexico.*, 249. A Carranza decree on oil shows that 20% of the total tax collected went to the states, and 20% went to the municipality where the wells were located: "Decreto 31, artículo 13, julio 1918," AGN PPM 104, P-P12, 17 febrero 1919. Also John W. F. Dulles, *Yesterday in Mexico; A Chronicle of the Revolution, 1919-1936* (Austin, 1961), 106-108; *Current History* (New York), 13, 1, January 1921, 289.

8.Frederick Starr, "The Mexican Situation: Manuel Gamio's Program," *The American Journal of Sociology* 24 (2), September 1918, 130-131.

9.Benito Javier Pérez Verdía, "The Foreign Policy of Carranza and Obregón," *El Mundo* (Tampico), 11 diciembre 1921, 2. See Thomas E. Gibbon, *Mexico Under Carranza* (Garden City, 1919), and Carlos Díaz Dufoó, *La cuestión del petróleo* (México, D.F., 1921). For Mexican-American relations see Stuart Alexander MacCorkle, *American Policy of Recognition Towards Mexico* (Baltimore, 1933); Luis G. Zorrilla, *Historia de las relaciones entre México y los Estados Unidos de América, 1810-1958* 2 vols., (México, D.F., 1965); Robert D. Gregg, *The Influence of Border Troubles on Relations Between the United States and Mexico, 1867-1910* (Baltimore, 1933); Josefina Z. Vázquez y Lorenzo Meyer, *México frente a los Estados Unidos. Un ensayo histórico, 1776-1980* (México, D.F., 1982); Berta Ulloa, *La Revolución Intervenida. Relaciones diplomáticas entre México y los Estados Unidos (1910-1914)* (México, D.F., 1971).

10.José López Portillo y Weber, *El petróleo de México* (México, D.F., 1975), 54-54; Douglas W. Richmond, "Carranza: The Authoritarian Populist as Nationalist President," George W. Wolfskill and Douglas W. Richmond (eds), *Essays on the Mexican Revolution y Revisionist Views of the Leaders* (Austin, 1979), 64-65. Also see Douglas W. Richmond, *Venustiano Carranza's Nationalist Struggle, 1893-1920* (Lincoln, 1984); Carlos Díaz Dufoó, *México y los capitales extranjeros* (México, D.F., 1918); Barbara W. Tuchman, *The Zimmerman Telegram* (London, 1958); J. Fred Rippy, *The United States and Mexico* (New York, 1926); Friedrich Katz, *The Secret War in Mexico, Europe, the United States and the Mexican Revolution* (Chicago, 1981).

11.Robert E. Quirk, "Liberales y radicales en la Revolución Mexicana," *Historia Mexicana* 2, (4), abril–junio 1953, 525; Wilfrid H. Calcott, *Liberalism in Mexico, 1857-1929* (Stanford, 1931); Richard N. Sinkin, *The Mexican Reforms, 1855-1876. A Study in Liberal Nation–Building* (Austin, 1979); Martin V. Scholes, *Mexican Politics During the Juarez Regime (1855–1872)* (Columbia, Mo., 1957).

12.Cumberland, *The Constitutionalist...* y 326; Richmond, "El nacionalismo de Carranza y los cambios socio–económicos, 1915–1920," *Historia Mexicana* 26 (1), julio- septiembre 1976, 107-131; Richmond, "Carranza...," 64.

13.Luis Cabrera, "The Purposes and Ideals of the Mexican Revolution," *Supplement to the Annals of the American Academy of Political and Social Sciences*, 69, January 1917, 13.

14.Federico Cervantes M., *Francisco Villa y la Revolución* (México, D.F., 1960); Cumberland, *The Constitutionalist...*, 340-341.

15.Cervantes M., 130; Arnaldo Córdova, *La ideología en la Revolución* (México, D.F., 1973), 26. An English translation can be found in Mexican Government, *English Translation of the New Mexican Constitution Effective May 1st., 1917* (México, D.F., 1926). For a comparison see Tena Ramírez, *Leyes fundamentales de México*, 817-881.

16.Juan B. Rojo, "The Meaning of the Mexican Revolution," *Supplement to the Annals...*, 29.

17.Córdova, *La ideología...*, 27. Article 27 is analyzed in Manuel de la Peña, *Estudio jurídico, político y económico sobre el Artículo 27 Constitucional* (México, D.F., 1921); Merril Rippy, *Oil and the Mexican Revolution* (Leyden, 1972); Cumberland, *The Constitutionalists...*, 328-360; Pastor Rouaix, *Génesis de los artículos 27 y 123 de la Constitución Política de 1917* (Puebla, 1946); Meyer, 107-149.

18.Cumberland, *The Constitutionalist...*, 364; Quirk, *Mexico...*, 94-95; Córdova, 27.

19.Quirk, 91-92.

20.Ernesto de la Torre y Villar, 519-520.

21.Katz, 363. Also De La Torre, 520-521; López Portillo y Weber, 57-62.

22.Katz, 350-383; López Portillo, 62; José D. Lavin, 104.

23.López Portillo, 36; *POET* 40, 37, 3 julio 1915, 3; *POET* 40, 35, 26 junio 1915, 2-3. Carranza's decrees on oil were made in 1915, but could not be enforced until 1917, except in those states where Carrancista governors attained power.

24.*México's Oil*, 12.

25.Heather Fowler Salamini, "Caciquismo and the Mexican Revolution: The Case of Manuel Peláez," paper, V Conference of Mexican and U.S. Historians, Chicago, 10 September 1981. Also Gabriel A. Menéndez, *El Cacique de las Huastecas* (México, D.F., 1957).

26.Díaz Dufoó, *La cuestión...*, 267-276; Ronald C. Hansis, *Alvaro Obregón: The Mexican Revolution and the Politics of Consolidation, 1920-1924* (Ph.D. diss., University of New Mexico, 1971, 168; Meyer, *Mexico...*, 68, 96, 99-103, 127; Ray C. Gerhardt, "Inglaterra y el petróleo mexicano durante la Primera Guerra Mundial," *Historia Mexicana* 25 (1), 95, julio–septiembre 1975, 126; Dennis J. O'Brien, "Petróleo e intervención: relaciones entre los Estados Unidos y México, 1917-1918," *Historia Mexicana* 27 (1) julio–septiembre 1977, 103-104.

27.Ludwell Denny, *We Fight for Oil* (New York, 1928), 54.

28.The APPM included the following companies: Standard Oil (Indiana), Sinclair Consolidated Oil Corp., Mexican Petroleum Co. (Huasteca and Pan American Petroleum), The Texas Co., Atlantic Refining Co., "El Aguila" Mexican Oil Co., and "La Corona" Oil Corporation (Royal Dutch Shell). See Meyer, 115; Marcial E. Ocasio-Meléndez, "Conflict and Truce. Alvaro Obregón's Oil Policy, 1921–1923," (manuscript).

29.Cumberland, *The Constitutionalist...*, 402-414.

30.Richmond, "Carranza...," 74-75; Dulles, 17. See Pindaro Urióastegui Miranda, *Testimonios del proceso revolucionario de México* (México, D.F., 1970), 409-411.

31.Dulles, 59.

32.López Portillo y Weber, 68-70; Meyer, 154-164.

33.López Portillo y Weber, 73-74.

34.*CACT*, 21, 439, 1921.

35.*CACT*, 21, 439, 1921.

36.Meyer, 19, note 69; *CACT* 18, 442, 1921, "Minutes of the Local Managers Association, 8 February 1921; *Current History* (New York) 14, 1, April 1921, 146; *NYT* 22 January 1921, 23:4; 31 March 1921, 12:7; 30 April 1921, 17:3; 3 May 1921, 4:3; 4 July 1921, 17:1; AGNPPM, 104, P1-P13, "Decreto presidencial 1921"; AGNPPM, 104, P1-P9, "Report of Special Agent Joseph B. Cheston on August 15, 1921;" *CACT* 14, 422, 2 July 1920, "Letter Mexican Gulf to Dawson;" Gobierno de México, Secretaría de Hacienda y Crédito Público, *La Hacienda Pública a través de los informes presidenciales* (México, D.F., 1951), 425; *CACT* 14, 438, 1921, "Letter H. Cook to Dawson, 14 July 1921," "Letter Christopher C. Pyre to Dawson, 13 July 1921," "Dawson to American Embassy in México, 13 July 1921."

37.*CACT* 14, 438, 1921, "Intercontinental Corporation to Dawson, 15 July 1921;" *NYT*, 17 July 1921, 15:1; *Current History* (New York) 14, 6, September 1921, 1076.

38.*CACT*, 14, 438, 1921, "Report to the Secretary of State #1192, n.d.;" *San Antonio Light* (San Antonio) 17 July 1921, 7:2; *NYT* 6 July 1921, 1:6.

39.*CACT* 14, 438, 1921, "Monthly Report to the Secretary of State, 18 August 1921;" AGNPPM, 104, P1-P13, "Telegram of heads of oil companies to Obregón;" *Current History* (New York) 15, (2) October 1921, 361; 15 (1) October 1921, 170; AGNPPM 104, P1-P8, 9 March 1922, "Letter to J.C. Kemp Van Ee;" AGNPPM, 104, P1-P13, "Decreto 30 agosto 1921."

40.*CACT*, 13, 437, 1921, "Thomas W. Lamont, Declarations, 19 October 1921;" *Current History* (New York) 15, (3) December 1921, 514; 16 (5) August 1922, 911; *NYT*, 10 July 1921, VII, 4:1; 6 October 1921, 24:3; 8 December 1921, 28:4; 10 December 1921, 5:1; 18 December 1921, 23:1; 20 December 1921,26:4; 21 December 1921, 22:6; 20 February 1922, 24:2; AGNPPM, 104, P1-P13, "J.P. Flynn to Obregon, 4 June 1921," "Kirby Petroleum to Obregon on behalf of Gulf Coast Producers Association, 15 June 1921;" Dulles, 149-160; Meyer, 173-174, 181-189; Harold E. Davis, "Mexican Petroleum Taxes," *HAHR* 12, 4, November 1932, 405-419.

41.Meyer, 136, 141, 157, 181; Pierre L'Espagnol de la Tramerge, *La lutte mondiale pour le petrole* (Paris, 1921); Albert D. Brokaw, "Oil," *Foreign Affairs* 6, October 1927, 93-114; James J. Horn, "Mexican Oil, Diplomacy and the Legacy of the Teapot Dome," *West Virginia College Studies in the Social Sciences* 17, 1978, 49-112. Also see Alfred Vagts, *Mexiko, Europa und Amerika unter besonderer Berücksichtung der Petroleumpolitik* (Berlin, 1928).

42.*NYT*, 21 May 1923, 6:1.

43.Dulles, 218-263. On Obregón see Miguel Alessio Robles, *Historia política de la Revolución* (México, D.F., 1946); Emile J. Dillon, *President Obregón: A World Reformer* (Boston/London, 1923) and *Mexico on the Verge* (New York, 1921); *Discursos del General Obregón* 2 vols. (México, D.F., 1932); Alvaro Obregón, *Ocho mil kilometros de campaña* (México, D.F., 1924); Juan de Dios Bojórquez, *Obregón, apuntes biográficos* (México, D.F., 1929); James E. Hindman, "¿Confusión o conspiración? Estados Unidos frente a

Obregón," *Historia Mexicana* 25 (2) octubre–diciembre 1975, 271-301. On De La Huerta and his 1923 rebellion see: Alvaro Obregón *Documentos oficiales relativos al convenio De La Huerta–Lamont* (México, D.F., 1923); Adolfo De La Huerta, *Memoria de Don Adolfo De La Huerta según su propio dictado* (México, D.F., 1957); Luis Monroy Durán, *El último caudillo, apuntes para la historia de México acerca del movimiento armado de 1923* (México, D.F., 1924); Alberto J. Pani, *Las conferencias de Bucareli* (México, D.F., 1953).

44.Jack London, "Our Adventures in Tampico," *Collier's* 53, 15, 22 June 1914, 6.

45.Joseph Hergensheimer, *Tampico* (New York, 1926), 32.

46.*CACT*, 13, 437, 1921, "Consular District Report for 1921;" Lief Adleson, 95; *Boletín Municipal* (Tampico) 6, 37, 31 diciembre 1911, 314; AMT, *Programa de las fiestas organizadas con motivo del Primer Centenario de la Fundación del Puerto de Tampico. 12 de abril de 1823-1923* (Tampico, 1923).

47.Alanís de Salazar, 43; Hamilton, 240-242.

48.Alanís de Salazar, 62-63, 67-68.

49.Adleson, 114-155; Santos Llorente, "Tampico en 1920," *Nosotros los Petroleros* 3, 17, 1981, 22; *The Pulse of Mexico* (México, D.F.) February-March 1922, 92; *RDRIAM* 274, 151, 610, 14 December 1922, Tampico, Consul James B. Stewart to Secretary of State.

50.Torrea y Fuentes, 341. Opium parlors are mentioned in the *Actas* of 1920. Moreover, ads placed in the *Boletín Municipal* against marijuana and other hallucinogens point to a drug problem in the city, AMT, *Boletín Municipal* 1920, 1921, 1922; also *Actas* 1920, 1921.

51.Santos Llorente, 27.

52.AMT, *Actas*, junio 1886; 1 enero 1887; 6 septiembre 1911; Adleson, 117; *Boletín Municipal* 7, 16, 22 junio 1922, 449; 10, 15, 24 junio 1925.

53.*Terry's Guide to Mexico*, 50b.

54.AMT, "Dictamen de la Comisión de Hacienda," 10 marzo 1913; Adleson, 108.

55.Adleson, 105.

56.By March 1913, the National Railways of México owned 534 houses rented to its employees at $2.69 pesos per unit per week. The rent could be raised unilaterally. By 1918, Doña Cecilia and Talleres alone had a population of 3,309 inhabitants. The number grew to 15,298 by 1921. AMT, "Censo de Doña Cecilia y Talleres, 1918," and Gobierno de México, *Censo general de 1912* (México, D.F., 1928). Also AGN, Fondo de Gobernación, Secretaría de Comunicaciones y Transportes, Marina, 385-35-1, 1917-1918, "Contrato con el H. Ayuntamiento de Tampico para la introducción de mejoras al servicio e aguas y aumento de los pasajes;" AMT, "Documentos relativos a la Compañía Mexicana de Pavimentos y Asfaltos y Construcción, S.A." 1914; Expediente 49, "Relativo a los contratos que tiene la Compañía de Ferrocarriles Nacionales de México sobre los terrenos de este municipio que son de su propiedad. 14 de mayo de 1913."

57.*RDRIAM*, 274, 135, 1065, Copy of *Diario Oficial* 18 octubre 1920.

58.AMT, Expediente 40, 1918; González Salas, *Tampico. Crónicas de una ciudad* (México, D.F., 1977), 91; *RDRIAM*, 274, 136, "Letter K. Zabriskie to Secretary of State" 16 November 1917; *Enciclopedia Espasa-Calpe* Vol. T (Madrid, 1923); Torrea y Fuentes, 132-133, 299-300, 333; Covián Martínez, 89; *RDRIAM*, 274, 135, 19106, Copy of *Diario Oficial* 4 noviembre 1920; Gobierno de México, *México* (México, D.F., 1929), 389. The 1913 dredging of the Pánuco did not occur until 1917. It provided a deeper berth for the ships arriving at the port.

59.AMT, "Expediente La Isleta," 204, 25 septiembre 1918, 1920. In 1923, Obregón expelled Buckley from México, who was the lawyer and most outspoken member of the APPM.

60.L.J. De Bekker, *The Plot Against Mexico* (New York, 1919), 23.

61.Jack London, 5.

62.*Terry's Guide...*, 50b,50 c.

63.*Terry's Guide...*, 1923, 50d.

64.Santos Llorente, 24.

65.Interview with Héctor Hernández Avilés, Public Relations Director of *El Sol de Tampico* on 17 September 1981; *CRUSE*, II, 149, 28 June 1921, 1809; *CACT*, 7, 415, 1920, 2 September 1920; 13, 437, 1921; Torrea y Fuentes, 305-306; *CACT*, 13, 437, 1921.

7

THE TWO TAMPICOS

> Tampico's workers believed that good salaries and jobs would last forever, and they spent accordingly during the Great Oil Boom days.
>
> Torrea y Fuentes, 1940.

> Tampico's Mexican and American businessmen are and have been on the friendliest terms. The Mexican and American Chambers of Commerce have worked together on every important project before the community.
>
> *San Antonio Light*, 1921.

Any visitor to México can get the impression, from the communications media, that Tampico is the only city on the Pánuco, notwithstanding the emergence and growth of other nearby urban centers in the last seventy years. The closest is Ciudad Madero, the former Tampico borough of Doña Cecilia, which gained considerable economic importance and national reputation as one of PEMEX (Petróleos Mexicanos) most important centers.[1] Oil for Ciudad Madero is what automobiles are for Detroit, yet, Tampico continues to dominate the politics and economy of the region and of people's imagination. Most of the wealth remains in Tampico as well as its outward symbols: banks, department stores, shopping malls, finest hotels, airport, piers, and the most luxurious residential developments and social clubs of the region.

On 1 May 1924, Tampico's municipality was officially divided in two different jurisdictions. The city lost its old boroughs of Doña Cecilia, Arbol Grande, and La Barra, which were formed into a new municipality named at first Villa Cecilia, and changed to Ciudad Madero in 1930.[2] This action apparently curtailed Tampico's growth, but in reality it was the result of a combination between the powerful forces that were trying to control the city, and México's oil. The division allowed the realignment of forces which had built up for the last ten years both locally and nationally. Tampico remained the powerful economic, social and political center, while Ciudad Madero, the other city, solved the immediate concerns of its residents by giving them an access to political power and influence in local, state and national forums.

The city and the oil boom

Tampico's population reached one hundred and fifty thousand people by 1923. Yet, the 1930 census shows the city with only 68,126 inhabitants.[3] This spectacular loss of population in seven years had at least two major causes. One was the slowdown and rapid decline of the oil industry in the Tampico area which began in late 1923. It caused a large emigration from the city, especially a number of its floating population. The other reason was the division of the municipality because a good number of those registered in 1923 were residents of the new Ciudad Madero municipality in 1930. The demographic change, however, did not lessen Tampico's role as the region's most important city, which had continued to attract businesses as the nation's largest export town, and as an excellent doorway into the Mexican market. Yet, why was Tampico divided? Who profited from it? Answers cannot be found easily.

Oil was king in Tampico, but it helped attract a diversified number of enterprises that served both industry and the large population, that began to arrive by late 1918. Some of these service industries arrived before oil, others made a strong presence in México after the 1920s. In the late 1890s, a soft drinks and ice plant had been founded, and in 1922, Herbert Fleishman, who held the first Coca Cola franchise in México, inaugurated his first plant in Tampico. It served the Mexican market, eventually opening other bottling plants across the nation. Tampico was the home of the first Mexican – fourth in the world – airline. Planes were the answer for the safe transport of payrolls from the oil companies' headquarters to the camps located within a 150 kilometer radius. In 1919, Jorge L. Rikle, American businessman and banker resident in Tampico, bought two used Lincoln Standard airplanes from the Air Division of the U.S. Army. An airfield was hastily prepared on **Moralillo** Island, and air service began between Tampico and the oil fields taking the payrolls - gold coins and dollars - to avoid the long journeys through the bandit-infested Huastecan jungles. The success of this service brought other investors to the company. Manuel Bulnes bought the airline, and renamed it **Compañía Mexicana de Transportación** (Mexican Transportation Company) on 12 July 1921. By 1924, the new airline enlarged its services including cargo and passengers, and with a new name **Compañía Mexicana de Aviación** offered flights between Tampico, México City, and Matamoros, and later to Brownsville and other border cities. Tampico became the airline's headquarters until its growth forced its move to México City.[4]

The automobile increased Tampico's accessibility to the Huasteca and the nation, just like the railroad had opened its port in the 1890s. Cars, owned by wealthy Mexicans and foreigners, appeared in Tampico during the first years of the new century. Once the 1916 oil boom began, more residents were able to buy automobiles, and also businesses began to use trucks for cargo services. The city council found a new source of revenue granting permits to drive and own cars and trucks. The money received was especially useful to comply requests of repairing the streets, pave others and build new highways and roads. Drivers wanted a highway connecting Tampico with La Barra and Miramar Beach that would bypass Doña Cecilia and workers' housing areas. Finally, in 1924, two major highways were built with the economic aid of the northern colonias' residents and of the large industries located along the road towards La Barra. The Jason Martin Company, American construction firm, headquartered in Tampico, was in charge of both projects.[5]

The automobile also allowed for greater urbanization and mobility, strengthening Tampico's commercial center now more accessible to residents of the new "colonias", the old boroughs, and the nearby Huastecan towns. Private cars, and a growing number of "route" cars and taxis provided service throughout the city. A service also taxed by the city council. But, modernization took its toll on the trolley. The old tram system suffered from the competition. It could not be as fast nor deliver passengers or cargo directly to their destinations. The trolley service lost customers and money rapidly. In 1923, 48,393 passengers rode the trolley, dropping to 30,062 in 1924, and to only 3,011 by 1927. The company was forced to eliminate most routes by 1926, leaving only the profitable Miramar Beach-Tampico line in service. Workers' resentment against the line's directors actions led to a strike that almost destroyed the company. Pearson's reaction was to sell the debt-ridden company to a cooperative of its workers in 1928.[6]

By 1924, no other city within a two hundred-mile radius could compete with Tampico's commerce. Cars and trucks helped it keep this prominence strengthening the marketing and trading opportunities of the new businesses and industries begun in the city when oil was already weakening as the major source of income. The city was Southern Tamaulipas center for federal and state bureaucracies, helping it maintain regional and national political importance. Therefore, the explanation for the municipality's division must be found in local social or political conflicts and not in national or economic problems.

Labor and oil

The 1917 Constitution followed closely most of the basic rules of its 1857 predecessor, yet differed on its basic philosophy about government's role in the nation. The new charter proposed a government that would be deeply involved in the social and economic problems of the people. It was to be the authoritative agent of change for a society that demanded modifications in its civil life. Necessarily, the federal government became a major actor, if not the most important, in the process of change. One social area in great need of change was labor.

"The most enlightened statement of labor protective principles in the world to that date" was Article 123 of the new Constitution.[7] It provided workers with a maximum of eight hours for regular work, less hours for night shifts, and for working children. It granted one day of rest a week, and a minimum wage that was to be determined by local conditions. It also stipulated wage payments in legal tender, double pay for overtime, equal pay for more work regardless of nationality or sex, and the right to organize and strike. It forced employers to observe job safety precautions, to provide housing at low cost, and schools when the factory or enterprise was located in isolated areas. Moreover, employers had to justify firing employees, and had to accept responsibility for accidents and job-related illnesses. The Article also established arbitration procedures for settling labor disputes requiring the presence of a board made up of representatives from the employer, workers, and the government whenever it was necessary.[8]

Labor problems increased with the growth of Mexican industrialization. A multitude of specialized workers became more active in their search for better working conditions and salaries using the Constitution as a useful tool for their demands, once the armed conflicts abated. Yet, most Mexican employers were unhappy with the prospect of labor struggles and with Article 123. They tried to coerce the government into canceling the article by firing thousands of workers all over México, who joined those idled by the revolutionary unrest. This situation was accompanied by continued inflation and food shortages. Official blame was immediately placed on the agents of international labor groups, such as anarcho-syndicalists from Europe, Bolsheviks, and especially the North American Industrial Workers of the World (IWW). Mexican radical labor groups were also blamed for the turmoil in the country.[9]

The Carranza government and the nation's capitalists, whether Mexicans or foreigners, were afraid that workers – now with the support of the Constitution – could paralyze production and help labor achieve political power. Therefore, plans were devised to steer away this threat. Carranza, and later Obregón, persecuted the independent labor groups. It was planned to create a state-controlled labor movement that would truly serve "revolutionary policies." Thus, after 1916, México's labor independent movement was under siege; it played the official tune or was destroyed. The government's official position was ambivalent toward the labor movement, and it gave hope to the capitalists and employers that they would eventually win versus the "radical" leaders and the Constitutional guarantees. However, workers' situation in Tampico deviated somewhat from what happened at the national level.[10]

Tampico's workers had moved ahead of the nation when they tried to take advantage of Carranza's constitutional plans for labor before these were included in Article 123. Although affected by food shortages and some unemployment, the city did not fare as bad as the rest of the country in 1916. Some labor leaders believed that Tampico could be a testing ground for the validation of any Constitutional guarantee. They asked the government to include three important issues in the Constitutional guarantees: the unjustified firing of workers, the illegal punishments for organizing strikes or unions, and compliance with the eight hour day.[11]

The 1871 Mexican Criminal Code stated that unions were illegal, and considered their organizers as criminals. During the Díaz regime, only mutualist and cooperative organizations were allowed. The mutualist movement appeared in Tampico in the 1880s, seeking the cultural and educational development of workers and their families, yet it had a tendency to attract the highest paid workers or artisans who could have enough money for dues and to pay for their activities. The **Sociedad Mutualista Benito Juárez** was Tampico's first, organized on 20 October 1888. Other mutualist societies were formed, but their importance and success began to falter as industries appeared, and were replaced by labor unions.

The success of the petroleum industry affected labor's situation. The growing migration of workers into the city increased their urban importance. Their presence multiplied the need for city services, housing, social control, and political participation. Slowly, workers became aware of their importance, not only to the oil industry, but to the city itself. Without them, there would be no economic life at the port. Their awareness came at a moment when world-wide demand for oil also increased. Then, industry leaders, businessmen, and city and federal officials came to a non-written, non-verbal - yet understood - agreement to keep workers under control whether by force, appeasement or coercion.

Up to 1915, Tampico officials had embodied the Porfirian positivist commercial ideals. Once the Constitutionalists took the city, workers entered city government. Their presence was small, but significant. A resolution passed by the council ordered the payment of salaries to the mayor and the councilmen, heretofore non-existent in Tampico, but which made them responsible to the taxpayers. Yet, these labor representatives did not have much substantive power. They were mostly standard bearers of the Constitutionalist ideals, but the commercial and industrial leaders saw to it that their power would be restricted. However, these labor leaders realized that workers' radical activities in Tampico would have local, national and international consequences because of the growing dependence of the nation on the oil industry, and owing to the Allies need for oil to fight in Europe. Nowhere in México did workers seem to be in a better suited position to strive for job-related aspirations versus both government and capital.[12]

Tampico's government had to comply with Federal assurances to protect foreigners' lives and properties, and to continue oil exports uninterruptedly. In order to carry out this compromise, it had to use the local police force and the federal troops stationed in the city. It also had to overlook the activities of the "white guards," and the paid armies, both existing thanks to the financial support of the oil companies. The city council was also powerless against the strong military presence of the Constitutionalist Army, whose commanders carried out official orders at their own will and interfered in many aspects of local concern. The councilmen also had to accept, reluctantly, the presence of U.S. naval vessels both in the Pánuco and offshore which, notwithstanding diplomatic excuses, violated México's sovereignty. Thus, the labor spokesmen in the city's administration had to yield to the extenuating circumstances of the period, and help keep their comrades under control, but it was not easy.[13]

The 1917 oil workers' strike against "El Aguila" Oil Company was an example of how Tampico could set national models and be an experimental setting for Article 123. Workers demanded a salary raise - to be paid in dollars or Mexican gold - and guarantees that no dismissals would be made by the company against strikers. One of these demands was included in Article 123, and the other - payment in gold - contravened one of Carranza's decrees stating that salaries had to be paid in national script. Tampico's **Casa del Obrero Mundial** organized a series of public discussions of the proposed Article 123, of its principles and consequences; and after its approval, more meetings were held to survey workers' responses to it.[14]

Tomás R. Morales, Tampico's labor mayor, had to promise both companies and state authorities that the IWW local group would be prohibited from holding public meetings, and had three of its leaders arrested. As "El Aguila" strike continued, Tamaulipas' governor, General Luis Caballero, had three other labor leaders placed under arrest. Sympathy strikes erupted at other oil installations in town, and the threat of a general strike hung up in the air. Rumors suggested that foreign agitators from the United States and Germany - anarchists, Bolsheviks, and German agents - were behind the strike. Therefore, Tampico's German merchant Gerhard Empler and U.S. IWW agent J. Anderson were arrested and deported.

The strike at 'El Aguila" was settled when the British government pressured company officials to satisfy workers' demands. Mexican oil was too important for its navy. Nevertheless, the strikes at other installations continued because workers believed that the settlement was based on the company's compliance to Article 123, and to the validity of workers' demands. The U. S. government advised American companies not to accept workers' requirements, and pressured Carranza to support General Caballero's actions in Tampico carried out in response to the October 1917 celebration in Tampico of the First Socialist Congress. It provoked great distrust and fear among foreign businessmen, and was kept under strict surveillance by local, national, and international authorities. By November, however, the federal government decided to end all strikes and allowed Generals J. Guerra and Alfredo Ricaut to arrest the leaders of the remaining strikes, and to force about 8,000 workers to return to their jobs under military vigilance. There on, strikes would become a routine in Tampico's labor life.[15]

This confrontation between labor and employers had a complex significance. First, it allowed workers to acquire knowledge and techniques for pressuring their adversaries. Second, it created some puzzling political questions. If workers were successful by imposing Article 123, the municipal council could be under their control, therefore, companies could face a threat to their historically-held power over the port. The situation, therefore, called for cautious dealing with both workers and city government. Third, workers's success in any aspect of the local economy was to be checked by both city officials supportive of federal policies and by the companies overtly complying with national laws. Coercion and co-option were to be tools for such control. An example of this scheme occurred in 1918 when the oil companies accepted to participate in a strike settlement through a Labor Relations Board. Workers wanted to have Mayor Tomás R. Morales as the federal representative on the Board, but the companies objected and left the negotiations. The national government named Enrique de Keratry, a Tampico company lawyer and oilman, as its representative, and the companies returned to the talks. Thus, two of the Board's three members were pro-capital.[16]

Workers in Tampico also joined forces to secure land titles for the plots where most of them had built shacks or houses, especially in the boroughs of Arbol Grande, Doña Cecilia, Talleres and La Barra. The lots were on lands owned originally by the city or the Federal governments that were granted to the oil companies or to the railroad (now partly owner of the National Railways of México.) Workers had pressured city council seeking essential services such as water, electricity, telephone, paved streets, a market, a cemetery, and sanitation. Although, the council refused allegedly for lack of funds to serve the needs of the fast-growing city and its citizens, it gave priority to the renewal and maintenance of the urban core and the new "colonias."

Few services were provided to the outlying communities; only two primary schools and a police station were built. Tampico's downtown supplied all health care services, commercial enterprises, and even burials. Furthermore, charitable organizations, as well as the local and foreign Chambers of Commerce, were not much interested in helping these outlying communities. Thus, land titles and municipal services became a problem of great relevance to all residents, mostly workers, and their concerns were somehow linked to their labor rights. These problems became real political issues when General César López de Lara, a powerful military man, sided with Tampico's workers, and the Carrancista mayor of Tampico - a socialist champion of workers' rights - considered their plight as radical, anti-nationalist and Bolshevik-oriented.[17]

The land problem

Tampico had increased the area around its urban center after closing and filling up the branch of the Tamesín River that flowed between the islands and the shore across from the city. But, most of these new lands were given to new businesses, warehouses and factories. On the other hand, the invasion of vacant lands by workers and others in all city boroughs revived the problem of the municipal ejidos. The Lerdo Law on 25 June 1856, later incorporated into Article 27 of the 1857 Constitution, abolished all communal lands owned or administered by the Catholic Church, by civil corporations such as municipalities, and by Indian village councils. Thus began one of México's most excruciating problems.

Until 1876, the Lerdo Law had not been fully enforced owing to national unrest, but Porfirio Díaz began to carry it out when he ordered the survey of millions of hectares of communal and Church lands. These were sold to the highest bidders, usually wealthy hacendados, who increased their already large haciendas or created new ones. The Constitution also protected those haciendas by protecting individual property rights.

The 1910 Revolution, however, had agrarian reform as one of its prime movers. It was proposed by Francisco Madero in his **Plan de San**

Luis, and by Emiliano Zapata in his **Plan de Ayala**, leading many to believe that it was the "fundamental cause of all the problems of México and its inhabitants." Although an unwilling Carranza began to deal with this issue, he was still too much of a Liberal at heart to solve it much more successfully than his predecessors had tried to do.[18]

The Tamaulipas State Congress gave ejidos to Tampico on 23 September 1826 which originally made up all the municipal jurisdiction. However, lack of residents in the rural areas of the municipality, and the commercial emphasis of the city gave these lands a limited agricultural importance permitting their division and use as private landholdings, an anomaly accepted by the authorities for a long period of time. By 1871, Tampico's ejidos were reduced to the areas called Tancol, Las Flores, Las Piochas, Limonal, Arenal, and the river islands of Zapotal, Pitahaya and Moralillo. The former ejido of La Barra was claimed as personal property by Ramón Obregón and his heirs, and the ejido of Doña Cecilia was also claimed as property by the heirs of José María Castillo Iberi. After the Porfirian decree enforcing the Lerdo Law, the city council distributed the remaining ejidos among its members, some wealthy residents, and the incoming railroad companies. Some of these land grants were increased through leases or fraudulent acquisitions of adjacent lands. The value of these municipal lands increased after oil became the city's main industry, and as new commercial and urban expansion occurred, and squatting became a major legal, social and economic problem for the Mexican government and the Tampico industrial-business complex.[19]

Land squatters' actions had some legal support from the Carranza decrees of 1915, and were strengthened by the 1917 Constitution. On 6 January 1915, Carranza ordered the nullification of all land concessions; of all sales, concessions or agreements made on ejidal lands, of all legal recourse made to take over ejido lands by any authorities; of all land concessions made by town or rancho (small rural unit) neighbors - valid only if two thirds of the ejido owners accepted - and also asserted that any town in need of ejidos could receive them from the national government by expropriation. Moreover, the 1857 Constitution was reformed on 3 February 1915, making municipalities, the basic political unit of the nation. It also eliminated the states' control of city governments.[20]

Furthermore, the new Article 27 states that the nation can impose limitations on private property on behalf of the public interest, and

> measures shall be taken to divide large landed estates; to develop small landed holdings; to establish new centers of rural population with such lands and water as may be indispensable to them...Pueblos, hamlets situated on private property and settlements which lack lands or water or do not possess them in sufficient quantities for their needs shall have the right to be provided them from the adjoining properties always having due regard for small landholdings. All contracts and concessions made by former governments from and after the year 1876, that shall have resulted in the monopoly of lands, waters and natural resources of the Nation by a single individual, or corporation, are declared subject to revision, and the Executive is authorized to declare those null and void which seriously prejudice the public interest.[21]

Supported by these legal positions, the squatters of Llanos del Golfo and Doña Cecilia sent petitions to the city council asking for the recovery of the municipal ejido lands. To do so meant the violation of the acquired rights of companies and individuals, some which dated back to the 1820s. The squatters reasoned that once the lands were recovered, the city could redistribute them. Many of these families had been allowed to remain on these lands because companies preferred to have their workers at a close distance to their work-place. But as Tampico grew in importance, some of these lands, especially those along the Pánuco River, became highly valuable. By 1921, most squatters were in lands leased to or owned by the National Railways, the Pierce-Sinclair Oil Company (Standard Oil), and the "El Aguila" Oil Company (Shell-Dutch Oil).[22]

The composition of the city council between 1915 and 1923 made that body appear as an apparent supporter of workers and poor residents' grievances. Mayors Tomás R. Morales (1915-16) a former carpenter, and engineer Antonio Prieto Laurens (1918-20), a socialist ideologue, were both strongly in favor of the pro-labor measures of Carranza and the Constitution. Moreover, other members were elected from among labor candidates or sympathized with labor's struggle. In response to workers and squatters' grievances, the council took several actions. One of these was to plan and urbanize Doña Cecilia under a commission headed by engineer Urusástegui. Streets were paved and straightened both in Doña Cecilia and Arbol Grande. It also ordered the distribution of lots on municipal lands. However, conflict arose because in order to carry out the urbanization plans, the National Railways had to move its fences, and its officers in Tampico refused to do so. On 11 September 1918, President Carranza informed Congress that an agreement had been reached with the National Railways over land titles that would benefit Tampico's poorest workers. The company was willing to give up seventy hectares (174 acres) in the Andonegui area - near Arbol Grande - in exchange for the right of way over twenty four hectares (52.8 acres) of lands on the planned Carpintero Lagoon desiccated area. The lagoon was never drained, and the railroad company together with another individual, who claimed to have bought lands in Andonegui, started a lengthy court litigation against the government for its insistence on claiming the validity of the agreement. The federal court finally decided against the company in 1921, and only then, was the State governor, able to grant provisional land titles to the 1917 petitioners. The same parties, however, went back to court to challenge the titles. Hence, a different solution for the problem had to be found.[23]

State politics and Tampico

Politics in Tamaulipas were the subject to controversies and confrontations between revolutionary leaders after 1917. These struggles were based either on ideological or greedy personal terms, and these politicians used all possible forces under their control to fight among themselves. For many, the Revolution was nothing but a step up for their personal goals, and did not care much for ideals or people. A large historiography of the policies, values, and actions of the revolutionary leaders has appeared that indicates a puzzling situation where they are seen shifting rapidly to adjust to new circumstances - the Revolution had a fast pace of change - and where the only real policy seems to have been the protection of the nation against foreigners whenever it did not hurt personal gains and ambitions.

Two such men were the Tamaulipas State governor candidates for the 1917-1920 period. Both were Constitutionalist generals, who had supported Carranza and were rewarded with commands of importance. Luis Caballero served as provisional governor of the State, and Commander of the Northeastern armies. He was considered an anti-labor man, although he tried for some time to court Tampico's workers. César López de Lara served as Military Governor of the Federal District, and had Carranza's trust. He accomplished the closing of the Casa del Obrero Mundial in México City under his orders, but later became a strong supporter of workers' rights. By 1917, both men wanted the governorship of Tamaulipas, and Tampico, richest and most important city in the state, made the difference in such elections. Caballero had the support of the oil companies, of the wealthy oligarchy, and of the legal establishment. López de Lara was backed by many Tampico workers and revolutionaries, who believed him to be faithful to the principles of the Revolution, notwithstanding his actions in México City. This conflicting situation interfered with Tampico's government decision-making process, and probably become one of the reasons for the municipal division of Tampico. One of this contest's outcomes was the break-up of the city's jurisdiction.

General Caballero's popularity among Northern Army troops, state Constitutionalists, and Tampico's elite did not help him in his relationship with Carranza, which reached its lowest point in 1917. Caballero received the support of the **Partido Liberal Constitucionalista** (Constitutionalist Liberal Party) or PLC, whose members had started to desert Carranza for political reasons. The party newspaper was closed by General López de Lara while in México City. Obviously, the President favored him for the governorship of Tamaulipas.

López also courted Tampico's workers, and had two valuable labor activists helping him in the city. Emilio Portes Gil, a corporate lawyer - President of México in 1928 - and pharmacist Juan Gual Vidal. His first visit to Tampico brought bloodshed when Caballero's brother-in-law attempted to kill him, and many were wounded in the resulting turmoil. Similar incidents occurred throughout the state because Caballero controlled most of it. Meanwhile in Tampico, the city council, although with a pro-labor attitude and at odds with the Interim State governor, Gregorio Osuna, prohibited all activities of the López de Lara organization. Chaos engulfed the state as the two groups fought against each other. Carranza named General E. Ricaut as new provisional state governor, and ordered him to Tamaulipas with more federal troops in order to put down the rebellious factions, and to oversee the elections, postponed by Ricaut until February 1918. Meanwhile, he remained in Tampico and carried out strong anti-strike actions already mentioned. He reasoned that a U.S.- British invasion was a more serious threat to the port and the nation if the workers did not go back to work, or if they won their demands.

Antonio Prieto Laurens, a Carranza supporter won the December

1917 municipal elections in Tampico. He believed in a national labor movement controlled by the federal government, a position in complete disagreement with Tampico workers' experience of independent unions supported by Portes Gil and Vidal. However, Prieto Laurens scared the city's capitalists, who also feared a labor movement controlled by the government, thus making it too powerful. López de Lara agreed with the Prieto and the Portes-Gual positions as long as he could win workers' support and the state governorship.[24]

General Caballero decided to organize his own government after losing the February gubernatorial elections to López de Lara. He set up a legislature of delegates in a building across the State Congress in Ciudad Victoria. Fighting followed and Carranza annulled the elections. On 19 April 1918, Caballero took up arms against Carranza, and called for a national rebellion. The President named López de Lara provisional governor of Tamaulipas with headquarters in Tampico, and ordered General Manuel Diéguez to advance with troops and restore order in Ciudad Victoria.[25]

Caballero was eventually defeated, but the presence of López de Lara in Tampico disrupted city's affairs and terrified the capitalist community owing to his personal views toward labor. In June 1918, he was named Chief of Military Operations for the Huasteca, with the purpose of destroying General Manuel Peláez' rebels, who had little to do with Tamaulipas' elections. London and Washington, however, were concerned about López because of his alleged pro-German position, and feared that his actions could affect the region's oil supply. Washington placed a Marines' unit in readiness for any sudden takeover of Tampico if necessary.[26] But, workers were enthusiastic with López' presence and of his support for their demands; and also welcomed the arrival of General Diéguez, who had been a former leader of the Casa del Obrero Mundial. They could now continue their strikes because state and federal troops in town were on their side. The situation lasted for most of 1919, but was altered when political changes occurred at the national level.

U.S. Consul Claude G. Dawson panicked when Generals Alvaro Obregón and Plutarco E. Calles rose up against Carranza in 1920. Obregón had visited Tampico as part of his presidential campaign, and was received by a crowd numbering over 10,000 at a rally in the Plaza de la Libertad. Dawson told Washington that Obregón was a tool of the Bolsheviks, who were members of his staff. Dawson was a strong supporter of capitalism, of the oil companies, and of the American government, in that order. He had accused General López of being pro-German, and after Germany's defeat, he accused him and Tampico workers of Bolshevism. For him, anyone who stood for México's sovereignty over American interests or was in favor of communal rights or even supported workers' rights had to commune with whatever was the most loathsome ideology at the time. Dawson feared all Mexican activities, and was constantly cabling Washington to send in the warships; an unnecessary action because U.S. warships constantly patrolled the Tampico Gulf coast. He supported all anti-labor and pro-capitalist groups or individuals as was the case of Colonel Carlos S. Orozco, Tampico's Chief of Police, who on 1 May 1920 closed the Tampico branch of the Casa del Obrero Mundial, and Dawson lauded him for it. However, Orozco, the "good revolutionary," seven days later opted to follow the Obregón rebellion, and Dawson immediately called him a Bolshevik. Clearly disheartened, the Consul wrote the State Department petitioning that before any U.S. recognition was granted to the "de facto government" in México, "the local government (Tampico) must be rid of its pronounced Bolshevik elements responsible for the past difficulties."[27]

Yet, the most important event for the city's political power struggle came from México City, and determined the trend to be followed. The 1920 rebellion against Carranza was successful. Emilio

Portes Gil was named Tamaulipas provisional governor, and General Lucas González, also a pro-labor Obregonista, was named military commander of Tampico. Prieto Laurens and his councilmen were forced to resign, and new officers with Obregonista tendencies replaced them. Finally, López de Lara was elected governor in the February 1921 state elections. Now, he could use his office to help Tampico's workers attain some of their goals.[28]

López wanted to give workers political and economic power using the cooperative movement. In 1922, he granted a state loan to the **Gremio Unido de Alijadores** to buy the equipment and machinery needed to control the Tampico port facilities. He also helped the trolley and electrical workers cooperative buy the Compañía Eléctrica de Luz, Tracción y Fuerza (Electric Co.) from its former owner. Interestingly, by April 1923, electric service was finally inaugurated at Arbol Grande, a workers' borough. A trend had developed elsewhere in México, whereby local governments acquired municipal services, but in Tampico, these services were now taken by workers for profitable purposes.[29]

It was López, who on April 1921, proposed the creation of a new municipality dividing Tampico's jurisdiction, to be named Doña Cecilia. The new town would take from Tampico the industrial and workers' boroughs of Llanos del Golfo, Arbol Grande, Talleres, Refineria, La Barra, and Miramar. Although his reasons for this action were not clearly stated, it is inferred that he wanted workers to acquire legal titles over the lands they had been bickering over since 1917. Furthermore, the creation of a new labor municipality would force companies, especially oil refineries and services, to deal with a local government of workers, thus undermining the power formerly held in Tampico.

López began his plan in September 1922, proclaiming a new State Expropriation Law for Public Safety and Use after a meeting held in México City with the Secretary of the Treasury, a representative of the

National Railways, and a delegate from the Tampico resident's association. Article 77 of the law stated that a new town could be formed if the government considered it necessary, and the State Congress could expropriate private lands for that purpose. Furthermore, Article 78 declared that expropriated lands were never to be considered as urban, but as rural, for rural property was cheaper and the government was capable of paying only for such value. These lands could then be sold more cheaply to workers, who had already built on them or were in the process of doing it. The México City meeting discussions were never disclosed, but López' commentaries indicate that a plan was discussed to expropriate over 2,000 hectares (4,400 acres) of lands in Tampico.[30]

By April 1923, General López declared his intention to solve the land problem of Tampico's workers in a message to the State Congress. He affirmed that population growth was at the root of the problem, and had forced the masses to take over private and government lands. However, it was not easy to implement the plan nor was it good timing to protect workers and squatters' position versus the oil companies, the National Railways and the federal government. Some weeks earlier, a federal court had ruled in favor of the National Railways, which continued to refuse selling or parting with any lands in Tampico. Additional problems arose when squatters' leaders quarreled among themselves for control of the movement. Besides, the federal government was in the midst of solving its international debt difficulties, including the payments to the National Railways bondholders, who opposed selling any of the company's lands in Tampico. It was also the moment when Obregón was still trying to force the oil companies to accept the taxes and provisions of Article 27.

General César López de Lara could not give a successful conclusion to his plan, neither was he able to complete his term in office. He joined the Adolfo de la Huerta's rebellion in December 1923. The importance of Tampico and Tamaulipas for the nation moved a quick response from Obregón, who immediately despatched General Benancio López Padilla as Tamaulipas' new provisional governor with headquarters in Tampico. The imminent threat to Tampico by the rebels who controlled Veracruz, most naval units, and close to half of the Federal Army was in Obregón's mind. That explains why he also sent General Manuel Peláez as commander of the federal force in Tampico. Thus, a certain accommodation was sought with the oil companies, and a willingness to play on their court at a dangerous time.[31]

Rebels were defeated by February 1924 with the military aid provided by the United States. The revolution opened a new chapter of economic difficulties for México, and retained oil as a most important item for national revenues. Under these circumstances Tampico could not be overlooked. Professor Candelario Garza of Tampico replaced General López Padilla as provisional governor, and moved to Ciudad Victoria. Tampico held elections during the rebellious days of December. Mayor Manuel Villaverde and his council were not amicable toward labor and had three objectives: capitalism, Obregón, and privatization. They feared the cooperative movement among workers, the independent unions, and the constant strikes that began after the rebellion was over. Moreover, they were concerned over the close relations which had existed between the former governor López de Lara and Tampico's workers.

The position of the federal government was presented by engineer Samuel González Cordero, a high official of the Department of Petroleum, who wrote that the continued strikes in the oil fields and at the terminals in Tampico had deeply affected government relations with the oil companies and with the unions. He also stated that companies such as Standard Oil and Shell could easily close their Mexican operations or pull out of México with no real damage to their world-wide revenues. He feared that this action would have deep economic consequences for

México. However, this new situation led to a most interesting alliance in Tampico. The threat of continued public disturbances and what they could represent financially for the federal government, plus the accompanying fears of the oil managers about workers and their damage to installations and productivity seem to have been the most powerful reasons behind the alliance of these two apparently opposite sectors: the oil companies and industry, and the federal–state governments. Both joined in their support for the state plan prepared by the ex-governor López de Lara to create a new municipality out of Tampico.[32]

Ciudad Madero: A Labor Experiment?

On 1 May 1924, Governor Garza decreed the creation of the new municipality named Villa Cecilia. It included the boroughs of Doña Cecilia, Arbol Grande, Refineria, "El Aguila," La Barra, and Miramar, as well as some small plots north of Tampico. The new town had a jurisdictional area of 57 square kilometers (44 square miles), and a population that neared 50,000. Its first presidente municipal (designated) was José Luis Herrera, a worker and teacher. Furthermore, the decree was proclaimed on labor's traditional international holiday of May 1.[33]

Tampico was divided by a combination of political and economic forces that coincided on one issue: consensus in attaining local power was far more productive than fighting over it. The city council and mayor agreed to have Tampico divided for four main reasons. First, the city would save expenses on services provided to the residents of those boroughs. Second, residents could now have their own government to complain to and to provide services. However, since those were not possible without an infrastructure, Villa Cecilia officials would have to ask Tampico for those services, and pay for them. Third, many of the marches supporting strikes and citizens' movements would be transferred to the new town, leaving Tampico alone. Yet, Villa Cecilia residents would have to continue buying in the old downtown. Finally, it can be suggested that fear of workers gaining more political power in Tampico was somehow offset because now they had their own local political structure where they could practice politics, making them more conscious and mature as to urban and regional problems.

For the oil companies, Villa Cecilia represented the possibility of dealing with workers' directly without state interventionists, Tampico revolutionary ideologue, or professional bureaucrats. If government and labor were one, then it would be easier for the companies to co-opt officials or to work with them in "collaboration."

The state government conformed to the federal position, which saw the new town as fulfilling a political promise to aid workers, as a method to make workers see the federal government as their only protection, and to ease the tension that had occurred in Tampico and caused problems with the oil companies. For workers and squatters, residents of Villa Cecilia, this event was a somewhat revolutionary victory. It meant Workers' Power! It was the accomplishment of many years of struggle to have homes and lands, and the possibility of receiving decent public services. They were encouraged to make Villa Cecilia a true workers' city that could be an example for workers all over the world.[34]

All these various elements made the Tampico division an accepted deed. It was the historical conjuncture of the pro-social reforms of Governor López de Lara, of the conflicts generated between workers and oil companies between 1921-1924, often supported by the Obregón regime, that led to a slowdown in oil production and to the loss of jobs and investments, and of the needs of local, state, and federal governments for power and money which created and supported this jurisdictional division. However, it also implied the possible destruction of Tampico's "spirit." The old alliance between labor, capital, and society born in 1823 had lasted almost one hundred years. The revolution as interpreted by the federal government, and the ideals of a workers' world, had interfered in the dreams of Tampico's residents. Most of them were no longer Tampiqueños, that is, born in town; and the city was just a place to make a living or to survive.

Since 1930, Villa Cecilia continues to exist as Ciudad Madero. Tampico continues to be México's major import-export port, and the oil industry is no longer headquartered in the city, though, it still plays an important role in the national and state economy. Oil workers, however, made Ciudad Madero their most important center in the Republic, but Tampico is still the business, sports, entertainment, and educational center for the Huasteca.

Tampico is a good example of the business town that appeared in Latin America after independence. It shows how the collective dreams of the controlling social group determined the trend and outcomes of urban life, thus creating a definite "collective spirit," that continued to assert itself with continued faith, some luck, and prowess to make things happen. Railroads, port facilities, and oil helped Tampiqueños attain their dream of economic power, yet, even without them, the port was already México's second by 1870. The actions carried by its citizens gave direction and re-asserted the "city spirit," and the success or collapse of their collective dreams. Tampico's municipal division proclaims the triumph of the nation over the regional and urban autonomy it had, but it does not imply the destruction of Tampico's spirit. It continues to live now divided among the twin sisters of the Pánuco: Tampico and Ciudad Madero.

NOTES

1.Ciudad Madero became the oil workers' center after President Lázaro Cárdenas nationalized petroleum in 1938. On 13 December 1923, "El Aguila" Oil Refinery workers organized the first oil workers' union. See Francisco Javier Martínez Hernández, *Historia de la Sección Uno* (Ciudad Madero, 1960); Emilio Portes Gil, *Raigambre de la Revolución en Tamaulipas* (México, D.F., 1972), 71-77; González Salas, *Acercamiento a la historia del movimiento obrero en Tampico, 1887-1983* (Ciudad Victoria, 1987), 168.

2.The State Congress changed the name to Ciudad Madero by Decree 91 of 11 September 1930; Covián Martínez, 93.

3.Meade, *Huasteca Tamaulipeca*, II, 229.

4.*El Mundo* (Tampico) 9, 33, 5 mayo 1927, 2:1.; José Santos Llorente, "Fortunas del auge," *Nosotros los petroleros* 3, 18, 1981, 25; Covián Martínez, 84, 93; *Revista Ahorro y Trabajo* (Monterey) 61, 2824, 28 agosto 1981, 6.

5.The highway to the north is still the city's major thoroughfare, named Avenida de los Heroes (Heroes Avenue); the other is a seven kilometer highway, Carretera del Golfo, which connects Tampico to Miramar Beach. The total cost for this last road was over $200,000 dollars, mostly provided by the refineries and other industries along the way. See *Informe del Gobernador César López de Lara* (1922), 17; *RDRIAM*, 274, 76766, July 1922, Consul James B. Stewart to Assistant Secretary of State; *CACT*, 14, 438, 1920, 3, Minutes Meeting Tampico Local Managers Association, 17 August 1920, 863-865.

6.*RDRIAM*, 274, 664, 27 April 1922, Consul James R. Stewart to Assistant Secretary of State; Interview with Mr. Francisco Salas García, former treasurer of the Trolley Cooperative Company of Tampico, March 1983 (Tampico); *El Mundo* (Tampico) 9, 33, 3098, 3 mayo 1927, 1; Torrea y Fuentes, 321.

7.Cumberland, *The Constitutionalist...*, 347.

8.Adolfo Gilly, " La guerra de clases en la Revolución Mexicana," en Adolfo Gilly et al., Interpretaciones de la Revolución Mexicana (México, D.F., 1979), 46.

9.*RDRIAM* 274, 243, 26139, Tampico 50, 12 May 1922; Cumberland, *The Constitutionalist...*,247-248. Also see Ramón Eduardo Ruíz, *Labor and the Ambivalent Revolutionaries. México 1911-1923* (Baltimore, 1976), 26-72; Barry Carr, *El movimiento obrero y la política en México, 1912-1929* (México, D.F., 1985); Jacinto Huitrón, *Orígenes e historia del movimiento obrero en México* (México, D.F., 1980).

10.Barry Carr, "The Casa del Obrero Mundial, Constitutionalism and the Pact of February 1915," in Frost, Meyer and Vázquez (eds), *El trabajo y los trabajadores en la historia de México* (México, D.F., 1979), 603-632; John M. Hart, "The Urban Working Class and the Mexican Revolution, The Case of the Casa del Obrero Mundial," *HAHR* 58 (1),

February 1978, 1-20; Ruíz, *Labor..*, 70-71. For Tampico see: González Salas, *Acercamiento...*, 137-138; Adleson, 264. Also Pablo González Casanova, *La clase obrera en la historia de México en el primer gobierno constitucional, 1917-1920* (México, D.F., 1980).

11.José Santos Llorente, "La ley y los trabajadores," *Nosotros los petroleros* 3, 19, 1981, 18; Cumberland, *The Constitutionalist...*, 398-399.

12.AMT, *Actas*, 1 enero 1917.

13. *RDRIAM*, 274, 17388, Tampico, Telegram 11 a.m., 3 February 1916; Adleson, 382 (note 140), 443 (note 64), 493, 497 (note 272), 445, 501.

14.Lorenzo Meyer, 141-142; Adleson, 428-29, 430-39, 458-460.

15.*RDRIAM*, 274, 154, Navy Department, 11 February 1917; 274, 115, 22 July 1917, Consul Dawson to Assistant Secretary of State; 274, 141, Navy Department, 15 October 1917; 274, 118, Telegram Tampico, 2 August 1917; 274, 127, Telegram, 27 August 1917; 274, 140, Telegram, 10 October 1917; Gruening, *Mexico*, 576.

16.Adleson, 452, 460-466, 487 (note 98); Charles Rayner's testimony, *American Petroleum Interests in Foreign Countries*, 15 October 1946, U.S. Senate, 79th. Congress, 1st. Session (1946), 19.

17.Covián Martínez, 51; *El Universal* (México), 16 noviembre 1917; *RDRIAM* 274, 136, 16 November 1917; 28, 156, México 49, 30 March 1917; AMT, "Dictamenes de 1917," 8133, 30 abril 1917.

18.See Jesús Silva Herzog, *Breve historia de la Revolución Mexicana* (México, D.F., 1972), 8-9, 253.

19.Meade, *Huasteca Tamaulipeca* II, 48; AMT, *Actas* 1881. See Table 5 for a list of owners of ejido lands remaining in Tampico.

20.*POET*, 40, 17, 27 febrero 1915, 4; 40, 18, 3 marzo 1915, 2-3.

21.Article 27, "The Mexican Constitution of 1917," *The Mexican Yearbook* (Los Angeles, 1921), 121.

22.AMT, "Dictamen de 1917," Expediente 8133, 30 abril 1917; González Salas, *Del reloj...*, 127-129.

23.Andrés Araujo and Guadalupe Jeréz Lara were two councilmen who came from a labor background; González Salas, "Los anarquistas en acción," *El Mundo* (Tampico) 9 enero 1984, 11; Javier Santos Llorente "Cerro Azul, Veracruz," *Nosotros los petroleros* 2, 13, 1980, 30; Adleson, viii; AMT, "Dictamen de 1917," Expediente 8133, 30 abril 1917.

24.Covián Martínez, 55, 89; Cumberland, *The Constitutionalist...*, 361-362, 368-369; Adleson, 292, 294-295.

25.*RDRIAM* 274, 21702, Monterey, Telegram 4 February 1918; 274, 21734, Tampico, Telegram 12 February 1918; 21893, Nuevo Laredo, Telegram 19 April 1918; Heriberto García Ríos, *Breve historia de la Revolución Mexicana* (México, D.F., 1964), 155; Cumberland, *The Constitutionalist...* 370; Covián Martínez, 50.

26.*RDRIAM* 274, 22098, Tampico 427, 29 June 1918; 22199, War Department, 7 June 1918.

27.*CACT*, 9, 419, Dawson to Secretary of State, 11 May 1920. Also see González Casanova, *La clase obrera*... 104-138; *RDRIAM*, 247, 25040, Tampico 1164, 6 June 1921; *CACT*, 14, 438, Dawson to Secretary of State, March 1921.

28.*RDRIAM*, 274, 23324, Tampico 874, 2 November 1920; 274, 222, Tampico, Telegram 9 July 1920; 274, 224, Tampico 936, 14 July 1920; *CACT* 9, 413, Dawson to Secretary of State, May 1920; Meade, *La Huasteca Tamaulipeca*, II, 224.

29.*Informe del Gobernador C. López de Lara a la XVIII Legislatura de Tamaulipas* (Ciudad Victoria, 1923), 16, 17, 27-29. *CACT*, 18, 1921, 439, Letter from William H. Cook, officer of the International Petroleum Company to Consul Claude I. Dawson, 14 July 1921.

30.Gobierno de Tamaulipas, *Ley sobre expropiación forzosa. Expedida por el XXVII Honorable Congreso Constitucional el dia 13 de diciembre de 1922, sancionada por el Ejecutivo el 15 del mismo mes y año* (Ciudad Victoria, 1923), 27.

31.*Informe del gobernador*... 37-40.

32.Covián Martínez, 12; R. Hansis, "The Political Strategy of Military Reform: Alvaro Obregon and Revolutionary México, 1920-1924," *The Americas* 36, October 1979, 2, 227; Leif Adleson, "Coyuntura y conciencia: factores convergentes en la fundación de los sindicatos petroleros de Tampico durante la década de 1920," in Elsa C. Frost, Michael C. Meyer y Josefina Z. Vázquez (eds) *El trabajo y los trabajadores en la historia de México* (México, D.F., 1979), 633. AGNPPM, Obregón–Calles 104, P1P6, "Memoria del Ingeniero S. González Cordero, Sub-Jefe del Departamento de Petróleo," 20 abril 1925, 2-3.

33.Torrea y Fuentes, 329; *New York Times* January 8, 1924, 6:3; January 9, 1924, 3:4; Adleson, "Coyuntura..., 555; AMT, *Actas*, 16 abril 1924.

34.González Salas, *Del Reloj*..., 233.

APPENDIX

TABLE 1

POPULATION OF TAMPICO BETWEEN 1823 AND 1877

Year	Population
1823	64[1]
1825	1676[2]
1831	1957[3]
1834	3707[4]
1839	3425[5]
1845	5078[6]
1855	5412[7]
1859	6168[8]
1860	6337[9]
1873	5847[10]
1877	5700[11]

1.There were sixty four land-grantees during the ceremony to present the lots in 1823. *Documentos de fundación de Tampico* (Ciudad Victoria, 1898).

2. Meade, *Huasteca Tamaulipeca*, I, 43.

3. AMT, legajo 6, Expediente 29 "Padrón de Tampico" (1831).

4. AMT, Expediente 126, Tampico, 1835.

5. AMT, *Padrón General de 1839*.

6. González Salas, *Tampico, mi ciudad*, 51.

7. *Ibid*, 74.

8. AMT, *Padrón de Tampico dividido por cuarteles* (1859).

9. AMT, *Padrón de esta municipalidad dividido en secciones y ejidos de Tancol y Tamesín*, Expediente 76, 15 de agosto de 1860. Out of 6,337 residents in the municipality, 5,171 lived within the city limits.

10. Alejandro Prieto, *Historia geográfica y estadística del Estado de Tamaulipas* (1873), 279.

11. Edmund Johnson, "Report upon the Trade and Commerce of Tampico for the year ending September 30, 1877." in *RUCRF* (Washington, 1878), 746.

TABLE 2

NORTH AMERICANS IN TAMPICO - 1867

Name	From	Age	Occupation
Eduardo de la Torre	New Orleans	36	Businessman
Ulises Labourdette	U.S.	31	Businessman
Alejandro Labourdette	U.S.	28	Businessman
Miguel P. Soto	Mobile, Ala.	43	Businessman
José Antonio Eduardo	Baltimore	49	Carpenter
Manuel Maples	Jacksonville	21	Store Sales
Simón Romero	U.S.	29	Businessman
Juan R. Menéndez Quiles	U.S.	23	Businessman
Julio Cavelier	New Orleans	30	Businessman
Eduardo Welder	New Orleans	38	Artisan
Antonio Sánchez Zamora (naturalized Spaniard)	U.S.	36	Businessman
Adolfo Alberone	New Orleans	39	Businessman
Luis de Poche	New Orleans	34	Teacher
Pedro Hernández	New Orleans	50	Mason
Julio Alvarez	New Orleans	48	Mason
Bernardo Miguel	New Orleans	50	Carpenter
José Setle	Philadelphia	49	Artisan
Manuel Castilla	U.S.	45	Businessman
Clemente Fúnez	U.S.	27	Artisan
Dionisio Ricahi	Pensacola	31	Businessman
Santiago Sanders	U.S.	31	Businessman
Mateo Belfort	U.S.	49	Artisan
Antonio Collins	U.S.	46	Businessman
Ricardo Gagnet	U.S.	40	Tailor
Francisco Esteban	U.S.	27	Tailor
Francisco Dastigue	U.S.	54	Painter
Tomás Herrién	U.S.	29	Sailor
Pablo Mandila	U.S.	54	Mason
Jorge Heill	U.S.	54	Carpenter
Francisco Martin	U.S.	44	Watchmaker
Otelo Cupidón	U.S.	32	Wallbuilder
Luis Bernard	U.S.	51	Wallbuilder
José Lange	U.S.	38	Wallbuilder
Hipólito Grandpé	U.S.	55	Businessman
Ricardo Romain	U.S.	48	Artisan
Epifanio Ralio	U.S.	32	Artisan
Francisco Bono	U.S.	22	Businessman
Benito Bono	U.S.	45	Shoemaker
Leopoldo Lavigne	U.S.	47	Mason

Name	From	Age	Occupation
Emilio Robert	U.S.	49	M.D.
Julio Abelard	U.S.	40	Artisan
Julián Wel	U.S.	38	Carpenter
J.O. Alford	U.S.	29	M.D.
José Lavigne	U.S.	25	Artisan
Ramón Toussain	U.S.	19	Shoemaker
Gustavo Lavigne	U.S.	20	Artisan
Juan Bernardino	U.S.	20	Carpenter
Pedro Chalback	U.S.	24	Shoemaker
Pablo Bernardino	U.S.	22	Carpenter
Teófilo Bagneris	U.S.	56	Mason
Alberto Souchet	U.S.	26	Blacksmith
Andrés P. Rodríguez	U.S.	23	Businessman
Alejandro Collins	U.S.	30	Barber
Agustín M. Dorestan	U.S.	42	Artisan
José Roche	U.S.	19	Artisan
José Chalback	U.S.	25	Carpenter
Ernesto Levafseur	U.S.	35	Watchmaker
Félix Ruíz	U.S.	28	Carpenter
Teófilo Populus	U.S.	23	Carpenter
Enrique Populus	U.S.	46	Mason
J. Julián N. Dufart	U.S.	34	Businessman
P. E. Percy	U.S.	43	Mason
Robert Panton	U.S.	56	Carpenter
Bernardo Collins	U.S.	47	Businessman
Pedro A. Tonaul	U.S.	56	Fencing tchr.
Joseph Hunt	U.S.	19	Carpenter
Edward Morris	U.S.	19	Tobacco worker
Clay St. Andra	U.S.	19	Tobacco worker
Marcos L. Fio	U.S.	38	Businessman

Source: AMT, Registro de extranjeros domiciliados en Tampico y solicitud al Supremo Gobierno para las cartas de Seguridad. Libro 75, Año de 1867. The register lists many other foreigners, but the above were selected for having born in the United States or claimed its citizenship. Those names associated with Texas, Florida or Louisiana have Spanish or French origins. Also notice that most were skilled workers or professionals.

TABLE 3

MEXICAN EXPORTS BY CUSTOM HOUSES, 1885-86

Port	Annual Average Five Years Ending 6-30-1885	Ending 6-30-1885	Ending 6-30-1886
Acapulco	180,166 (16)	190,695 (17)	104,178 (22)
Altata	60,105 (23)	71,372 (23)	40,105 (26)
Bahía Magdalena	48,117 (26)	55,852 (25)	7,120 (30)
Cabo San Lucas	4,005 (34)	4,755 (32)	6,077 (31)
Camargo	56,229 (25)	47,206 (27)	39,208 (27)
Coatzacoalcos	179,600 (17)	193,014 (16)	184,879 (15)
Frontera*	366,091 (11)	443,127 (9)	245,252 (14)
Guaymas	349,682 (12)	400,551 (11)	463,075 (10)
Guerrero	25,822 (30)	33,578 (29)	25,524 (28)
Isla del Carmen	468,194 (9)	562,935 (8)	568,103 (9)
La Paz	496,734 (8)	399,651 (12)	392,821 (12)
Laredo*	828,459 (6)	1,152,722 (5)	1,070,333 (5)
Manzanillo	204,084 (15)	141,178 (18)	163,441 (17)
Matamoros*	520,738 (7)	355,737 (13)	411,725 (11)
Mazatlán	3,589,934 (2)	3,214,951 (3)	2,874,586 (3)
Mier*	93,737 (20)	102,487 (20)	169,976 (16)
Nogales*	291,501 (13)	662,615 (7)	372,658 (13)
Palominos	27,147 (29)	78,104 (22)	52,787 (23)
Paso del Norte*	2,129,722 (4)	7,871,245 (2)	8,462,340 (2)
Piedras Negras*	175,165 (18)	404,186 (10)	630,628 (7)
Presidio del	47,918 (27)	------	8,313 (29)
Progreso	2,907,874 (3)	3,426,769 (3)	2,650,319 (4)
Puerto Angel	16,965 (31)	19,369 (30)	108,190 (21)
Quitoraguita	1,741 (36)	2,880 (33)	977 (32)
Reynosa*	3,544 (35)	------	------
Salina Cruz	109,256 (19)	53,212 (26)	111,806 (20)
San Blas	253,969 (14)	233,443 (15)	132,821 (19)
Sasabe	43,263 (28)	43,325 (28)	44,164 (25)
Soconusco	93,637 (21)	84,127 (21)	------
Tampico	916,888 (5)	895,585 (6)	703,917 (6)
Tijuana*	5,574 (33)	8,632 (31) 1,392	45,633 (24)
Todos los Santos	9,350 (32)	(34)	88 (33)
Tonalá	74,509 (22)	104,412 (19)	137,980 (18)
Tuxpam	397,490 (10)	321,867 (14)	606,293 (8)
Veracruz	15,858,957 (1)	15,720,958 (1)	13,940,662 (1)
Zapaluta	59,161 (24)	57,920 (24)	------

Source: U.S.Department of State, **CRUSFC** 1886 and 1887 (Washington, D.C., 1888), 582–583. Figures include precious metals and othe exports. Gulf ports are highlighted, asterisks indicate border cities. Parenthesis represent their relative standing in each year.

TABLE 4

MEXICAN IMPORTS FROM MAJOR TRADING PARTNERS
(In United States dollars)

Country	**1893**	**1894**	**1895**
United States	26,236,963	14,351,785	15,130,367
Great Britain	5,680 990	5,754,523	6,668,327
France	4,781 023	4,359,395	5,576,750
Germany	2,874.801	2,665,707	3,301,643
Spain	3,630.608	1,948,929	1,913,660

Source: Department of State, *Commercial Relations of the United States with Foreign Countries During the Year 1895 and 1896*, I, (Washington, D.C.: Government Printing Office, 1897), 404.

TABLE 5

TAMPICO'S CUSTOM HOUSE MONTHLY RECEIPTS (1894–1895)
(In Mexican pesos)

Month	**1894**	**1895**
January	$ 85, 515.09	$ 152, 329.54
February	77, 756.62	108, 535.80
March	102, 362.04	157, 016.30
April	94, 667.14	158, 163.89
May	96, 821.80	204, 071.11
June	100, 989.89	229, 364.54
July	96, 191.07	250, 987.59
August	117, 922.29	296, 408.45
September	138, 296.37	389, 000.00

Source: C.P. Bond, "Tampico," *The Mexican Herald* (México, D.F., Saturday, 7 December 1895), 2.

TABLE 6

TAMPICO'S INCOME AND EXPENDITURES - 1894

(In pesos)

Income	Amount
Tax on warehouses	$ 3, 567.07
Tax on urban property	8, 115.18
Tax on businesses	9, 964.50
Late payments on professional taxes	1, 484.50
Late payments on property taxes	2, 386.72
Local taxes	16, 043.17
Leases on market-floor spaces	20, 965.00
Permits on dances and serenades	1, 352.00
Taxes on imports (all arriving articles)	12, 445.24
Health Bills on arriving ships	1, 184.00
Administrative fines (mayor's office)	1, 935.17
State taxes (collected by the city)	3, 540.77
Additional 3% tax on federal stamps	16, 392.96
Ejido land sales	1, 595.58
State taxes on food items	1, 204.18
Loan from Trápaga Bros. House	2, 000.00
	$104,116.14

Expenditures	Amount
Board of Education	$ 11, 250.00
Charities's Board	12, 150.00
Jail (assistance to prisoners)	5, 920.56
Street Lighting	12, 561.71
Office of the Municipal Secretary (salaries)	2, 859.00
Office of the Municipal Treasury (salaries)	2, 994.27
Municipal Police Department (salaries)	10, 438.97
Sanitation Department	5, 281.25
Extraordinary expenses	8, 596.52
State taxes	3, 540.77
Assistance to State Penitentiary	4, 220.71
Federal Stamp taxes	16, 392.96
State taxes on food items	1, 204.18
	$ 97, 410.90

Source: "Corte de caja general que practica esta oficina del movimiento de caudales habidos en los meses de enero a diciembre de 1894," Archivo Municipal de Tampico, Tesorería, Expediente 1895.

TABLE 7

TAMPICO'S INCOME AND EXPENDITURES (1895–1899)
(In pesos)

Year	Income	Expenditures
1895	$ 106, 181.01	$ 94, 914.41
1896	134, 647.32	125, 843.27
1897	307, 067.65	304, 571.35
1898	208, 293.12	210, 790.21
1899	214, 078.62	208, 618.33
	961, 500.89	944, 737.57

Source: *Periódico Oficial del Estado de Tamaulipas* (Ciudad Victoria). 31, 37, 26 marzo 1901, 3. Tampico's income was very important for the State for the benefits accrued from it. In 1896, the State's income was $129,984 pesos, while Tampico's was $134,647.32 pesos. See *Memoria Oficial del Gobierno del Estado de Tamaulipas* (Ciudad Victoria, 1896), 10.

TABLE 8

TAMPICO CITY COUNCIL MEMBERS, 1910–1914

1910

P.M. José María Maraboto
C. Joaquin Pazzi
Pablo Soules
Gonzalo N. Silva
Pedro Torres Grillo
Emilio Baldit
Sabás Prom
Gustavus A. Populus
Ramón Sottil
Vicente Fusco
Francisco Hernández Rábago
Santiago Bautista
Sin. Fernando Lachica y Flores, Esq.

1911

P.M. Dr. Antonio Matienzo
C. Joaquin Pazzi
Carlos Amado
Gonzalo N. Silva
Simon Torres Grillo
Ernesto López
Juan Zubiaga
N. Jauregui
Luis M. Vázquez
Sabino Gutiérrez
Adolfo A. Autrey
Eustorgio R. Ruiz
Sin. Fernando Lachica y Flores, Esq.

1912

P.M. Angel Boeta
C. Carlos B. Sahagón
José B. Valladares
Pafnuncio Padilla
Aquiles Castilla
José Etienne
Dr. Francisco Rivera
Cándido García
Donato Arteaga
Felipe Hernández
Sin. Francisco R. Zorrilla

1913 (Jan-Oct)

P.M. Carlos B. Sahagón
C. Matías Domingo
José B. Valladares
Herminio García
Luis F. Gómez
Tomás R. Morales
Dr. Juan F. Gual
Alejandro Labourdette
Manuel Caballero Govea
Gonzalo N. Silva
Sin. Morales Aguirre, Esq.

TAMPICO CITY COUNCIL MEMBERS, 1910–1914

1913 (Oct-Dec)

P.M.	Matías Domingo (one week)
C.Dr.	Mariano Treviño
	Juan Zubiaga
	Francisco R. Zorrilla
	Sabás Prom
	Emilio Baldit
	Gonzalo N. Silva
	Luis M. Vázquez
	Adolfo E. Balboa
Sin.	F. Lachica Flores, Esq.

1914 (Jan-May)

P.M.	Fernando Lachica Flores,
C.Dr.	Mariano Treviño
	Juan Zubiaga
	Benito Zorrilla
	Sabás Prom
	Emilio Baldit
	Cayetano Fuentes, Esq.
	Matías Domingo
	Adolfo E. Balboa
Sin.	Pafnuncio Padilla

1914 (May-Dec)

P.M.	Eustorgio R. Ruiz
C.	José B. Valladares
Dr.	Francisco Rivera
	Enrique Rendón
	Graciano Juárez
	Tomás R. Morales
	José Etienne
	Marcos Castañón
	Amador González
	Antonio P. Gómez
Sin.	Cayetano Fuentes, Esq.

Source: AMT, *Actas*, 1 enero 1910, 1911, 1912, 1913, 1914.
PM= Presidente Municipal; C=Councilman; Sin=Comptroller

TABLE 9

WORLD OIL PRODUCTION, 1910–1925
(in millions of barrels)

Year	U.S.	México	Russia	Persia	Dutch Indies	Venezuela
1910	209.6	3.6	70.3	-	11.0	-
1911	220.4	12.6	66.2	-	12.2	-
1912	222.9	16.6	68.0	-	10.8	-
1913	248.4	25.7	62.8	1.9	11.2	-
1914	265.8	26.2	67.0	2.9	11.4	-
1915	281.1	32.9	68.5	3.6	11.9	-
1916	300.8	40.5	65.8	4.5	12.5	-
1917	335.3	55.3	63.1	7.1	13.2	0.1
1918	355.9	63.8	27.2	8.6	12.8	0.3
1919	378.4	87.1	31.8	10.1	15.5	0.4
1920	442.9	157.1	25.4	12.2	17.5	0.5
1921	472.2	193.4	29.0	16.7	17.0	1.4
1922	557.5	182.3	35.7	22.2	17.1	2.2
1923	732.4	149.6	39.1	25.2	19.9	3.2
1924	713.9	139.7	45.4	32.4	20.5	9.0
1925	763.7	115.6	52.4	35.0	21.4	19.7

Source: Enrique Krause, Jean Mayer and Cayetano Reyes, *Historia de la Revolución Mexicana, 1924–1928. La reconstrucción económica* (México, D.F., 1981), 244.

TABLE 10

TAMPICO'S POPULATION (1860 - 1922)

Year	Population
1860	6,344 [1]
1879	6.996 [2]
1885	7,500 [3]
1890	8,045 [4]
1897	11,689 [5]
1900	17,569 [6]
1910	23,452 [7]
1917	40,192 [8]
1921	94,667 [9]
1922	120,000 [10]

1.Includes the ejidos, AMT, Expediente 65, "Lo referente a los Jefes de Cuartel de esta Municipalidad. 21 enero 1860."

2. AMT, Expediente 42, 1879.

3. AMT, *Actas*, 26 marzo 1885; Expediente 125, 21 julio 1886.

4. *PORT*, 22 marzo 1890, 1.

5. *The Two Republics* (México, D.F.) 44, 53, 3 March 1897; AMT, Expediente 128, 1 noviembre 1897.

6. A. Arguelles, *Reseña de Tamaulipas*, 100; González Salas, *Tampico, mi ciudad*, 79.

7. Torrea y Fuentes, *Tampico*, 408; Censo 1910, "Tamaulipas."

8. Adleson, 4.

9. Gobierno del Estado, *Censo de Tamaulipas* (Ciudad Victoria, 1921), 169.

10. *The Pulse of Mexico* (México, D.F.), February/ March 1922, 10.

TABLE 11

PETROLEUM'S SHARE OF THE MEXICAN FEDERAL INCOME, 1916–1925
(In pesos)

Year	Federal Income[1]	Oil Taxes[2]	Percent
1916	402,000,000	3,355,395	8.3
1917	117,000,000	7,553,295	6.5
1918	100,000,000	12,008,065	12.0
1919	157,000,000	17,321,542	11.0
1920	458,000,000	51,313,557	11.2
1921	264,000,000	69,028,711	26.0
1922	355,000,000	87,778,191	25.0
1923	253,000,000	62,393,357	25.0
1924	294,000,000	56,467,587	19.0
1925	291,000,000	46,798,312	16.0

1. Diego G. López Rosado, *Historia y pensamiento económico de México. Comercio interior y exterior. Sistema monetario y de crédito* (México, D.F., 1971), 164, 208.

2. Gobierno de México, *El Petróleo de México* (México, D.F., 1940), 18.

TABLE 12
LAND OWNERS OF THE ISLETA, TAMPICO 1920

Owner	**Lots**	**Area** (sq. mts)
E. L. Buckley and Company	7	8,032.54
Ice Company	1	1,598.10
"La Libertad" Packing Co. Ltd.	1	1,000.00
Compañía Refinadora AGWI, S.A.	3	3,940.80
Laguna Transportation Co. Ltd.	4	4,087.75
Continental Mexican Petroleum Co.	5	6,841.42
Y.B. Sutton	1	960.00
N.A. Moller	1	960.00
Tampico Marine Iron Works	4	4,721.63
Ravizé American Lumber Co., Ltd.	5	5,894.41
A. E. Collins	1	960.00
Martin F. Head Co., Ltd.	1	1,315.54
Ellis & Ryan, Ltd.	2	2,630.82
Manuel Morlote Peral	5	7,167.16
General Machinery Supply Co.	4	4,047.10
Van Bethem Van der Vergh	1	985.90
E. G. Mead	1	1,288.50
Tampico Foundry Machine & Supply Co.	7	8,666.78
Roberto Gayol	2	1,745.00
Monterey, S.A. Fund. Hierro y Acero	1	1,291.26
Streets and prepared lots	1	59,372.00

Source: AMT, Expediente "La Isleta," 204, 10 de agosto de 1920.

BIBLIOGRAPHY

Archival Sources

Archivo Municipal de la Ciudad de Tampico, Tamaulipas, México.
Catastro Municipal de la Ciudad de Tampico, Tamaulipas, México.
Instituto de Investigaciones Históricas, Ciudad Victoria, Tamaulipas.
Archivo General de la Nación, México, D.F.: Ramo de Gobernación.
Archivo de la Secretaría de Relaciones Exteriores, México, D. F.
Archivo Histórico de Matías Romero, Banco de México, México, D.F.
National Archives of the United States, Washington, D.C., U.S.A.
Record Group 59: General Records of the Department of State Relating to the Internal Affairs of México, 1910–1929.
Record Group 84: Records of the Foreign Service Posts. Correspondence of the American Consulate in Tampico.
Despatches from U.S. Consuls in Tampico, 1824–1906.
Despatches from U.S. Consuls in Tuxpám, 1879–1906.
Despatches from U.S. Consuls in Veracruz, 1822–1906.

Newspaper and Journals

Boletín Municipal del R. Ayuntamiento de Tampico, (1912–1925), Tampico, Tamaulipas.
El Comercio de Tampico, Tampico, Tamaulipas.
El Faro de Tampico, Tampico, Tamaulipas.
Gaceta de Santa Anna de Tampico, Tampico, Tamaulipas.
El Mundo, Tampico, Tamaulipas.
La Opinión, Tampico, Tamaulipas.
El Porvenir, Tampico, Tamaulipas.
El Semanario, Tampico, Tamaulipas.
El Sol de Tampico, Tampico, Tamaulipas.
Tampico Times, Tampico, Tamaulipas.
Tampico Tribune, Tampico, Tamaulipas.
Gaceta del Gobierno del Estado de Tamaulipas, Ciudad Victoria, Tams.
Periódico Oficial del Estado de Tamaulipas, Ciudad Victoria, Tamaulipas.
La Reconstrucción, Ciudad Victoria, Tamaulipas.
Revista Trabajo y Ahorro, Monterey, Nuevo León.
Boletín del Archivo General de la Nación, México, D.F.
Diario Oficial del Superior Gobierno de los EE. UU. Mexicanos, México.
Excelsior, México, D.F.
Mexican American Review, México, D.F.
The Mexican Herald, México, D.F.

Mexican Life, México, D.F.
El Municipio Libre, México, D.F.
Novedades, México, D.F.
The Pulse of México, México, D.F.
The Two Republics, México, D.F.
El Universal, México, D.F.
The Daily Times Picayune of New Orleans, New Orleans, Louisiana.
San Antonio Light, San Antonio, Texas.
New York Times, New York, New York.
The World's Work, New York, New York.

Printed Documents

Actas Municipales de Tampico, 1840–1930.

Alba, Rafael de. *Tamaulipas. Reseña geográfica y estadística.* México, D.F.: Libreria de la Viuda de C. Bouret, 1910.

Album of the America Club. City of Mexico. Its Origin, History, and Roster of Members (1895-1910). México, D. F.

American Chamber of Commerce. *Business Directory of Tampico*, 1921.

Andrade, Manuel (ed.). *Leyes y reglamentos sobre aguas, bosques, minas, colonización y petróleo.* 2 vols. México, D.F.: Ediciones Andrade, S. A., 1962.

Arguelles, Adalberto J. *Reseña del Estado de Tamaulipas.* Ciudad Victoria: Gobierno del Estado, 1910.

______. *Compendio de geografía del Estado de Tamaulipas.* Ciudad Victoria, Tamaulipas, 1895.

Arriola, Enrique. "Los intereses petroleros, Calles y los conflictos de 1924." *Boletín del Archivo General de la Nación* México, D.F. (1977), (1): 26–30.

Bureau of the American Republics. *Mexico* No. 9. Washington, D.C., July 1891.

Bustamante, Miguel. *El petróleo en la República Mexicana.* México, D.F.: Secretaría de Comunicaciones, 1917.

Carreño, Alberto María. *Archivo del General Porfirio Díaz. Memorias y Documentos.* 24 vols. México, D.F., 1947–1963.

Covián Martínez, Vidal. *Cronología histórica de Tampico, Ciudad Madero y Altamira, Tamaulipas y de la expropiación petrolera.* Ciudad Victoria: Ediciones Siglo XX, 1969.

Davis, H.W.C and R.H. Weaver (eds). *Dictionary of National Biography, 1912 - 1921.* London: Oxford University Press, 1927.

Enciclopedia Espasa-Calpe. Madrid, 1923.

Encyclopaedia Britannica. London, 1910–11.

Estados Unidos Mexicanos. Dirección General de Estadísticas. *Anuario Estadístico del comercio exterior de los Estados Unidos Mexicanos, 1920–1928*. México, D.F., 1960.

Estados Unidos Mexicanos. Dirección General de Estadísticas. *Censo General de la República Mexicana*. México, D.F.: Oficina Tipográfica de la Secretaría de Fomento, 1897–99.

______. *Censo General de la República Mexicana, 1900*. México, 1901.

______. *Censo General de la República Mexicana, 1910*. México, 1918–1920.

______. Departamento de la Estadística Nacional. *Censo General de habitantes, 1920*. México, D.F.: Talleres Gráficos de la Nación, 1925–28.

______. *Aspectos estadísticos de un quinquenio, 1921–1925*. México, D.F., 1926.

______. Secretaría de la Economía Nacional. Dirección General de Estadísticas. *Quinto censo de población, 1930*. México, D.F.: Talleres Gráficos de la Nación, 1932–1936.

______. Secretaría de Fomento, Colonización, Industria y Comercio. *La crisis monetaria. Estudios sobre la crisis mercantil y la depreciación de la plata*. México, D.F.: Tipografía de la Secretaría de Fomento, 1886.

Estados Unidos Mexicanos. Secretaría de Relaciones Exteriores. *Correspondencia oficial entre los Estados Unidos y México con relación...Artículo 27 de la Constitución. Primera parte*. México, D.F., 1926.

Estados Unidos Mexicanos. Secretaría de Fomento. *Memoria presentada al Congreso de la Unión por el Secretario de Estado y del Despacho de Fomento, Colonización, Industria y Comercio de la República Mexicana Vicente Riva Palacio, correspondiente al año transcurrido de diciembre de 1876 a noviembre de 1872*. México, D.F., 1877.

______. *Memoria presentada al Congreso de la Unión por el Secretario de Estado General Carlos Pacheco. corresponde a los años transcurridos de diciembre de 1877 a diciembre de 1882*. 4 vols México, D.F., 1885.

______. *México*. México, D.F.: Talleres Gráficos de la Nación, 1929.

______. *El Petróleo de México. Recopilación de documentos oficiales del conflicto de orden económico de la industria petrolera, con una introducción que resume sus motivos y consecuencias*. México, D.F.: Editorial Cultura, 1940.

Gardiner, C. Harvey (ed). *Mexico, 1825-1828. The Journal and Correspondence of Edward Thornton Wallace*. Chapel Hill: University of North Carolina Press, 1959.

Gobierno Municipal de Tampico. *Programa de las fiestas organizadas con motivo del Primer Centenario de la Fundación del Puerto de Tampico, 1823–1923*. Tampico: Imprenta El Arte, 1923.

Gobierno Municipal de Tampico. *Contratos y documentos concernientes a la introducción de agua potable y drenaje de la ciudad de Tampico*. Tampico: Imprenta Hidalgo, 1903.

Gobierno de Tamaulipas. *Informe del Gobernador César López de Lara del Estado a la XXVIII Legislatura de Tamaulipas*.Ciudad Victoria, 1923.

Gutiérrez Zamora, Manuel. "El salvamento de Don Porfirio Díaz frente a la barra de Tampico (1876), " *Historia Mexicana* 5, 17: 62–85.

Hammond, George P. and Edgar F. Good (eds). *A Scientist on the Trail. Travel Letters of A. F. Bandelier, 1880-1881*. Berkeley: The Quivira Society, 1949.

Instituto de Derecho Comparado. *Constituciones vigentes en la República Mexicana con las leyes Inorgánicas de los Territorios Federales y del Departamento del D.F.* 2 vols. México, D.F.: Imprenta Universitaria, 1962.

Lyon, G.F. *Journal of a Residence and Tour in the Republic of Mexico in the Year 1826 with some account of the mines of that country*. 2 vols. London: John Murray, 1828.

Meyer, Brantz. *Mexico as it was and as it is*. New York: J. Winchester, 1844.

Norman, B. M. *Rambles by Land and Water or Notes of Travel in Cuba and Mexico; Including a Canoe Voyage up the River Panuco, and Researches Among the ruins of Tamaulipas, etc.* New York/ New Orleans: Paine & Burgess Pub., 1845.

Ober, Frederick A. *Travels in Mexico*. Boston: Estes and Lauriat Pub., 1883.

Parte oficial de la toma de Tampico por las fuerzas del Supremo Gobierno al mando del C. General Saturnino Rocha. México,D.F.:Imprenta del Gobierno, 1871.

Poinsett, Joel R. *Notes on Mexico made in the Autumn of 1822 accompanied by an historical sketch of the Revolution and translations of official reports on the present state of that country*.Philadelphia: H.C. Carey and I. Lea, 1824.

Prieto, Alejandro. *Discurso pronunciado en Tampico...en la noche del 14 de septiembre de 1902*. Ciudad Victoria: Oficina Tipográfica del Gobierno, 1902.

_____. *Historia geográfica y estadística del Estado de Tamaulipas*. México, D. F.: Tipografía Escalerillas 13, 1873.

Tena Ramírez, Felipe (ed). *Leyes fundamentales de México, 1808–1964*. México, D.F.: Editorial Porrúa, 1964.

La Universal. *Informe.Compañía Explotadora de Petróleo, S.A.* Tampico, 1916.

Union of the American Republics. *Bulletin of the Pan American Union* (December).Washington, D.C., 1925.

United States. Department of Commerce. *Commerce Reports. Daily Consular and Trade Reports*.Washington, D.C.: Government Printing Office, 1890–1900.

_____. Bureau of Foreign and Domestic Commerce. *Commercial Relations of the United States with Foreign Countries for the Year 1893. Annual Reports of the Consusls of the United States on the Commerce, Manufactures, Industries, Etc., of Their Several Districts*. Washington, D.C.: Government Printing Office, 1894.

United States. Department of Commerce. *Commercial Relations of the U.S. with Foreign Countries for the Year 1911*.Washington, D.C.,1913.

_____. *Commercial Relations of the United States with Foreign Countries for the Year 1912*. Washington, D.C., 1914.

United States Department of Commerce and Labor. Bureau of Manufactures. *Commercial Relations of the U.S. with Foreign Countries* (1907). 2 vols. Washington, D.C., 1908.

_____. *Commercial Relations of the United States with Foreign Countries* (1908). 2 vols. Washington, D.C., 1909.

_____. *Commercial Relations of the United States with Foreign Countries* (1909). Washington, D.C., 1911.

United States. Fuel Administration. *Final Report of the United States Fuel Administration, 1917–1919*. Washington, D.C., 1921.

United States. Department of State. *Reports from the Consuls of the United States on the Commerce, Manufactures, etc., of their Consular Districts* (1890). Washington, D.C., 1891.

_____. *Report Upon the Commercial Relations of the United States with Foreign Countries for the Year 1876.* Washington, D.C., 1877.

_____. *Report Upon the Commercial Relations of the United States with Foreign Countries for the Year 1877.* Washington, D.C., 1878.

_____. *Report Upon the Commercial Relations of the United States with Foreign Countries for the Year 1878.* Washington, D.C., 1879.

_____. *Report Upon the Commercial Relations of the United States with Foreign Countries for the Year 1879.* Washington, D.C., 1880.

United States. Department of State. *Report Upon the Commercial Relations of the United States with Foreign Countries for the Years 1880 and 1881.* Washington, D.C., 1883.

_____. *Commercial Relations of the United States with Foreign Countries during the Years 1882 and 1883.* Washington, D.C., 1884.

United States Deparment of State. *Commercial Relations of the United States with Foreign Countries during the Years 1886 and 1887.* Washington, D.C., 1888.

_____. *Commercial Relations of the United States with Foreign Countries during the Years 1890 and 1891.* Washington, D.C., 1892.

_____. Bureau of Statistics. *Commercial Relations of the United States with Foreign Countries for the Years 1894 and 1895.* 2 vols. Washington, D.C., 1896.

United States. Department of State. *Commercial Relations of the United States with Foreign Countries during the Years 1895 and 1896.* 2 vols. Washington, D.C., 1897.

_____. Bureau of Foreign Commerce. *Commercial Rels. of the U. S. with Foreign countries during 1896 and 1897.* Washington, 1898.

_____. *Commercial Relations of the United States with Foreign Countries during the Year 1898.* Washington, D.C., 1899.

_____. *Commercial Relations of the United States with Foreign Countries during the Year 1899.* Washington, D.C., 1900.

_____. *Commercial Relations of the United States with Foreign Countries 1901.* 2 vols. Washington, D.C., 1902.

United States Senate. Foreign Relations Committee. *Investigation of Mexican Affairs. Reports and Hearings.* 2 vols. 66th. Congress, 1st. Session. Senate Document 62. Washington, D.C.: Government Printing Office, 1919.

_____. *Restrictions on American Petroleum Prospectives in Certain Foreign Countries* 66th Congress, 2nd. Session. Senate Document 272. Washington, D.C., 1919–1920.

_____. *Investigation of Mexican Affairs. Preliminary Report and Hearing...to Investigate the Matter of Outrages on Citizens of the United States in México* 2 vols. 66th. Congress, 2nd. Session. Senate Document 285. Washington, D.C., 1920.

_____. *Oil Concessions in México. Message from the President of the United States transmitting Report of the Secretary of State in Response to Senate Resolution No. 330. Submitting Certain Information Respecting Oil Lands or Oil Concessions in Mexico* 69th. Congress, 2nd. Session. Senate Document 210. Washington, D.C., 1927.

United States Senate. *American Petroleum Interests in Foreign Countries. Hearings of the U.S. Senate, October 15, 1945* 79th. Congress, 1st. Session. Washington, D.C., 1946.

Ward, George. *Mexico. Second edition enlarged with an account of the mining companies, and of the political events in that Republic to the present day* 2 vols. London: Henry Colburn, 1829.

Unpublished Studies and Dissertations

Adleson, Lief S. *Historia social de los obreros industriales de Tampico, 1906–1919*. Ph.D. diss., El Colegio de México, 1982.

Baldridge, Donald Carl. *Mexican Petroleum and the United States-Mexican Relations, 1919–1923*. Ph.D. diss., U. of Arizona, 1951.

Collins Rojas, Carlos. *Estudio del puerto de Tampico y desarrollo futuro* Engineering Thesis, Universidad de Veracruz, 1969.

Cott, Kenneth S. *Porfirian Investment Policies, 1876–1910*. Ph.D. diss., University of New Mexico, 1979.

French, John D. *A United States Merchant Consul and the Foreign Community: Franklin Chase and His Friends and Enemies at Tampico, Mexico, 1861-1865*. M.A. Thesis, University of Pittsburgh, 1978.

Gray, Sister Gertrude M. *Oil in Anglo-American Relations, 1920–1928*. Ph.D. diss., University of California, Berkeley, 1950.

Hansis, Ronald C. *Alvaro Obregón, the Mexican Revolution and the Politics of Consolidation, 1920–1924*. Ph.D. diss.,University of New Mexico, 1971.

Hernández Sotomayor, Laura. *Guadalupe Mainero, Gobernador de Tamaulipas, 1876–1901* Tesis de Licenciatura en Historia, Universidad Iberoamericana, 1981.
Ignasias, Charles Dennis. *Reluctant Recognition: the United States and the Recognition of Alvaro Obregón of México, 1920–1924.* Ph.D. diss., Michigan State University, 1967.
Montoto Guevara, José A. *Mercado municipal y central de abastos. Ciudad Madero, Tamaulipas.* Tesis de arquitectura, Universidad Autónoma de Tamaulipas (Tampico), 1979.
Ocasio Meléndez, Marcial E. *Conflict and Truce. Alvaro Obregón's Oil Policy, 1920–1923.* 1981. (Unpublished paper).
Prevot, Marie France. *Tampico:Geographie Urbaine.* M.A. Thesis,Centre Nationale de la Recherche Scientifique, 1972.

Books and Articles

Ackerman, Carl W. *Mexico's Dilemma.* New York, 1918.
Adleson, Leif S. "Coyuntura y conciencia: factores convergentes en la fundación de los sindicatos petroleros de Tampico durante la década de 1920," in Frost, Elsa, Michael Meyer and Josefina Z. Vázquez, eds. *El trabajo y los trabajadores en la historia de México.* México, 1979: 632–666.
Alzati, Servando. *Historia de la mexicanización de los Ferrocarriles Nacionales de México.* México, 1946.
Apostle, Paul and Alexandre Michelson. *La lutte pour le petrole et la Russie.* Paris, 1922.
Araiza, Luis. *Historia del movimiento obrero mexicano.* México, 1964.
Atkin, Ronald. *Revolution! Mexico, 1910–1920.* London, 1969.
Baldizan, E. *La Huasteca Potosina.* 2 vols. México, 1946.
Barker, E. C. "Tampico Expedition," *Quarterly of the Texas Historical Association.* VI (1902–03): 169–186.
Barnes, John K. "The Crisis in Our Oil Policy," *World's Work.* May 1920: 30.
Barragán Rodríguez, Juan. *Historia del ejército y de la revolución constitucionalista.* 4 vols. México, 1946.
Barron, Clarence W. *The Mexican Problem.* Boston/New York, 1917.
Bazant, Jan. *Historia de la deuda exterior de México, 1923–1946.* México, 1968.
Beals, Carleton. *Porfirio Díaz. Dictator of Mexico.* Philadelphia, 1932.

Bell, Samuel E. *The Zona Libre, 1856–1905. A Problem in American Diplomacy*. El Paso, 1982.

Bernstein, Harry. "Regionalism in the National History of Mexico," *Acta Americana*. II, (October-December 1944): 305–314.

Bethell, Leslie, ed. *The Cambridge History of Latin America*. Vols. III, IV, and V. Cambridge, England, 1985–86.

Bigelow, John. "The Railway Invasion of Mexico," *Harper's Magazine*. LXV, (1882) 747–748.

Bonilla, Juan de Dios. *Historia marítima de México*. México, 1963.

Boracres, Paul. *El petróleo mexicano...¿Es cosa robada?* Paris, 1939.

Boyer, R. E. "Las ciudades mexicanas: perspectivas de estudio en el siglo XIX," *Historia Mexicana* XII, 2, (Octubre–diciembre 1972): 142–159.

Bulnes, Francisco. *Los grandes problemas de México*. México, 1926.

Cabrera, Luis. "The Purposes and Ideals of the Mexican Revolution," *Annals of the American Academy of Political and Social Sciences*. Supplement. LXIX, (January 1917): 1–17.

Calcott, Wilfrid H. *Liberalism in Mexico, 1857–1929*. Stanford, 1931.

Calderón de la Barca, Frances. *La vida en México durante una residencia de dos años en ese país*. México, 1959.

Callahan, James M. *American Foreign Policy in Mexican Relations*. New York, 1932.

Calleja, Carlos A. "Tampico sigue siendo el primer puerto marítimo de la República,' *Todo* (México) 870, 50, 11-5-1950: 36–37, 40.

Cardoso, Ciro, ed. *México en el siglo XIX, 1821–1910. Historia económica y de la estructura social*. México, 1983.

Cardoso, Fernando H. *Elites in Latin America*. London/New York, 1967.

Carleton Millan, Verna. *Mexico Reborn*. Boston, 1939.

Carpizo, Jorge. *La Constitución Mexicana de 1917*. México, 1969.

Carr, Barry. "The Casa del Obrero Mundial, Constitutionalism and the Pact of February 1915," Frost, Meyer and Vázquez, eds. *El trabajo y los trabajadores en la historia de México*. México, 1979: 603–632.

Carr, Barry. "Recent Regional Studies of the Mexican Revolution," *Latin American Research Review*. XV, 1, (1980): 3-4.

Casados, Alfonso. "En mis archivos y viejos relatos," El Sol de Tampico. Weekly articles from February to May 1985.

Chase, Stuart. *Mexico: A Study of Two Americas*. New York, 1931.

Charterins, Stewart. "The Petroleum Industry in México," *Engineering and Mining Journal*. 110, 15, (October 9, 1920): 725-726.

Chipman, Donald E. *Nuño de Guzman and the Province of the Pánuco,1518–1533*. Glendale, California, 1967.

Clark, Marjorie R. *Organized Labor in Mexico*. Chapel Hill, 1934.

Cleland, Robert G. *The Mexican Yearbook. The Standard Authority in Mexico, 1920–1921*. Los Angeles, 1922.

Coatsworth, John H. *Growth Against Development: The Economic Impact of Railroads in Porfirian Mexico*. De Kalb, 1981.

_____. "Railroads and the Concentration of Landownership in the Early Porfiriato," *Hispanic American Historical Review*. 54, 1, (February 1974):48–71.

Coerver, Don M. *The Porfirian Interregnum: The Presidency of Manuel González of Mexico, 1880–1884*. Fort Worth, 1979.

Coerver, Don M. "The Perils of Progress: The Mexican Department of Fomento During the Boom Years 1880–1884," *Interamerican Economic Affairs*. 31, 2 (July 1977):41–62.

Colmenares, Francisco. *Petróleo y lucha de clases en México:1864-1982*. México, 1982.

Corthell, E.L. *A History of the Jetties at the Mouth of the Mississippi River*. New York, 1881.

Cosío Villegas, Daniel, ed. *Historia Moderna de México*. 10 vols. México, 1957–1972.

Creel, George. *The People Next Door. An Interpretive History of Mexico and the Mexicans*. New York, 1926.

_____. *Estados Unidos contra Porfirio Díaz*. México, 1955.

Cumberland, Charles. *Mexican Revolution. Genesis Under Madero*. Austin, 1952.

_____. *The Constitutionalist Years*. Austin 1972.

_____. *Mexico: The Struggle for Modernity*. Oxford, 1968.

Cuevas, Mariano S.J. *Historia de la Nación Mexicana*. México, 1940.

Dallal, Alberto. "Urbanismo y planificación," *Cuadernos Americanos*. I, (enero–junio 1969):107–130.

Davenport, E.H. and Sydney R. Cooke. *The Oil Trusts and Anglo-American Relations*. New York, 1924.

Davis, Harold E. "Mexican Petroleum Taxes," *Hispanic American Historical Review*. XII, 4 (November 1932):405–419.

De la Garza Treviño, Ciro R. *La Revolución Mexicana en el Estado de Tamaulipas. Cronología 1885–1913*. México, 1973.

De la Peña, Manuel. *Estudio jurídico, político y económico sobre el Artículo 27 Constitucional.* México, 1921.

_____. *El petróleo y la legislación frente a las compañías petroleras.* México, 1920.

Denny, H. S. "The Oil Excitement in Mexico," *Mining Journal.* 89, (June 1910):4.

Díaz Duffoó, Carlos. *México y los capitales extranjeros.* México, 1918.

Dorbecker, Narno. 'Laguna del Carpintero," *Boletín de la Sociedad Mexicana de Geografía y Estadística.* 59 (1944): 225–233.

Dulles, John W. F. *Yesterday in Mexico: A Chronicle of the Revolution, 1919–1936.* Austin, 1961.

Escobar y Rivera, Manuel. "Campaña de Tampico de Tamaulipas, año de 1829," *Historia Mexicana.* IX, 1, (julio-septiembre 1959):44–96.

Falcón, Romana. "¿Orígenes populares de la revolución de 1910? El caso de San Luis Potosí," *Historia Mexicana.*XIX, 2, (octubre-noviembre 1979):32–70.

Filisola, Vicente. *Memoria para la historia de la Guerra de Tejas.* 2 vols. México, 1924.

Forbin, Victor. *Le Petrole dans le Monde.* Paris, 1940.

Foster, John W. *Las memorias diplomáticas de Mr. Foster sobre México.* México, 1924.

Francis, F. "A Glimpse of Mexico," *Twentieth Century Studies.* XII, (1882):591-600.

Galindo y Villa, Jesús. *Geografía de la República Mexicana.* 2 vols. México, 1926.

Gálvez, Enrique. "Desarrollo económico de Tampico," *Revista de Economía.* (México). (Abril 1951):52.

García Granados, Jorge. *Los veneros del diablo.* México, 1941.

García Granados, Ricardo. *Historia de México desde la restauración de la República en 1867 hasta la caída de Porfirio Díaz.* v.1 México, 1928.

_______. *Historia de México desde la restauración de la República en 1867 hasta la caída de Huerta.* v.2 México,1956.

El General Rosencranz y el ferrocarril de Tuxpám al Pacífico. México, 1870.

El General Rosencranz, la "Doctrina Monroe," el "Destino Manifiesto" y el ferrocarril de Tuxpám al Pacífico. México, 1870.

Gerhardt, Ray C. "Inglaterra y el petróleo mexicano durante la Primera Guerra Mundial," *Historia Mexicana*. XXV, 1, (julio–septiembre 1975):118–142.

Gibbon, Thomas Edward. *Mexico under Carranza; a Lawyer's Indictment of the Crowning Infamy of Four Hundred Years of Misrule*. Garden City, 1919.

Gilly, Adolfo. *The Mexican Revolution*. London, 1983.

Gómez Serrano, Jesús. *Aguascalientes: Imperio de los Gugenheim*. México, 1982.

González Casanova, Francisco. *México: economía, sociedad y política. De la República Restaurada a la Constitución de 1917*. Antología. 2 vols. México, 1985.

González Casanova, Pablo. *La clase obrera en la historia de México en el primer gobierno constitucional 1917-1920*. México, 1980.

González Salas, Carlos. *Tampico, mi ciudad*. Tampico, 1981.

_____. *Los seis municipios conurbados de la desembocadura del Río Pánuco*. Ciudad Victoria, 1980.

_____. *Del reloj en vela*. Tampico, 1983.

_____. *Acercamiento a la historia del movimiento obrero en Tampico, 1887-1983*. Ciudad Victoria, 1987.

González Treviño, Luis. Indices de geografía, economía y sociedad del Estado de Tamaulipas," *Boletín de la Sociedad Mexicana de Geografía y Estadística*. LIX, 1–6, (septiembre–diciembre 1944):315-342.

Grieb, Kenneth J."Standard Oil and the Financing of the Mexican Revolution," *California Historical Society Quarterly*. XLIX, 1 (March 1971):59–72.

Gruening, Ernest. *Mexico and Its Heritage*. New York, 1928.

Halleck, H. W. ed. *A Collection of Mining Laws of Spain and Mexico*. San Francisco, 1859.

Hamilton, Charles W. *Early Days Oil Tales of Mexico*. Houston, 1966.

Hart, John M. "The Urban Working Class and the Mexican Revolution: The Case of the Casa del Obrero Mundial," *Hispanic American Historical Review*. 58, 1, (February 1978):1-80.

Henderson, Peter V. N. *Felix Díaz. The Porfirians and the Mexican Revolution*. London/Lincoln, 1981.

Hergesheimer, Joseph. *Tampico*. New York, 1926.

Hidy, Ralph and Muriel. *Pioneering in Big Business, 1882-1911*. New York, 1955.

Hoffmann, Fritz L. "Edward L. Doheny and the Beginnings of Petroleum Development in Mexico," *Mid-America.* XXIV, 13 (April 1942) :94–108.

Humboldt, Alejandro de. *Ensayo político sobre el Reino de la Nueva España.* (1811) 6 vols. México, 1941.

Icaza, Xavier. *Panchito Chapapote. Retablo tropical o relación de un extraordinario sucedido de la heróica Veracruz.* México, 1961.

Katz, Friedrich. *The Secret War in Mexico. Europe, the United States and the Mexican Revolution.* Chicago, 1981.

Kemmerer, Edwin W. *Inflation and Revolution: Mexico's Experience of 1912–1917.* Princeton, 1940.

Kemper, Robert V. and Anya P. Royce. "Mexican Urbanization Since 1821: A Macro-historical Approach," *Urban Anthropology.* VIII, 3–4 (1979):267–289.

Knight, Alan. *The Mexican Revolution.* 2 vols. Cambridge, England, 1986.

Lavin, José Domingo. *Petróleo. Pasado, presente y futuro de una industria mexicana.* México, 1950.

Lazo, Carlos. "Planificación de Tampico," *Espacios.* XIV, 31–32 (Octubre 1952):87–110.

Leal, Juan Felipe. "La política ferrocarrilera de los primeros gobiernos porfiristas y las compañías ferroviarias norteamericanas (1876–1884)," *Relaciones Internacionales.* (México) V, 14, (jul-sept. 1976):8–49.

Lewis, Cleona. *America's Stake at International Investment.* Washington, D.C., 1938.

Liceaga, Luis. *Félix Díaz.* México, 1958.

London, Jack. "Our Adventures in Tampico," *Collier's Magazine.* 53, (June 27, 1914):5–7.

López Rosado, Diego. *Historia y pensamiento económico de México.* 4vols. México, 1968.

Ludwell, Denny. *We Fight for Oil.* New York, 1928.

MacElwee. Roy S. *Port and Terminal Facilities.* New York/London, 1926.

_____. *Port Development.* New York, 1926.

MacHugh, R. J. *Modern Mexico.* London, 1914.

Martínez, Andrea. *La intervención norteamericana en Veracruz, 1914.* México, 1982.

Martínez, Oscar J. *Border Boom Town: Ciudad Juarez Since 1848.* Austin/London, 1975.
Martínez Hernández, Francisco Javier. *Historia de la Sección Uno del Sindicato de Trabajadores Petroleros de la República Mexicana S.T.P.R.M.* Ciudad Madero, Tamaulipas, 1960.
Meade Saínz, Joaquín. *La Huasteca. Epoca antigua.* México, 1942.
_____. *La Huasteca Tamaulipeca.* 3 vols. México, 1977.
_____. *La Huasteca Veracruzana.* 2 vols. México, 1962–1963.
Menéndez, Gabriel A. *Doheny el cruel.* México, 1958.
Meyer, Jean. *La revolución mexicana, 1910-1940.* Barcelona, 1975.
_____. "Los obreros en la revolución mexicana: los Batallones Rojos," Historia Mexicana. 21, 1, (julio-septiembre 1971): 57.
Meyer, Lorenzo. *México y los Estados Unidos en el conflicto petrolero, 1917–1942.* México, 1968.
Meyer, Lorenzo. *Los grupos de presión extranjeros en el México revolucionario, 1910–1940.* México, 1978.
Middleman, Robert Keith. *The Master Builders.* London, 1963.
Miller, Robert Ryan. *Mexico. A History.* Norman, Oklahoma, 1985.
Moreno Toscano, Alejandra. "Cambios en los patrones de urbanización de México, 1810–1910, "*Historia Mexicana* XXII, 2, 86 (1972):160–187.
Morgan, F. W. *Ports and Harbours.* London/New York, 1952.
Muir, John M. *Geology of the Tampico Region. Mexico.*Tulsa, 1936.
O'Gorman, Edmundo. *Historia de las divisiones territoriales de México.* México, 1966.
Ordoñez, Ezequiel."La industria petrolera de México, 1870–1910," *Revista Mexicana de Ingeniería y Arquitectura.* 14, 12 (Diciembre 1936):2.
Ortíz de Casas, M. *El problema del petróleo.* Tampico, 1920.
Pan American Petroleum Co., *Mexican Petroleum.* New York, 1922.
Perry, Laurens B. *Juárez and Díaz. Machine Politics in Mexico.* De Kalb,1978.
Pletcher, David M. "The Fall of Silver in México, 1870–1910," *Journal of Economic History.* 18 (Spring 1958):33–55.
Portes Gil, Emilio. *Autobiografía de la Revolución Mexicana. Un tratado de interpretación histórica.* México, 1964.
Portes Gil, Emilio. *Raigambre de la Revolución en Tamaulipas. Autobiografía en acción.* México, 1972.
Pratt, Joseph A. *The Growth of a Refining Region.* Greenwich, CT,1980.

Quirk, Robert E. *An Affair of Honor. Woodrow Wilson and the Occupation of Veracruz.* Lexington, 1962.

Reed, St. Clair Griffin. *A History of Texas Railroads and of Transportation Conditions Under Spain and Mexico and the Republic and the State.* Houston, 1941.

Richmond, Douglas. *Venustiano Carranza's Nationalist Struggles, 1893-1920.* Lincoln, 1983.

Richmod, Douglas W. and George Wolfskill, eds. *Essays on the Mexican Revolution. Revisionist Views of the Leaders.* Austin, 1979.

Rippy, Fred J. *The United States and Mexico.* New York, 1926.

_____. *British Investments in Latin America, 1822–1949: A Case Study of Private Enterprise in Retarded Regions.*Minneapolis, 1959.

Rippy, Fred J. "The British Investment Boom of the 1880's in Latin America," *Hispanic American Historical Review.* XIX, 2, (May 1949): 281–286.

_____. José Vasconcelos and Guy Stevens. *American Policies Abroad: Mexico.* Chicago, 1928.

Rippy, Merrill. *Oil and the Mexican Revolution.* Leiden, 1972.

Rives, George L. *The United States and Mexico, 1821–1848.* 2 vols. New York, 1913.

Rodríguez, Antonio. *El rescate del petróleo. Epopeya de un pueblo.* México, 1975.

Rogers, Thomas L. *México? Sí, Señor.* Boston, 1894.

Romero, José Luis. *Latinoamérica. Las ciudades y las ideas.* México/Buenos Aires, 1976.

Romero, Matías. "The Free Zone in Mexico," *The North American Review.* 154, 459 (May 1892):459–471.

Rosenzweig, Fernando. "El desarrollo económico de México de 1877 a 1911, "*El Trimestre Económico.*32, 127, (julio–septiembre 1965):404–454.

Ross, Stanley R. *Francisco I. Madero: Apostle of Mexican Democracy.* New York, 1970.

Ruiz, Ramón Eduardo. *The Great Rebellion: Mexico, 1905–1924.* New York, 1980.

_____. *Labor and the Ambivalent Revolution:México, 1911–1923.* Baltimore, 1976.

Saldívar, Gabriel. *Historia Compendiada de Tamaulipas.*México, 1945.

Solano, Francisco de. *Estudios sobre la ciudad iberoameriana.* Madrid,1983.

Soto, Julio. *El México de Porfirio Díaz.* Valencia, Spain, 1909.

Soto, Manuel Fernando. *Proyecto de comunicación interoceánica por el centro de la República Mexicana* México, 1869.

Soto, Manuel Fernando. *El nuevo Estado. Necesidad de formarlo inmediatamente de parte de Tamaulipas, Hidalgo y Veracruz.* México, 1856.

Spender, J. A. *Weetman Pearson: First Viscount Cowdray, 1856–1927.* London, 1930.

Squier, E. L. "Tampico," *Ladies Home Journal.* 45, (August 1928):18–19.

Sweetman, Jack. *The Landing at Veracruz: 1914. The First Complete Chronicle of a Strange Encounter in April 1914, when the U.S. Navy Captured and Occupied the City of Veracruz, México.* Annapolis, 1968.

Tannenbaum, Frank. *Peace by Revolution: An Interpretation of Mexico.* New York, 1933.

Tarbell, Ida M. *A History of Standard Oil.* 2 vols. New York, 1904.

Thompson, Craig. *Since Spindletop: A Human Story of Gulf's First Half Century.* Pittsburgh, 1951.

Thompson, Wallace. *Trading with Mexico.* New York, 1921.

Thorup, Cathryn. "La competencia económica británica y norteamericana en México, 1887–1910," *Historia Mexicana.* XXXI, 4, 124, (abril–junio1982):599–641.

Tischendorf, Alfred. *Great Britain and Mexico in the Era of Porfirio Díaz, 1876–1910.* Durham, North Carolina, 1961.

Torrea, Juan Manuel and Ignacio Fuentes. *Tampico. Apuntes para su historia.* Tampico, 1942.

Toussaint, Manuel. *La Conquista del Pánuco.* México, 1948.

Traven, B. *The Treasure of the Sierra Madre.* New York, 1935.

Unikel, Luis, Crescencio Ruiz Chapetto and Gustavo Garza Villareal, eds. *El desarrollo urbano de México: diagnóstico e implicaciones futuras.* México, 1976.

Uribe Rubalcava, Alfonso. *Breve historia de Ciudad Madero.* Ciudad Madero, 1980.

Vagts, Alfred. *Mexiko, Europa und Amerika unter besonderer Berüchsichtung der Petroleumpolitik.* Berlin, 1928.

Van Oss, S.F. *American Railroads as Investments.* New York,1893.

Vincent, Ralph W. *Mexico Today and Tomorrow. An Outline of the Present Economic Power and Possibilities of Her Railroad Systems.* New York, 1906.

Wilkins, Mira. *The Emergence of Multinational Enterprise: American Business Abroad From the Colonial Era to 1914.* Cambridge, MA, 1970.

Wilkins, Mira. *The Maturing of Multinational Enterprise: American Business Abroad From 1914 to 1970.* Cambridge/London, 1975.

Womack, John R. "The Mexican Economy During the Revolution, 1910–1920: Historiography and Analysis," *Marxist Perspectives.* 1, 4, (1978):80–123.

Wright, Marie. *Mexico. A History of Its Progress and Development in the Hundred Years Between 1810 and 1910.* Philadelphia, 1911.

Young, Desmond. *Member for Mexico. A Biography of Weetman Pearson. First Viscount of Cowdray.* London, 1966.

Zischka, Antoine. *La guerra secreta por el petróleo.* Paris. 1934.

Printed by
CPI books GmbH, Leck

FSC
www.fsc.org
MIX
Papier | Fördert
gute Waldnutzung
FSC® C083411

Kolibri 360 GmbH
Ferdinand-Jühlke-Straße 7
99095 Erfurt, Deutschland
produktsicherheit@kolibri360.de